Participatory Critical Rhetoric

Participatory Critical Rhetoric

Theoretical and Methodological Foundations for Studying Rhetoric In Situ

Michael Middleton, Aaron Hess,
Danielle Endres and
Samantha Senda-Cook

LEXINGTON BOOKS
Lanham • Boulder • New York • London

Published by Lexington Books
An imprint of The Rowman & Littlefield Publishing Group, Inc.
4501 Forbes Boulevard, Suite 200, Lanham, Maryland 20706
www.rowman.com

Unit A, Whitacre Mews, 26-34 Stannary Street, London SE11 4AB

British Library Cataloguing in Publication Information Available

Library of Congress Control Number: 2015952181
ISBN: 978-1-4985-1380-7 (cloth)
ISBN: 978-1-4985-1382-1 (pbk.)
ISBN: 978-1-4985-1381-4 (electronic)

To the many participants we have danced, protested, hiked, grieved, celebrated, and become friends with during our projects.

Contents

Acknowledgments

This book represents an equal collaboration between the four of us. The arguments that we develop in our efforts to advance participatory critical rhetoric are the product of both our individual efforts in the area, as well as our collaboration over the last eighteen months. The author order on the front of the book is a necessity and is the result of a randomized number generator on Michael's phone. However, this book is the result of equal contributions by each author and we consider ourselves to be co-first authors.

We want to start by acknowledging each other and the process of collaboration. This book would not have been possible without each other and the beautiful blend of collective thinking and contributions from our individual perspectives and experiences.

We also want to thank all of the participants that we have worked with in our varied fieldwork projects. We dedicated the book to our participants because they are essential to the practice of participatory critical rhetoric, and we could not have come to the arguments we make in this book without our relationships with our participants in the field. We have learned so much from our participants and hope that we have also offered something back (however modest) to them and the broader communities in which they/we have devoted time and energy.

Participatory Critical Rhetoric also responds to a groundswell of research in the field of rhetoric over the past several decades. We are thankful for the various articles, conference presentations, workshops, and other events in which we have presented, discussed, and learned from others about field-based approaches to critical rhetoric. In particular, we would like to thank: Carole Blair, Phaedra Pezzullo, Greg Dickinson, and Dan Brouwer for providing inspiration, encouragement, and feedback to this and other participatory critical rhetoric projects in various stages of development.

We are also grateful to Nicolette Amstutz and Alison Pavan, the editorial and production staff at Lexington Press, and the reviewers who helped strengthen this manuscript; our departments and universities who supported research and writing efforts to produce this book; and our families and friends who support us. In the remainder of this section, we each offer some personal acknowledgments.

To Kristy, Grayson, and Benson, many thanks for your support on the many, many projects that I undertake. You three not only tolerate all my writing endeavors, but often come along for a protest in the Phoenix heat, a documentary in Lower Manhattan, or a late-night dance in the desert. To my parents, thank you for the love and support, especially when state lines separate us. Additionally, over the years, I've been blessed to meet and work with many great minds, including my coauthors for this book. I am grateful to them, and many others including Karen Stewart, Miriam Sobre-Denton, Roberta Chevrette, erin mcclellan, Art Herbig, and Lisa Menegatos. Finally, many additional thanks to my department at Downtown Phoenix, whose commitment to community engagement sustains my intellectual curiosities and participatory research.

—*Aaron*

My colleagues at the University of Utah have provided a wealth of support and intellectual stimulation for this project and others, particularly Kent Ono, Helene Shugart, Kevin DeLuca, and Marouf Hasian. I am also grateful to Leah Ceccarelli, Barbara Warnick, Gerry Philipsen, Tarla Rai Peterson, and Leah Sprain who supported and challenged me through my path to bring rhetoric and fieldwork together in my own projects. Most of all I am immensely appreciative of the love, encouragement, and sustenance I get from my family—Wayne, Rosa, Owen, Mom, my late Dad, and Nick.

—*Danielle*

I am grateful to my colleagues at the University of Utah for their support of this collaborative effort, as well as for the ongoing supportive feedback and collegiality of the Rhetoric & Writing Research Interest Group supported by the generosity of the Tanner Humanities Center at the University of Utah. In addition to my coauthors, I would like to thank my mentors Leonard C. Hawes, Mary S. Strine, and Karen Rasmussen for their supportive conversations and feedback on the arguments developed in this text and in countless other ways. To my friends and family, thank you for the ongoing support you provide. Finally, to my partner, Ashley, thank you for supporting the long hours dedicated to this collaboration that all too often intervened on our time together.

—*Michael*

This book is the product of many hands and minds, each contributing with their conversations, guidance, encouragement, and distractions. First, I feel privileged to have had the honor to write once again with Danielle and Mike, and for the first time with Aaron. (Go team!) Next, I am grateful to my coworkers at Creighton, especially Chad, who never fail to listen and always provide good company at lunchtime. Also, I appreciate the colleagues I see in person only a few times a year, who question, speculate, and debate ideas intensely and joyfully. Finally, to my friends and family, especially James, thank you for drawing me in and tethering me to many worlds.

—*Samantha*

Introduction

On April 14, 2007, thousands of climate change activists decided to "step it up" by engaging in a national day of climate change that included both traditional and nontraditional protest events organized in over 1,400 places around the USA.[1] From 2008 until the present, homeless citizens and their allies have lobbied their local community leaders in Sacramento both in meetings at City Hall and through collective actions taken in the streets to create new solutions to an old, but increasingly dire, set of political and economic conditions faced by Sacramento's homeless citizens.[2] Daily in national parks, wilderness enthusiasts, tourists, and passers-by navigate—and sometimes resist—efforts by park officials to normalize the ways of interacting with and, as a consequence, coming to know the environments they encounter.[3] And, health advocacy groups attend raves aiming to find new spaces and tactics to effectively shape perspectives on recreational drug (ab)use and of the War on Drugs.[4] These and countless other fields where communities form, engage in collective action, and disperse are brimming with the insights to be gained from examining everyday localized rhetorical practices.

Viewed individually, these vastly different fields of rhetorical action seemingly share little in common. Yet, they provide examples of the forms of rhetorical invention that increasingly capture the attention of rhetorical theorists and critics.[5] They point toward the significant rhetorical exigencies that rhetors tackle in the spaces of everyday life, they highlight the important challenges with which communities struggle, and they demand that scholars rethink what can be learned from the everyday rhetorical practices that are often dismissed as too mundane to warrant critical attention. Engaging with these *in situ* fields of rhetorical invention highlights the significance of the embodied, emplaced, material, visual, affective, processual, and vernacular dimensions of rhetorical practice that intersect in these places inhabited by activists, speakers, audiences, and observers to shape shared understandings of significant phenomena.[6] Accessing, documenting, enacting, and analyzing these extratextual forms of *in situ* rhetoric calls for new ways of doing rhetorical scholarship that involve the critic's presence in the moment of rhetorical invention and draw from the tools of fieldwork and qualitative inquiry to participate with and interpret these embodied and emplaced performances of rhetoric. Encounters with these rhetorical fields goad rhetorical scholars to recognize the significance of shifting and nontraditional notions of texts, rhetor, audience, critic, and context.[7]

In this book, we develop a set of theoretical and methodological perspectives that we collectively refer to as participatory critical rhetoric. In doing so, we embark on a programmatic effort to theorize *in situ* critical rhetorical scholarship as a trend with important consequences for the discipline. A deliberate and extended effort to tease out the challenges and opportunities presented by this approach helps clarify its focus and strengthen the foundation on which future participatory critical rhetoric research is conducted.

Participatory critical rhetoric describes a set of research practices that bring qualitative methods of data collection such as participant observation, interviewing, and oral history into the process of doing rhetorical criticism. Grounded in the intellectual tradition of critical rhetoric, participatory critical rhetoric affords critics the opportunity to stand with, for, and among the people whose rhetoric we study.[8] As a participatory research praxis, participatory critical rhetoric reconsiders the relationship between critic, rhetor, text/context, and audience by placing the critic in direct contact with audiences and rhetors, inviting new perspectives on these complex rhetorical processes. It provides a means to account for the rhetoric of the everyday, to locate rhetoric in relationship to broader cultural discourses, and to open space for critics to analyze, participate with, and contribute to an emancipatory form of critique. By naming and theorizing participatory critical rhetoric, we also hope to contribute to a programmatic and sustained study of the potential offered by this critical approach. To that end, we highlight how participatory critical rhetoric draws on and expands the theoretical and critical exploration of scholars who are already pursuing efforts to better understand vernacular, everyday, and live(d) rhetorics through field-based approaches to rhetorical inquiry.[9] Further, through our own experiences with fieldwork, we attend to how we have struggled to determine the impact of the forms of rhetorical action encountered in the field. Throughout the book, we provide, by way of vignettes and references to extant rhetorical scholarship, examples of practical efforts to engage with these problematics of participatory rhetorical fieldwork.

We use this introduction to develop our definition of participatory critical rhetoric by synthesizing previous *in situ* rhetorical research and theory, and to examine each of the key terms: rhetoric, critical, and participatory. We also offer a brief glimpse into our own experiences with using the approach. Finally, we sketch the key questions that guide subsequent chapters and that illuminate critical considerations that are activated in unique ways when one undertakes *in situ* rhetorical research.

TOWARD A PARTICIPATORY CRITICAL RHETORIC

The argument throughout this book is that field-based approaches to rhetorical criticism raise generative questions and provoke new discussions that are at the core of theorizing rhetorical practice. Put simply, participatory critical rhetoric theorizes field-based rhetoric. In practice, it signals that a rhetorical critic engages in fieldwork as a part of the critical process, where the critic enters a naturalistic field in which rhetoric occurs in order to observe, participate with, document, and analyze that rhetoric in its embodied and emplaced instantiation. Participatory critical rhetoric furthers efforts to theorize these practices on the part of critical rhetoricians and rhetorical critics.[10] While we recount the development of field-based approaches to rhetorical criticism in chapter 1, here we focus on describing the participatory critical rhetoric approach as a critical framework that rhetoricians can use to investigate live(d), locally situated rhetoric in its immediate manifestation. This approach emerged from a synthesis and enhancement of our previous work on the topic, including "critical-rhetorical ethnography" and "rhetorical field methods."[11] On the one hand, participatory critical rhetoric draws on Aaron Hess's efforts to theorize critical-rhetorical ethnography, which combines critical rhetoric, ethnography, and the classical rhetorical concepts of invention, *kairos*, and *phronesis*. He contends that a need exists in rhetorical criticism for a method that would allow scholars to "advocate alongside vernacular organizations, arguing for their causes."[12] Foregrounding advocacy and activism, critical-rhetorical ethnography privileges access to locally situated, vernacular rhetorics and seeks to partner with rhetors rather than merely study them. On the other hand, participatory critical rhetoric also draws from Michael Middleton, Samantha Senda-Cook, and Danielle Endres's theorization of rhetorical field methods. They argue that rhetorical field methods provide a means to identify emancipatory potential in the communities that rhetoricians study and a way to better understand live(d) rhetoric. They contend that, "Rhetorical field methods offer a productive articulation of the careful textual analyses characteristic of CR [critical rhetoric] with the provocative insights uncovered by *in situ* research common in ethnography and performance studies."[13] Synthesizing and expanding on these two efforts to theorize *in situ* rhetorical study provides a means by which to develop the theoretical groundings that can guide the proliferation of field-based studies being undertaken by rhetorical scholars.

Both approaches seek to understand everyday rhetoric as well as extraordinary rhetoric as it happens in its naturalistic field, and both present the voices of marginalized communities by attending to vernacular discourses. Participant observation that produces fieldnotes, interviews (ranging from informal conversations to collected oral histories), and other techniques that result in recordings and transcripts allow rhetoricians to access (otherwise) undocumented, embodied, emplaced, material, and ephemeral rhetorical practices. Moreover, both critical-rhetorical ethnography and rhetorical field methods aim to create durable artifacts that provide insights into the lived experiences of the communities they study and, as a consequence, expand the archive of rhetorical activity in ways that add to conventional "after-the-fact" forms of textual criticism familiar to the discipline.[14] Yet, they also illuminate elements of rhetoric that are difficult to ascertain from a textual (particularly already documented texts) purview, including insights into the judgments that underpin the production and reception of rhetoric within a community and the variety of rhetorical forms (affective, sensorial, emplaced, embodied) that can be difficult to capture with textualization.

Participatory critical rhetoric is an umbrella term to describe a range of research practices in which rhetoricians engage—depending on the type of projects they conduct and the kinds of questions they pursue—in extended forms of interaction, participation, and observation with the rhetorical communities they study. Participatory critical rhetoric, however, does not simply take up the mantle of ethnography or claim to offer the same sorts of evidence and analysis. For example, whereas ethnographers tend to be in the field for extended periods of time to gain insight into cultural practices, rhetoricians could be in the field for only a few hours during a political rally or public performance to understand the rhetorical culture of the event. Moreover, while ethnography may seek a holistic picture of culture, participatory critical rhetoric is mainly interested in how symbols are deployed to construct, maintain, and challenge cultures, identities, movements, and place/space.[15] Participatory critical rhetoric maintains a focus on rhetorical interaction by inquiring into community advocacy, symbolic contestation, deliberative practices, and other elements of rhetorical culture.

The kinds of artifacts privileged by and the questions asked by rhetoricians influence how the boundaries (temporal, spatial, etc.) of participatory critical rhetoric are negotiated. Some participatory rhetoricians enter the field with the aim of gathering texts (e.g., speech transcripts or photographs) that lend themselves to approaches more aligned with conventional textual criticism; others enter the field with a focus on embodied, emplaced, and material artifacts and experiences that require different critical approaches (e.g., taking fieldnotes, attending to extratextual dimensions of corporeality); and still other participatory rhetorical critics seek to put both types of artifacts into conversation with one another. Likewise, how rhetoricians imagine the role of the critic has consequences for the analytical approach. Participatory critical rhetoricians must choose the degree to which they privilege the perspectives of the participants in their research vis-a-vis the critic's expertise, deciding whether to maintain control of the interpretive process or share it with participants. In other words, within the common set of practices named by participatory critical rhetoric, a spectrum of approaches can emerge based on the length of time in the field, ways of negotiating textualization and its implications, analysis processes, perspectives on the role of the critic, types of advocacy enacted, levels of organizational membership, and involvement with participants that each participatory rhetorical critic adopts. And, to the extent that each of these elements is emphasized in a particular project, participatory critical rhetoric presents a number of vexing considerations to be interrogated by its practitioners, each of which is taken up over the course of this book. However, there are some baseline critical commitments that are evoked by each of the key terms that name this approach.

Rhetoric

As we suggest above, participatory critical rhetoric, despite its intellectual debt to qualitative communication scholarship, ethnographic practice, and performance studies, maintains a *rhetorical focus*. For us, this means it is concerned with how symbolic practices articulate disparate identities, ideas, values, beliefs, images, meanings, bodies, and communities with some effect on immanent (and future) symbolic practice within, at minimum, the communities where those practices emerge. That is to say, participatory critical rhetoric casts its net broadly when it comes to the question of what constitutes rhetoric or rhetorical practice. We draw from Carole Blair, Greg Dickinson, and Brian Ott's definition of rhetoric as: "discourses, events, objects and practices [whose] character [is] meaningful, legible, partisan, and consequential."[16] When entering the field, the critic is faced with the messy multimodality of rhetoric. Intersectionality, therefore, becomes an important move toward explaining how multiple forms of rhetoric engage in intertextual relationships in the field. In this respect, Darrel Enck-Wanzer's theorization of intersectional rhetoric provides a useful grounding for how participatory critical rhetoric conceptualizes its rhetorical focus. It endeavors to understand how different forms of rhetoric—words, images, bodies—work together without privileging one over another.[17] Participatory critical rhetoric promotes consideration of "the confluence of forms in a radically fragmented vernacular rhetoric."[18] This confluence is important to field-based rhetorical practices where a variety of (rhetorical) forces are colliding with one another at once to create an embodied and emplaced rhetorical encounter. For instance, in addition to verbal texts, images, and bodies, place and space are also crucial rhetorical forms at play in many *in situ* rhetorical performances. So, while participatory critical rhetoric draws on the efforts of Enck-Wanzer and others to theorize the viability of an intersectional rhetorical approach, it aims to further develop these insights from their focus on already documented texts to explore their promise for *in situ* rhetoric.[19]

Critical

Participatory critical rhetoric is closely aligned with a *telos* of *critical praxis* that informs its approach to rhetorical scholarship. By critical praxis we mean a practice in which critics not only analyze rhetoric, but also seek to intervene in structures of power and engage with communities by doing rhetoric. On the one hand, this critical commitment aligns with the already developed commitments of critical rhetoricians who aim to expose how power is sustained through the mystifying force of discourse. Accordingly, participatory critical rhetoric shares the recognition that power is contingent, that it is made material through discursive practice, and that it is communicated by both presence and absence of rhetorical action by both privileged and subordinated rhetorical communities. Like other practitioners of critical rhetoric, it recognizes that new forms of freedom are as likely to mask the discursive operations of power as effectively (if not more so) than the forms of domination which they intend to upend. On the other hand, participatory critical rhetoric endeavors to emphasize the role of the critic as an activist both in their scholarly efforts and in their embodied engagements with the rhetorical communities they examine. It aims to trouble the way in which much critical rhetoric scholarship is focused on efforts to shape future political actions distanced from immediate political struggles in which the critic and the communities they research are located. Specifically, participatory critical rhetoric recognizes that critics who participate with communities in the field cannot restrict their political efforts to objective commentary alone, but rather that claims are made on critics to take immanent political action, which we outline in further detail in chapter 2. And, whether critics desire it or not, those claims will be answered as much by the lack of action or silence of critics in the moment of those encounters as by any other action they choose to take. In this regard, participatory critical rhetoric aligns with the "commitment to a telos," for which Kent Ono and John Sloop argue.[20] However, we contend that the moment when action must be taken and the political horizon that informs that action is not defined by when pen is put to paper. Rather, it is defined by what the embodied, emplaced critic chooses to do (or not do) when claims are made on the critic's body by the communities that have shared their fears, their trust, their insights, and (sometimes) their resources with the critic.

Participatory

Most essentially, participatory critical rhetoric demands the *participation* of the critic with the rhetorical fields and practices that inform their research and critical praxis. For this, there is no substitute. Intimate engagement with the rhetorical communities that inform one's scholarly efforts through fieldwork is the link to both the critical praxis to which participatory critical rhetoric commits itself, as well as the intersectional rhetorical interactions and practices that it seeks to privilege as an object of analysis. As we suggest throughout the following chapters, participation can take many forms and mean many things, but it evokes a few minimal criteria to fulfill our conceptualization of participatory. At minimum, it requires that the critic be present as the rhetorical practices under examination unfold. In other words, participatory critical rhetoric eschews the notion that the critic can or should occupy a third position outside of rhetor or audience. It, instead, insists that to begin to capture insight into the embodied, emplaced experience of live(d) rhetoric, the critic must make efforts to erode the critical distance that places rhetoricians above or outside the rhetorics they examine. In its most thorough enactment, participatory critical rhetoric invites critics to experiment with the creation of rhetoric alongside the rhetorical community they examine, to become a full participant and intimately know the challenges, successes, failures, and metrics for measuring effects in the rhetorical dynamics of that community. In between these two roles, participatory critical rhetoric invites and values a range of other forms of participation, each of which recognizes that to gain intimate insights into the rhetorical processes that shape any rhetorical community, the boundaries that found traditional rhetorical criticism (i.e., the critic as separate from the rhetorical practice) must be made porous. Such a critical move affords the critic insight into what are otherwise often fleeting, ephemeral moments of rhetorical creativity.

It is this synthesis of rhetoric, critical praxis, and participation that defines participatory critical rhetoric, laying bare some of the underlying assumptions of this approach that we discuss further in chapter 1. Our emphasis on critical praxis in particular situates participatory critical rhetoric within a particular subset of rhetorical theory and criticism. While it is possible to undertake forms of rhetorical ethnography, rhetorical fieldwork, or participatory rhetoric that are not informed by critical rhetoric, the approach we put forth in this book narrows the scope with our commitment to a critical praxis. Nonetheless, we believe the issues we raise in subsequent chapters are of importance to all practitioners of field-based rhetorical criticism, whether one addresses those issues with a critical rhetoric lens or not. Further, as we argue, these issues are also of importance to larger conversations in the field of rhetorical theory and criticism.

PARTICIPATORY CRITICAL RHETORIC IN PRACTICE

As we outlined thus far, participatory critical rhetoric encompasses differing degrees of participation and a variety of tools but is always accented with a critical rhetorical sensibility. To illustrate the scope of possibility within the approach, over the course of this book, we often refer to our own work. Between the four of us, we have engaged in a number of projects that fall under the umbrella of participatory critical rhetoric. Each of these projects informs our current and collective thinking about the theoretical nature and methodological scope of the approach. Throughout the chapters, we offer our own tales from the field in the form of personal vignettes, which provide moments of insight from conducting this work including unexpected outcomes, striking interactions with participants, and the lessons learned from placing our bodies in the field. Taken together, the scope of our research has been quite broad and has included a variety of methodological choices. We hope that the inclusion of vignettes shows that participatory critical rhetoricians take up a number of tools to explore fundamental questions of rhetoric.

For example, Michael's efforts with the framework of participatory critical rhetoric have been focused on the social movement practices of homeless communities. During his graduate study and presently, Michael has spent several months conducting periodic research embedded with activists forming the homeless advocacy group, SafeGround Sacramento. His research included participant observation, interviewing, and the collection of vernacular texts produced by the activists with whom he worked. This research informs his current publication efforts while he is laying the groundwork for a related study of the criminalization of homelessness and responses to that criminalization via research in alternative "homeless courts."[21]

Aaron has also conducted a number of projects that have included a range of methods including participant observation, interviews, focus groups, and documentary filmmaking. While his work at the intersection of rhetoric and qualitative methods began with his undergraduate honor's thesis using observational methods at a Promise Keepers rally, his long-term ethnographic engagement with a health advocacy group called DanceSafe was the foundation of his dissertation work on critical-rhetorical ethnography. Working with Art Herbig, he has also been involved with two documentary projects, one in Washington, DC covering Jon Stewart and Stephen Colbert's "Rally to

Restore Sanity and/or Fear" and another in Lower Manhattan during the tenth anniversary of 9/11. In Phoenix, he has worked with a local birthing center to explore health advocacy and the politics of natural birth through interviews and focus groups.[22]

Danielle's interest in field-based rhetorical approaches began in graduate school where she was trained in both ethnography of communication and rhetorical theory/criticism. Although her dissertation analyzed a set of already documented texts related to nuclear waste siting decisions, that work was informed by fieldwork conducted with Native American and environmental activists opposed to the Yucca Mountain nuclear waste site. Over the years she has continued to build relationships, spend time in the field as a participant observer, and create an oral history archive on a variety of topics related to the Atomic West to inform her work on conceptions of place/space in the American West, nuclear colonialism, and environmental justice. Danielle also coheaded with Tarla Rai Peterson and Leah Sprain a team of scholars across the USA who studied the rhetorical tactics of the 2007 Step It Up climate change rallies using both participant observation and rhetorical methods, and shared their findings with key members of the Step It Up organization (now 350.org). Currently, Danielle and Peterson are leading a collaborative project that is examining the expert-to-expert internal rhetoric of low-carbon energy technology scientists and engineers, using multisited participant observation and interviewing at nuclear science, wind energy science, and carbon sequestration science conferences. This project has moved Danielle from the world of activists to the world of scientists and engineers (not necessarily mutually exclusive worlds), which has prompted thinking about doing critical work with a community that is not always aligned with her politics.[23]

Samantha wove participant observation and interviewing into her rhetorical research about outdoor recreation at Zion National Park. During this project, she spent a month camping and hiking through Zion, documenting and analyzing the different forms of material rhetoric present in this national park. As a graduate student, she collected oral histories for Danielle's nuclear colonialism research. She has also attended, as a researcher, a few one-day events such as Step It Up, PARK(ing) Day, and Elevate. As part of a research team, she attended two Step It Up rallies in Salt Lake City, gathering data that provided evidence of the rhetoric that places themselves perform. For a project about spatial argument, she participated in a PARK(ing) Day event in Omaha. This fieldwork informed the analysis but did not become part of the published essay. Again, in Omaha, she attended Elevate, which was an event aimed to challenge dominant food practices by making connections between food and transportation. Finally, focusing on urban environments, she has been using participant observation and interviewing to engage in a long-term study of constructions of place/space in neighborhoods in Omaha.[24]

Taken together, our experiences in the field may seem disparate; however, upon closer inspection, they reveal a fundamental focus on participating in intersectional rhetorical processes as they happen in the field. Across our works, we have maintained a critical focus on the dissemination, circulation, and contestation of meanings inherent to each respective rhetorical community. Whether nuclear science, drug culture, outdoor recreation, or homelessness, we examine the nature of symbolic identities and meanings forged and challenged in urban streets, national parks, desert raves, scientific meetings, and official memorials. These sites of invention and the people found therein inform our theories of rhetoric. We use them to illustrate the potential of participatory critical rhetoric in articulating new insights into the processes and products of rhetoric. We also hope that our collective experience indicates that participatory critical rhetoric is not a set of predetermined tools to be taken up, or a prescriptive, formulaic method. Rather, participatory critical rhetoric engenders a commitment to flexibility in participating with the immanent politics of emplaced and intersectional rhetorics, as comprehended through the critical embodiment of being present in the sites of invention and affected by the perspectives offered by those who participate in the production of rhetorical discourse.

ORGANIZATION OF THE BOOK

In the chapters that follow, we expand on the foundations and key assumptions of participatory critical rhetoric and develop some of its potential implications for rhetorical theorists and communication scholars working in ethnography and performance studies. In particular, we develop four interrelated *topoi* that open conversations about the theoretical and methodological implications of participatory critical rhetoric: immanent politics, critical embodiment, emplaced fields of rhetoric, and gaining perspectives from participants. Chapter 1 begins by tracing the theoretical foundations of participatory critical rhetoric. Specifically, we situate participatory critic rhetoric in the critical tradition of rhetorical theory, discussing how critical rhetoric itself demands a reexamination of texts, rhetors, critics, and audiences. In doing so, we argue that critical rhetoric provides the grounds for embodying participatory approaches to rhetorical criticism. This chapter also provides key assumptions of participatory critical rhetoric, expanding the definition we offer in this introduction. We contend that (1) texts are always embedded within social practices, performances, and contexts; (2) participation itself functions epistemologically to advance theory and criticism; and (3) when conceiving of rhetoric as embodied and emplaced, rhetoric itself is revealed as intersectional and multidimensional. We close this chapter by articulating some of the implications of apprehending rhetoric via participatory experience.

In chapter 2, we argue that participatory critical rhetoric provides the opportunity to position the critical rhetorician as an activist-scholar. In order to theorize this role for the critic, we focus on three dimensions of critical rhetoric that we believe are supplemented by participatory critical rhetoric: its focus on text or textual fragments, its deferral of politics by seeking to offer counsel relevant to future rhetorical engagements, and its risk of fostering political paralysis by privileging constant criticism over immanent engagement. We introduce the concept of immanent politics as a way to challenge the critic to engage directly with the rhetorical field that hosts their research, consider the importance of minor, often non-textual (or textualizable) rhetorical practices, and imagine how the critic might adopt the role of activist-scholar. We conclude by considering how these shifts enable critics to focus on and participate in productive criticism, utilizing their insights to sharpen the political edge of critical rhetoric.

In chapter 3, we theorize critics as embodied, contending that although critics embody their roles in conventional rhetorical criticism, physical presence at the site of rhetorical invention heightens the significance of critics' bodies in participatory critical rhetoric, which calls for increased reflexivity. We begin by arguing that although rhetorical critics increasingly attend to the body as a rhetorical entity itself, they rarely consider the body *in situ*, focusing instead on representations of bodies of rhetors or on how rhetors deploy the bodies of others. We enhance these perspectives by calling attention to the critical embodiment of the critic. As such, we suggest three ways of conceiving of critics' bodies: as critical, affective, and risky. By critical, we mean that critics' bodies function as research instruments, collecting multisensory information. We also advance theories of affective rhetoric, discussing how critics' bodies participate in a field of affect at once experiencing and contributing to it. Lastly, we explain that critics' bodies can raise suspicion, incur damage, or change unfolding rhetorical situations for the better and the worse. Throughout, we emphasize that reflexivity ought to become a routine practice not only among scholars using participatory critical rhetoric but also in rhetorical criticism more broadly.

In chapter 4, we argue that the field is not simply a different context for rhetoric. Rather, the field is a participant in rhetorical invention that takes on a range of meanings from a place of research to context to community of meaning to a rhetorical actor. In order to theorize the way the field participates in rhetorical invention in participatory critical rhetoric, we advance the argument that rhetoric is an emplaced phenomenon, meaning that rhetoric is always an embodied experience in relation to place and space. Participatory critical rhetoricians who enter the field are in a unique position to access and document emplaced rhetoric. We examine how four intersecting vectors of the field—place of research, context, community of meaning, and rhetorical actor—not only allow the participatory critical rhetorician to better understand emplaced rhetoric, but also how engaging with, attuning to, and evaluating emplaced rhetoric in the field enhances a critic's understanding of the complex and intersectional material experience of rhetoric.

In chapter 5, we turn our attention to the role of participants in field-based rhetorical research. By engaging those present in the rhetorical field, we encourage critics to take up a multiperspectival form of judgment. This judgment is attained through the consideration and elevation of the voices of participants. Participants in participatory critical rhetoric can range from audience members to rhetors, depending on the nature of the particular project. Engaging with participants means inquiring into the immediate moment of speaking as judgments on rhetorical invention and reception are shared between speaker and audience. We offer three conceptualizations of participants—as inventors and auditors of discourse, as rhetorical bodies, and as dialogic interlocutors—each of which provides complementary understandings of how participants can be understood within participatory critical rhetoric research and how they assist in forming multiperspectival judgment. Finally, we discuss the ethics of participant interaction and how it challenges and decenters the traditional role of the critic.

In the conclusion, we synthesize our discussion in each of these chapters and consider some of the implications of this approach for rhetorical study. We also use the conclusion to address practical and logistical aspects of doing participatory critical rhetoric. Although this book is not meant to be an instructional "how to" method book, we recognize the importance of sharing our insights into the actual practice of this approach. Finally, we identify some of the challenges that we continue to struggle with as we theorize our engagement with the field.

Ultimately, we hope that this book serves as both a resource and catalyst for continued engagement with fieldwork by rhetorical theorists and critics. Climate change and homelessness activism, performances of material rhetoric in national parks, health advocacy in drug communities, and the many other fields of everyday and extraordinary, embodied and emplaced rhetorical practice can offer valuable insights into the inner-workings of rhetorical communities. Participatory critical rhetoric offers an approach and set of interrelated tools and practices for tapping into these insights that have the potential to enhance the field's understanding of rhetoric's fundamental role in the lives of communities, large and small, that we inhabit.

NOTES

1. Danielle Endres, Leah M. Sprain, and Tarla Rai Peterson, eds., *Social Movement to Address Climate Change: Local Steps for Global Action* (Amherst, NY: Cambria Press, 2009).

2. Michael K. Middleton, "'SafeGround Sacramento' and Rhetorics of Substantive Citizenship," *Western Journal of Communication* 78 (2014): 1–15, doi:10.1080/10570314.2013.835064; Michael K. Middleton, "Housing, Not Handcuffs: Homeless Misrecognition and 'SafeGround Sacramento's' Homeless Activism," *Communication, Culture & Critique* (2014): 320–37, doi: 10.1111/cccr.12055.

3. Samantha Senda-Cook, "Rugged Practices: Embodying Authenticity in Outdoor Recreation," *Quarterly Journal of Speech* 98 (2012): 129–52, doi: 10.1080/00335630.2012.663500; Samantha Senda-Cook, "Materializing Tensions: How Maps and Trails Mediate Nature," *Environmental Communication: A Journal of Nature and Culture* 7 (2013): 355–71, doi:10.1080/17524032.2013.792854.

4. Aaron Hess, "Critical-Rhetorical Ethnography: Rethinking the Place and Process of Rhetoric," *Communication Studies* 62 (2011): 127–52, doi: 10.1080/10510974.2011.529750.

5. See, for example: Carole Blair, "Contemporary US Memorial Sites as Exemplars of Rhetoric's Materiality," in *Rhetorical Bodies,* eds. Jack Selzer and Sharon Crowley (Madison: University of Wisconsin Press, 1999): 16–57; Carole Blair, "Reflections on Criticism and Bodies: Parables from Public Places," *Western Journal of Communication* 65 (2001): 271–94, doi: 10.1080/10570310109374706; Carole Blair, Marsha S. Jeppeson, and Enrico Pucci Jr., "Public Memorializing in Postmodernity: The Vietnam Veterans Memorial as Prototype," *Quarterly Journal of Speech* 77 (1991): 263–88, doi: 10.1080/00335639109383960; Greg Dickinson, "Memories for Sale: Nostalgia and the Construction of Identity in Old Pasadena," *Quarterly Journal of Speech* 83 (1997): 1–27, doi: 10.1080/00335639709384169; Greg Dickinson, "Joe's Rhetoric: Finding Authenticity at Starbucks," *Rhetoric Society Quarterly* 32 (2002): 5–27, doi: 10.1080/02773940209391238; Greg Dickinson, "The Pleasantville Effect: Nostalgia and the Visual Framing of (White) Suburbia," *Western Journal of Communication* 70 (2006): 212–33, doi: 10.1080/10570310600843504; Greg Dickinson, Brian L. Ott, and Eric Aoki, "Memory and Myth at the Buffalo Bill Museum," *Western Journal of Communication* 69 (2005): 85–108, doi: 10.1080/10570310500076684; Greg Dickinson, Brian L. Ott, and Eric Aoki, "Spaces of Remembering and Forgetting: The Reverent Eye/I at the Plains Indian Museum," *Communication and Critical/Cultural Studies* 3 (2006): 27–47, doi: 10.1080/14791420500505619; Endres, et. al eds., *Social Movement to Address Climate Change*; Leah Sprain, Danielle Endres, and Tarla Rai Petersen, "Research as a Transdisciplinary Networked Process: A Metaphor for Difference-Making Research," *Communication Monographs* 77 (2010): 441–44, doi: 10.1080/03637751.2010.523600; Danielle Endres, Leah Sprain, and Tarla Rai Peterson, "The Imperative of Praxis-Based Environmental Communication Research: Suggestions from the Step It Up 2007 National Research Project," *Environmental Communication: A Journal of Nature and Culture* 2 (2008): 237–45, doi: 10.1080/17524030802141794; Danielle Endres and Samantha Senda-Cook,

"Location Matters: The Rhetoric of Place in Protest," *Quarterly Journal of Speech* 97 (2011): 257–82, doi: 10.1080/00335630.2011.585167; Mindy Fenske, "Movement and Resistance: (Tattooed) Bodies and Performance," *Communication and Critical/Cultural Studies* 4 (2007): 51–73, doi: 10.1080/14791420601138302; Mindy Fenske, "The Movement of Interpretation: Conceptualizing Performative Encounters with Multimediated Performance," *Text and Performance Quarterly* 26 (2006): 138–61, doi: 10.1080/10462930500517907; Mindy Fenske, "The Aesthetic of the Unfinished: Ethics and Performance," *Text and Performance Quarterly* 24 (2004): 1–19, doi: 10.1080/1046293042000239447; Marouf Hasian and Rulon Wood, "Critical Museology, (Post)Colonial Communication, and the Gradual Mastering of Traumatic Pasts at the Royal Museum for Central Africa (RMCA)," *Western Journal of Communication* 74 (2010): 128–49, doi: 10.1080/10570311003614484; Bryan Hubbard and Marouf A. Hasian Jr., "Atomic Memories of the Enola Gay: Strategies of Remembrance at the National Air and Space Museum," *Rhetoric & Public Affairs* 1 (1998): 363–85, doi: 10.1353/rap.2010.0084; Tamar Katriel, "Rhetoric in Flames: Fire Inscriptions in Israeli Youth Movement Ceremonials," *Quarterly Journal of Speech* 73 (1987): 444–59, doi: 10.1080/00335638709383818; Tamar Katriel, "'Our Future is Where our Past Is': Studying Heritage Museums as Ideological and Performative Arenas," *Communication Monographs* 60 (1993): 69–75, doi:10.1080/03637759309376296; Samuel McCormick, "Earning One's Inheritance: Rhetorical Criticism, Everyday Talk, and the Analysis of Public Discourse," *Quarterly Journal of Speech* 89 (2003): 109–31, doi: 10.1080/00335630308176; Phaedra C. Pezzullo, "Resisting 'National Breast Cancer Awareness Month': The Rhetoric of Counterpublics and Their Cultural Performances," *Quarterly Journal of Speech* 89 (2003): 345–65, doi:10.1080/00335 63032000160981; Phaedra C. Pezzullo, "Performing Critical Interruptions: Stories, Rhetorical Invention, and the Environmental Justice Movement," *Western Journal of Communication* 65 (2001): 1–25, doi:10.1080/10570310109374689; Phaedra C. Pezzullo, "Touring 'Cancer Alley,' Louisiana: Performances of Community and Memory for Environmental Justice," *Text and Performance Quarterly* 23 (2003): 226–52, doi:10.1080/10462930310001635295; Phaedra C. Pezzullo, "Tourists and/as Disasters: Rebuilding, Remembering, and Responsibility in New Orleans," *Tourist Studies* 9 (2009): 23–41, doi: 10.1177/1468797609360591; Senda-Cook, "Materializing Tensions"; Senda-Cook "Rugged Practices"; Peter Simonson, "The Streets of Laredo: Mercurian Rhetoric and the Obama Campaign," *Western Journal of Communication* 74 (2010): 94–126, doi:10.1080/10570310903466045; Kenneth S. Zagacki and Victoria J. Gallagher, "Rhetoric and Materiality in the Museum Park at the North Carolina Museum of Art," *Quarterly Journal of Speech* 95 (2009): 171–91, doi:10.1080/00335630902842087.

6. Dwight Conquergood, "Rethinking Ethnography: Towards a Critical Cultural Politics," *Communication Monographs* 58 (1991): 179–94, doi: 10.1080/03637759109376222; Dwight Conquergood, "Ethnography, Rhetoric, and Performance," *Quarterly Journal of Speech* 78 (1992): 80–97, doi: 10.1080/00335639209 383982; Fenske, "Movement and Resistance"; Kent A. Ono and John M. Sloop, "The Critique of Vernacular Discourse," *Communication Monographs* 62 (1995): 19–46, doi: 0.1080/03637759509376346; Kevin Michael DeLuca, "Unruly Arguments: The Body

Rhetoric of Earth First!, Act Up, and Queer Nation," *Argumentation and Advocacy* 36 (1999): 9–21; Kevin Michael DeLuca and Jennifer Peeples, "From Public Sphere to Public Screen: Democracy, Activism, and the 'Violence' of Seattle," *Critical Studies in Media Communication* 19 (2002): 125–51, doi: 10.1080/07393180216559; Steve Whitson and John Poulakos, "Nietzsche and the Aesthetics of Rhetoric," *Quarterly Journal of Speech* 79 (1993): 131–45, doi:10.1080/00335639309384025; Raymie E. McKerrow, "Critical Rhetoric: Theory and Praxis," *Communication Monographs* 56 (1989): 91–111, doi: 10.1080/03637758909390253; Ronald Walter Greene, "Another Materialist Rhetoric," *Critical Studies in Media Communication* 15 (1998): 21–40, doi: 10.1080/15295039809367031; Dana L. Cloud, "The Materiality of Discourse as Oxymoron: A Challenge to Critical Rhetoric," *Western Journal of Communication* 58 (1994): 141–63, doi: 10.1080/10570319409374493.

7. Bryant Keith Alexander, "Fading, Twisting, and Weaving: An Interpretive Ethnography of the Black Barbershop as Cultural Space," *Qualitative Inquiry* 9 (2003): 105–28, doi:10.1177/1077800402239343; Bryant Keith Alexander, *Performing Black Masculinity: Race, Culture, and Queer Identity* (Lanham, MD: AltaMira Press, 2006); Bryant Keith Alexander, "Performance Ethnography: The Reenacting and Inciting of Culture," *The Sage Handbook of Qualitative Research* 3 (2005): 411–42; Michael S. Bowman, "Killing Dillinger: A Mystery," *Text and Performance Quarterly* 20 (2000): 342–74, doi: 10.1080/10462930009366309; Frederick C. Corey and Thomas K. Nakayama, "Sextext," *Text and Performance Quarterly* 17 (1997): 58–68, doi: 10.1080/10462939709366169; Fenske, "Movement and Resistance"; Fenske, "The Movement of Interpretation"; Mindy Fenske, "The Aesthetic of the Unfinished: Ethics and Performance," *Text and Performance Quarterly* 24 (2004): 1–19, doi:10 .1080/1046293042000239447; Ragan Fox, "Skinny bones# 126–774-835–29: Thin Gay Bodies Signifying a Modern Plague," *Text and Performance Quarterly* 27 (2007): 3–19, doi: 10.1080/10462930601045956; Ragan Fox, "Re-membering Daddy: Autoethnographic Reflections of My Father and Alzheimer's Disease," *Text and Performance Quarterly* 30 (2010): 3–20, doi:10.1080/10462930903366969; Ragan Fox, "Tales of a Fighting Bobcat: An 'Auto-archaeology' of Gay Identity Formation and Maintenance," *Text and Performance Quarterly* 30 (2010): 122–42, doi: 10.1080/10462931003650153; Ragan Fox, "'Ragan Fox is a Gay Slam Poet': An Autobiographical Exploration of Performance Poetry's Performative Implications," *Text and Performance Quarterly* 30 (2010): 420–29, doi:10.1080/10462937.2010.508535; Elyse Pineau, "Nursing Mother and Articulating Absence," *Text and Performance Quarterly* 20 (2000): 1–19, doi: 10.1080/10462930009366280.

8. Michael Calvin McGee, "Text, Context, and the Fragmentation of Contemporary Culture," *Western Journal of Speech Communication* 54 (1990): 274–89, doi: 10.1080/10570319009374343; McKerrow, "Critical Rhetoric"; Philip Wander, "The Third Persona: An Ideological Turn in Rhetorical Theory," *Central States Speech Journal* 35 (1984): 197–216, doi: 10.1080/10510978409368190.

9. McCormick, "Earning One's Inheritance"; Ono and Sloop, "Critique of Vernacular Discourse"; Kent A. Ono and John M. Sloop, "Critical Rhetorics of Controversy," *Western Journal of Communication* 63 (1999): 526–38, doi:10.1080/10570319909374657; John M. Sloop, and Kent A. Ono, "Out-law Discourse:

The Critical Politics of Material Judgment," *Philosophy & Rhetoric* 30 (1997): 50–69; Kent A. Ono and John M. Sloop, *Shifting Borders: Rhetoric, Immigration, and California's Proposition 187* (Philadelphia: Temple University Press, 2002).

10. While we craft this approach with a foundation in critical rhetoric, we believe field-based approaches could prove useful for all rhetorical critics. That said, we also believe that theorizing outside of this critical rhetorical foundation is beyond the scope of this book.

11. Middleton et al., "Articulating Rhetorical Field Methods"; Hess, "Critical-Rhetorical Ethnography."

12. Hess, "Critical-Rhetorical Ethnography," 128.

13. Middleton et al., "Articulating Rhetorical Field Methods," 388.

14. Hess, "Critical-Rhetorical Ethnography," 128.

15. As we discuss in chapter 4, we use place/space to refer to the mutually constitutive relationship between semi-bounded places and more generalized spatial practices.

16. Carole Blair, Greg Dickenson, and Brian L. Ott, "Introduction: Rhetoric/Memory/Place," in *Places of Public Memory: The Rhetoric of Museums and Memorials,* eds. Greg Dickenson, Carole Blair, and Brian L. Ott (Tuscaloosa: University of Alabama Press, 2010): 2.

17. Darrel Enck-Wanzer, "Trashing the System: Social Movement, Intersectional Rhetoric, and Collective Agency in the Young Lords Organization's Garbage Offensive," *Quarterly Journal of Speech* 92 (2006): 174–201, doi: 10.1080/00335630600816920.

18. Ibid, 180.

19. Elinor Light, "The (Em)Placed Vernacular: Rhetorics of Control and Transgression in the American City," (PhD diss., University of Utah, 2015).

20. Kent A. Ono and John M. Sloop, "Commitment to a *Telos*: A Sustained Critical Rhetoric," *Communication Monographs* 59 (1992): 48, doi:10.1080/03637759209376248.

21. Middleton, "'SafeGround Sacramento'"; Middleton, "Housing, Not Handcuffs."

22. Daniel C. Brouwer and Aaron Hess, "Making Sense of 'God Hates Fags' and 'Thank God for 9/11': A Thematic Analysis of Milbloggers' Responses to Reverend Fred Phelps and the Westboro Baptist Church," *Western Journal of Communication* 71 (2007): 69–90, doi:10.1080/10570310701215388; Art Herbig and Aaron Hess, "Convergent Critical Rhetoric at the 'Rally to Restore Sanity': Exploring the Intersection of Rhetoric, Ethnography, and Documentary Production," *Communication Studies 63* (2012), 269–89, doi:10.1080/10510974.2012.674617; Hess, "Critical-Rhetorical Ethnography"; Aaron Hess and Art Herbig, "Recalling the Ghosts of 9/11: Convergent Memorializing at the Opening of the National 9/11 Memorial," *International Journal of Communication* 7 (2013): 2207–30.

23. Endres and Senda-Cook, "Location Matters"; Danielle Endres, Deborah Cox Callister, Autumn Garrison, Samantha Senda-Cook, Julie Kalil Schutten, "Step What Up?: The Rhetorical Framing of Salt Lake City's Step It Up Events," in *Social Movement to Address Climate Change: Local Steps for Global Action*, eds. Danielle Endres, Leah Sprain, and Tarla Rai Peterson (Amherst, NY: Cambria Press, 2009), 117–46; Endres, Sprain, and Peterson, *Social Movement to Address*; Endres, Sprain,

and Peterson, "The Imperative of Praxis-Based"; Danielle Endres, "Environmental Oral History," *Environmental Communication: A Journal of Nature and Culture* 5 (2011): 485–98, doi: 10.1080/17524032.2011.610810; Danielle Endres, Brian Cozen, Megan O'Byrne, and Andrea Feldpausch-Parker, "Putting the U in Carbon Capture and Storage: Performances of Rupture within the CCS Scientific Community, in *Communication for the Commons: Revisiting Participation and Environment,* eds., Mark S. Meisner, Nadarajah Sriskandarajah, and Stephen P. Depoe (Turtle Island: The International Environmental Communication Association, 2015), 320–31.

24. Endres and Senda-Cook, "Location Matters"; Endres et al., "Step What Up?"; Danielle Endres, Samantha Senda-Cook, and Brian Cozen, "Not Just a Place to Park Your Car: Park(ing) as Spatial Argument," *Argumentation and Advocacy* 50 (2014): 121–140; Samantha Senda-Cook, "Rugged Practices: Embodying Authenticity in Outdoor Recreation," *Quarterly Journal of Speech* 98 (2012): 129–52, doi: 10.1080/00335630.2012.663500; Samantha Senda-Cook, "Materializing Tensions: How Maps and Trails Mediate Nature," *Environmental Communication: A Journal of Nature and Culture* 7 (2013): 355–71, doi:10.1080/17524032.2013.792854; Samantha Senda-Cook and Danielle Endres, "A Place of One's Own," in *Environmental Rhetoric and Ecologies of Place*, ed. Peter Goggin (London: Routledge, 2013), 143–54; Samantha Senda-Cook, Michael Middleton, and Danielle Endres, "Interrogating the 'Field' of Rhetorical Field Methods," for *Connecting Textual Criticism and Field Work*, National Communication Association Conference, Washington, DC November 2013; Samantha Senda-Cook, Michael Middleton, and Danielle Endres, "Rhetorical Cartographies: (Re)Mapping Urban Spaces," Conference on Communication and the Environment, Boulder, CO, June 2015.

Chapter 1

Theorizing Participatory Critical Rhetoric

In recent years, rhetorical scholars have increasingly turned to fieldwork to access new forms of rhetorical practice. For example, rhetorical critics have explored how places/spaces of rhetorical interaction both act as a constraint on the rhetorical exchanges that happen in them, as well as how place/space itself can function rhetorically to shape the meanings made by its inhabitants.[1] Others have taken up questions of the rhetorical force of intensely affective, embodied, and aesthetic dimensions of rhetorical practices.[2] These varying forms of field-based rhetorical theory and criticism reveal the insights available to critics that enact an embodied presence, placing themselves at and in emergent sites of *in situ* rhetorical invention. Indeed, a review of contemporary rhetorical research would suggest that the discipline has become fixated on efforts to begin rethinking the purpose of rhetorical criticism, the subject of rhetorical action, the role of audiences in rhetorical exchange, the responsibilities of the critic, and other dimensions of rhetorical study that promise to alter the way scholars think about rhetorical theory and criticism.[3] The growing field-based turn in rhetorical theory and criticism plays a significant role in this rethinking.

At the same time, much of this move toward accounting for mundane, everyday, and (extra)ordinary rhetorical practice through field-based practices has developed in irregular flurries of activity and around an *ad hoc* set of critical experiments involving, in many cases, the use of qualitative and ethnographic research epistemologies and tools. While this critical mass of scholarship indicates that many rhetoricians recognize the value such practices can contribute to theorizing rhetoric, few efforts have been made to synthesize and develop programmatic approaches to, or sustained theoretical explorations of, this new form of critical inquiry, that is, field-based methods within rhetoric. As a consequence, rhetorical critics fashion critical practices by combining a menagerie of tools developed by qualitative, ethnographic, performance, and other scholars with the instruments of rhetorical criticism. An increasingly robust set of scholarship employs various forms of participatory methods to gain access to and analyze different forms of rhetoric. Yet, we see a need to enhance this scholarship with a more sustained inquiry into the methodological and theoretical possibilities and problems of field-based rhetorical approaches. Participatory critical rhetoric is our attempt to hone in on and expand on some of the unique contributions that come from the field-based turn in rhetorical studies.

In this chapter, we deepen our definition of participatory critical rhetoric by outlining its key theoretical underpinnings and underlying assumptions. We argue that critical rhetoric has prompted critics to reconsider the central elements of rhetorical criticism and in turn provides the foundation for participatory critical rhetoric. We retrace the shifts in understanding of basic elements of rhetorical theory (text, rhetor, critic, and audience) to establish a disciplinary context for participatory critical rhetoric. Then, we examine some of the key assumptions that orient participatory critical rhetoric as we conceive it. We conclude the chapter by considering the contributions that participatory critical rhetoric can offer to critical rhetorical studies.

CRITICAL TURNS: RETHINKING TEXTS, RHETORS, CRITICS, AND AUDIENCES

The critical turn in rhetorical studies initiated by Michael Calvin McGee, Raymie McKerrow, Phillip Wander and others activated a fundamental rethinking of the epistemological assumptions of rhetorical research.[4] Central to the theoretical foment generated by this turn have been efforts to grapple with basic elements of rhetorical theorizing, especially what constitutes rhetorical action (texts and contexts), who counts as and what is the relationship between the doers and scholars of rhetoric (rhetors and critics), and what role is played by those who are witness to rhetorical action (audiences). Theorizing participatory critical rhetoric necessitates that we traverse these same questions to interrogate how its practitioners engage with the ephemeral nature of everyday rhetoric, interact with the audiences of those emplaced rhetorical practices, and attempt to navigate the ethical and critical challenges posed by rhetorics that are encountered immanently in the field rather than as after-the-fact texts.[5] This section traces some of the lines of theoretical development that inform our thinking about these questions as they relate to participatory critical rhetoric.

The Text

A fundamental tension and a critical locus of theory development since the critical turn has been the nature of the text. Traditionally, a text was conceived as an oratorical speech and rhetorical scholars looked to the text with the belief that a close reading would reveal its intentions, persuasiveness, effect, and historical relevance.[6] Indeed, for Herbert Wichelns, although informed by history and extrinsic contextual elements, the text is a finite construction in the form of a speech provided at an occasion for a particular audience to be measured for its intrinsic form and content.[7] Following this lead, the text of a speech remained of preeminent importance for rhetorical scholars for decades as classical principles were applied through neo-Aristotelian criticism.[8] Lloyd Bitzer's and Richard Vatz's contributions to rhetoric through the examination of rhetorical situations reaffirm the commitment that the text of the speech, while understood in more robust ways through contextualization, is a relatively stable object on which rhetorical inquiry should be centered.[9] Critics seeking to understand the nature of a persuasive attempt or some other element of rhetoric would examine the text through close textual engagement while considering the conceptual context of the text as a contributing, but not central, focus of their analysis.[10] Moreover, traditional approaches to rhetoric examine (and appreciate) texts that represent the "great speakers" of a historical period, with the idea that exposure to such grand texts promises pedagogical outcomes ranging from career advancement to improving the citizenry.

However, beginning with rhetoric's ideological turn, theorists began to contend that the text it informed by a host of influences that exceed those isolated by close textual analysis and, as a consequence, the boundaries and characteristics of the "rhetorical text" became a contested topic. Bucking the traditional model of the stable rhetorical text, McGee theorizes the text's fragmentation in the midst of "radical change[s]" in the postmodern human condition, arguing that a text is merely a "dense reconstruction" of fragments—other bits of discourse—pulled together by critics.[11] The fragmentation of texts placed professional critics of rhetoric in the role of an inventor of "text[s] suitable for criticism."[12] This argument provoked a windfall of new approaches to rhetorical inquiry accented with postmodern and poststructural sensibilities and an expanded notion of texts beyond speeches. For example, Carole Blair, Marsha S. Jeppeson, and Enrico Pucci Jr. examine the Vietnam Veterans Memorial, which they argue does not constitute a stable text, but one that "changes materially over time" due to artifacts and objects left at the memorial that offer a form of "supplemental rhetorical activity."[13] In short, they and others develop McGee's notion that texts do not have natural, unproblematic, finite boundaries that define the beginnings, middles, and ends of discourse. They are, instead, messy, fuzzy, and incomplete, necessitating a critical approach that actively engages with the contexts of discourse in practice and that draws together a meaningful text for analysis.

As a consequence of these shifts, critics began to look to different locations for meaningful rhetorical activity warranting critical analysis. One strain of these efforts emerged from the focus on vernacular discourses advocated by a range of rhetorical critics.[14] For example, Kent Ono and John Sloop critique mainstream rhetorical criticism for its "critical focus on the discourse of the empowered, discourse of those who control, design, and create the public space."[15] In its place, they argue for increased critical attention to be given to vernacular discourses represented in "everyday speech, conversations in homes, restaurants, and 'on the corner.'"[16] Other critics joined this call for a reconsideration of the choices made about what texts ought to draw the attention of scholars by questioning whether a stable, public address could ever be properly isolated.[17] For example, Gerard Hauser argues that the text is not merely the performance of one speaker or author. Rather, he contends that the text "is the dialogue" found in response to a speaker or author, which is "often scattered and inchoate in its form."[18] These major shifts in thinking about the rhetorical text extend McGee's thesis and further reshape our understanding of the text of rhetorical criticism.

More recently, rhetoricians have problematized the dominance of verbal texts by engaging material forms of rhetoric; affective, aesthetic, embodied, and performative dimensions of rhetoric; and mediated bodily forms of rhetoric. One thread of this challenge emerges from critics concerned with the materiality of rhetoric. Materiality is a contested term in rhetorical studies. For some, a materialist approach to rhetoric refers to a set of concerns that form the cultural, social, political, and economic conditions of rhetoric, and in this view rhetoric variously inhabits, reveals, and obfuscates these conditions.[19] Others taking a constitutive approach see discourse as material in and of itself, insofar as it constructs the social realities inhabited by audiences and rhetoricians; that is, rhetoric makes material that which it names.[20] For others still, the answer lies somewhere in between; rhetoric is not exclusively material but it shapes the conditions of possibility with which material realities are engaged.[21] And, for some rhetorical scholars, rhetoric is always both symbolic and material—embedded in the structure of memorials, the movements of tourists, and the words of a speaker issued from a specific place at a specific time before a specific audience.[22] Taken together, the critical turn in rhetoric, then, has sensitized critics to the ways in which material dimensions of rhetoric shape everyday rhetorical practices and their consequences.[23]

Alongside this focus on materiality, the critical turn has also tuned rhetorical scholarship to the affective, aesthetic, embodied, and performative dimensions of rhetoric to challenge the dominance of the verbal rhetorical text.

Consistent with McKerrow's call for a "corporeal rhetoric" that presences "[rhetoric's] practice in . . . lived experience," scholars have pursued efforts to understand how rhetoric exerts influence through affect and pleasure as much as it does through argument and reason.[24] Several strains of theorizing contribute to reconfiguring conceptualizations of the text to account for its affective, embodied and performative dimensions.[25] Ronald Walter Greene summarizes the potential of an "aesthetic rhetoric" that "counts on, attends to, and takes into account the body and its senses"[26] when he argues that taking seriously such embodied practices reveals how rhetorical actions (embodied and textual) "generate 'fictions' or worlds that subjects might inhabit."[27]

Other critics have challenged the dominance of verbal texts in light of media systems. Kevin DeLuca sees the construction of "image events," bodily and visual displays often disseminated through mass media for public consumption, as inherent to the character of contemporary rhetoric. He argues that, "often, image events revolve around images of bodies—vulnerable bodies, dangerous bodies, ludicrous bodies, transfigured bodies. These political bodies constitute a nascent body rhetoric that deploys bodies as a pivotal resource for the crucial practice of public argumentation."[28] In expanding this bodily rhetoric, DeLuca and Jennifer Peeples turn toward the public screen as a concept that informs—eclipses perhaps—the public sphere. In this sense, bodily rhetoric was performed for the camera. In the public screen, texts are (re)mediated as bodily performance and rhetoric is understood through a logic of media spectacle.[29] Developing this idea further, Art Herbig and Aaron Hess call on rhetorical critics to include the nature of textual production through media within the act of criticism, saying that "scholarship must attempt to incorporate the production practices that are central to how these texts are created as part of our investigation of how they function in public discourses."[30] In this way, rhetorical criticism should not only reflect on media practices and how they contribute to textual production, but also participate in the media structures and production elements under investigation.

Although I was interested in "extra-textual" forms of rhetoric, as I thought of them then, I had little experience conducting fieldwork before I started my PhD program. The idea of rhetorically analyzing physical places, bodies, and behaviors appealed to me. And, accessing these material forms of rhetoric through fieldwork, interviews, focus groups, and oral histories made sense to me. When Danielle Endres invited me to join her research team to critique the Step It Up campaign, I saw it as a good opportunity to learn how to use these methods.

I had attended protests in the past, and my expectation for the Step It Up event at the Salt Lake City and County Building was that participants would be listening to speakers, holding signs, chanting or singing, and contributing to a visual spectacle in the hopes of getting Congress's attention. Therefore, I was surprised to find pizza vendors, beer tents, and a children's bounce house inside a fenced-off area with a sign that advertised the event as a "free concert." Our research team decided to attend Step It Up events all across the country because we suspected that they would provide insight into how contemporary social movements took different forms. Additionally, being present at the events would give us a chance to access a myriad of rhetorical discourses such as the spaces themselves and the actions of participants. Before we even entered the fenced-off area, we were all taking notes about what we saw, smelled, and heard. Although the whiffs of food and the hum of a generator were mere fragments of rhetorical messages, they came together with many other elements to create a meaning for this place and time, one that did not seem to align exactly with the stated goal of Step It Up actions.

Knowing that the recordings, fieldnotes, and photographs we gathered that day would be the artifacts that we analyzed later, I took care to write as much as I could about the stage, police, letter-to-Congress/T-shirt give-away tent, and hula-hoops. Everything seemed potentially important because we knew we were interested in many different kinds of rhetoric. Turning a critical eye toward not only the written and spoken messages, I recorded what the place looked like, who was present, what they were doing, where they gathered, and, how I felt.

Reflecting about this experience, I realize that documenting an ephemeral event like this makes me conscious of how my decisions shape a research project right from the beginning. Like in conventional rhetorical criticism, my attention was necessarily drawn to some things and not others. But, in this case, instead of only seeing the news reports that followed the event or the website that helped organizers get ready, I had singers and speakers to hear, a layout of the event to draw, and people to interview.

Being present at the event meant that I had a chance to check my perceptions against what other people said they perceived. Each of the members of the research team interviewed a number of people to get a sense of what "step it up," meant to them, why they attended the event, and what their expectations were going in. I talked to only one group of people who seemed ready for a protest event. Carrying their signs with sayings like, "no blood for oil," they seemed out of place. The incongruity between their embodied unmet expectations (i.e., slouched against a tree with their signs resting on the ground) and the material reality around them revealed not only all their assumptions about what protest events look like and do but also about the strategies of the organizers and what they hoped to accomplish.

At the end of the day, we had five researchers' worth of fieldnotes, photographs, recordings, and interviews that we then needed to analyze. Putting all of these documents in conversations with one another created a complex rhetorical picture, full of fragments and conflicts, of which we needed to make some sense. Although this was challenging, in this case, it exposed differences and nuances that we would have missed had we not had the opportunity to participate and observe.

—Samantha

Taken together, these lines of material, affective, aesthetic, and embodied rhetoric reveal a "text" that refuses to be pinned down and that exceeds the confines of "things made [merely] with words."[31] As Samantha experienced, this expanded notion of text provokes the need for a critical rhetorical practice that participates in and experiences everyday intersectional rhetorics, that engages with the force of rhetorical action that operates through visceral sensations of affect and pleasure, that relies on the body as a rhetorical asset, and that recognizes the meaningfulness of the improvisational choices of rhetors engaged in *in situ* rhetorical contexts. Doing so makes for a complex, multilayered critical challenge for rhetorical critics whose interests direct them away from traditional rhetorical texts and critical approaches. It highlights the challenge generated when attempting to answer to questions about how one textualizes ephemeral rhetorical activity. Participatory critical rhetoric provides a means to engage with this rhetorical space. In the chapters that follow, we highlight some of the ways that participatory critical rhetoric extends this challenge and offers examples of how critics might (con)textualize everyday rhetorical activity.

The Rhetor

Interrogating the nature of the text also problematizes the conventional origin of rhetorical texts: the rhetor. Traditionally, theorizing about the nature of a speaker led to an agent-centered focus in rhetoric. Rhetorical critics typically defined rhetors as particular speakers, located in history, and driven by particular motives.[32] These rhetor-agents are typically privileged, or at least well recognized.[33] The larger ideological turn in rhetoric marks one of the primary efforts to problematize this notion of the rhetor. Edwin Black, in his critique of neo-Aristotelian criticism, contends that a rhetor-centered approach does not "account for the influence of the discourse on its author: the future commitments it makes for him [*sic*], rhetorically and ideologically . . . the public image it portrays to which he [*sic*] must adjust."[34] In other words, contextualizing the rhetor within and against potential ideological influences or commitments changed the ways rhetoricians understood speakers' motives from unproblematically self-directed to a product of myriad influences.

Beginning in 2009, I embarked on the first of what would be several trips to spend time among those organizing against the conditions of homelessness they faced in Sacramento. Over the following eighteen months, I would spend several weeks with the organizers, participants, critics, and supporters of SafeGround whose efforts were aimed at improving the conditions faced by homeless persons. Their efforts were aimed both at changing public perceptions of homelessness and reforming municipal laws that harmed or, in their view, violated the human rights of the area's homeless population. They endeavored, as they put it, to ensure, "everyone has a place to be."

As I spent more time learning about SafeGround and from its members about their rhetorical and political struggle, the sheer complexity and expansiveness of their rhetorical campaign became increasingly evident. SafeGround members regularly contributed to local mainstream media, articulating their political agenda and their rhetorical campaign through editorials in the Sacramento Bee, *offering interviews on local AM radio programming, e.g., Capitol Radio, and developing content for the local homeless newspaper which was staffed by many of their current and former members and allies. In addition, members of SafeGround participated in the creation of independent media, including working with a filmmaker producing a documentary about homelessness and their particular efforts at forming a successful social movement aimed at addressing conditions of homelessness. Still other members of SafeGround lobbied city hall through a weekly campaign of public comments at regularly scheduled meetings; some members of SafeGround even served in advisory roles or as board members of local organizations working to improve services and other concerns related to the areas homeless population.*

The more time I spent talking to, marching with, and learning from members of SafeGround, the more apparent it became that their efforts challenged many of the more conventional assumptions of rhetorical inquiry. There was no single spokesperson or group of spokespersons who crafted and disseminated the group's message to a broader public (although, the members of the group did refer to some of their colleagues as "soapbox elder" as a way of indicating that they were particularly skilled or frequently engaged in helping spread the group's message). Instead, members of the group frequently moved in and out of roles of rhetor for the causes of the homeless community, audience to the efforts of other members and allies of SafeGround, and, sometimes, critics of the rhetorical efforts of some of their peers. In a similar fashion, others, like myself, who were drawn to SafeGround for various reasons, including academic inquiry, were often recruited to join the ranks of those speaking in support or on behalf of SafeGround's interest. In fact, during my time researching SafeGround, at least one other academic who lived in the local community spent significant amounts of time with the group, eventually becoming an official member and spokesperson for the group while continuing their academic pursuits.

After leaving the field and with the time to reflect on this vibrant and constantly shifting network of rhetorical productivity that fostered the efforts of SafeGround, it became apparent that the long-standing conventions of rhetorical inquiry would not adequately capture the rich and active rhetorical processes that sustained the homeless activists from which I had learned. Their rhetorical efforts could not be isolated to one, or even a few, central rhetorical texts, instead percolating through a network of different efforts, ranging from protest marches and rallies to editorials to interviews to other even more mundane interactions and enactments. Likewise, isolating a single or even a few key rhetors would be impossible in an organization where at least a dozen individuals had held leadership positions during the time I was present. In the time since, I have relied on the insights offered by my participation in the field into how this complex rhetorical network functioned as I have begun to try to unpack the significance and lessons to be learned from the rhetorical efforts of the community of homeless activists who shared their time with me. Each effort reinforces that the move into the field and the engagement with live(d) rhetorics undoes and requires a rethinking of many of the assumptions that guide our efforts as theorists and critics of rhetorical practice.

—Michael

Michael's vignette demonstrates the challenges of an agent-centered conceptualization of rhetorical criticism. Laying the groundwork for participatory critical rhetoric approaches, McKerrow frames critical rhetoric as further decentering the speaker-oriented notion of the rhetor by reconceptualizing rhetoric as "discourse that addresses publics" rather than "public address."[35] In doing so, the critic shifts from a focus on deducing the motivations of the speaker-rhetor to a concern with "illuminat[ing] otherwise hidden or taken for granted social practices" in which rhetorical acts participate.[36]

Likewise, many theorists began to examine the nature of the rhetor within larger social structures, and especially within the public sphere.[37] While a Habermasian model of the public sphere theorizes a critical-rational rhetor whose bracketed speech is designed to alter, represent, and form public opinion in service of public good, many feminist scholars shifted their attention to speakers bound by social context, power, and inequalities manifest in decorum and style.[38] These subaltern counterpublics are marked primarily through status or identity concerns; they are "subordinated social groups—women, workers, peoples of color, and gays and lesbians."[39] Rather than considering the primary speaking motivations as tied to what or who these speakers are, often these rhetors are understood in relation to their social exclusions, or what *they are not*. Eschewing the bracketing of identity, counterpublic discourse embraces its "counter" status, focusing on the "varying degrees of exclusion from prominent channels of political discourse and a corresponding lack of political power" that shapes rhetorical action.[40] In short, before examining the nature of his or her speech, the rhetor is examined within larger social structures, acknowledged for his or her positionality, and often conceptualized as co-constituted with audiences as resistant to dominant discourses.[41] This view of the rhetor expands the critical challenge faced by participatory critical rhetoric scholars. Endeavoring to theorize and critique everyday rhetoric can leave critics without a speaker or even set of speakers who can be easily isolated, and without a clearly demarcated text for which those speakers are responsible or that rhetoricians can examine. This reality necessitates that critics engage the networks of rhetorical practice—as opposed to a single rhetor—that generate vernacular, counterpublic, marginal, and everyday discourses. Participatory critical rhetoric, as we theorize it, begins to unpack the complexities of acknowledging these rhetoric-producing networks and, as we address when we consider questions of critical embodiment and relations with participants, places critics themselves in these networks of rhetorical productivity.

The Critic

Participatory critical rhetoric also requires analyzing the nature of the critic as a contested *topos* activated by the critical turn in rhetorical studies. In traditional rhetorical methods, the critic is revered as the expert who evaluates the motivations, morals, and effectiveness of rhetors as evidenced in their great works. Black argues for the critic's public responsibility in criticism to provide a moral understanding (read as: a judgment about its motives) of discourse.[42] This privileging of the critic's ethos orients the act of criticism as speaking from expertise and objectivity regarding persuasion and aesthetics. Since the critical turn in rhetoric, critics have moved away from this position, embracing subjectivity and a relativistic understanding of their positions within the act of criticism.

Both McKerrow and McGee endeavor to reposition the critic as an inventor of discourses, engaged in a constant critique of power.[43] McGee rejects the position of a critic as an "independent agent" who performs the pedagogical exercise of judging excellence and failure in oratory.[44] McKerrow expresses concern that traditional modernist approaches valorize standards of excellence through a position of elitism—as "high priests of antiquity," in McGee's words[45]—believing that such approaches perpetuate "sterile forms of criticism."[46] In response, McKerrow's critical rhetoric asks the critic to engage in a constant critique of power relations, "looking toward a future yet unrealized."[47] A critic's method, for McKerrow, rejects proscribed approaches (e.g., neo-Aristotelian, Burkian pentad) to discourse and engages in a sustained practice coupled with a critical orientation concerned with ethical and political commitments. However, whereas traditional critics judge discourse based on its fulfillment of a set of rational rhetorical principles, critical rhetoricians turn their judgment toward how discourse advances or stymies the interest of marginalized communities.

Following McGee, the critic, motivated by these commitments, draws together from a sea of rhetorical fragments a text that reveals how meanings are constructed, held in place by power, and disrupted by interventions.[48] In this vein, the critic does not simply encounter texts to be explained, but instead constructs "texts suitable for criticism" that enact the enlivened form of critique envisioned by McKerrow.[49] As such, the critic becomes both an active and a politicized participant in rhetoric when engaging in the practice of criticism. Being a politicized critic does not remove ethics from criticism, but rather shifts the locus of ethical evaluation from what is or is not represented in the *great text* to the critical implications of the text as constructed by the critic. Consequently, the role of the critic necessitates self-awareness of one's own ethics and politics. This shift is also animated by the belief that "the critic must not pretend the critical practice is separate from its cultural context. Critics must see their work *in situ*—related to the circumstance, situation, and history of the artifact and its world."[50] As a consequence, "criticism should be moved nearer to the social and cultural communities from which [it] derives."[51] Taken together, critics, following rhetoric's ideological and critical turns, are both reflective of their own social positions and obligated to more closely attend to marginalized communities. Speaking with and within these communities, McKerrow contends that the critic operates much like Michel Foucault's *specific intellectuals*, who work within specific sites to secure justice for the oppressed and underprivileged.[52]

Public intellectualism also provides a model for rethinking the nature of the critical endeavor and toward what ends it ought to be directed. The possibility of rhetorical scholars serving as intellectuals within local communities or even on larger national or international stages offers rhetoric an opportunity for civic engagement beyond the halls of academia. Yet, the debate over what constitutes public intellectualism vacillates on the role of the intellectual as being housed in the classroom, the public sphere, or on the street,[53] as well as whether the public intellectual serves as an agent of justice[54] by producing intellectual work within philosophical situations,[55] or by rhetorically engaging audiences outside of academic institutions.[56] In any case, the role of the critic exists beyond texts and arguably beyond academia. The desire, for many rhetorical scholars, is to be able to position rhetorical theorizing in such a way as to affect larger public concerns or to influence smaller-scale social problems. They seek to reclaim a way for rhetorical criticism to contribute to the political imagination of the citizenry.[57] Participatory critical rhetoric enters this discussion of the public intellectual by providing a critical approach that enables critics to work in and with the communities they research in practical ways that have effects beyond descriptive or evaluative critiques of those communities. As we articulate in chapter 2, this shifts the role of the critic from one of critical scholar to that of activist-scholar engaged in immanent and material ways with the communities they research.

Related to this movement toward a more engaged, politically self-conscious form of critical inquiry, many scholars have overtly recognized and proclaimed the need for rhetorical critics to embrace the activist edge of rhetorical criticism. McKerrow calls for a critical rhetoric that recognizes rhetoricians in the role of producers who perform criticism and do rhetoric, while others have argued that critics have an obligation to work to unmask the power relations that underpin inequality, to involve themselves in the practices of resistance engaged in by the oppositional communities one studies, and to revive (or invent) contributions to social justice as a necessary component of critical rhetorical research.[58] As Stephen John Hartnett observes, traditional approaches to rhetorical criticism that do otherwise are a potential liability that abdicate the contributions that rhetoricians can make toward social justice. Instead, he pleads that critics should endeavor to "create pieces of moral clarity and writerly elegance wherein we demonstrate our central roles in enhancing democratic life" and that critics "pledge . . . to work for social justice and for personal growth, to be both radical in our demands and gentle in our demeanor, both outraged by inequality and oppression and joyous in our commitments to end them."[59] By embracing such an approach, participatory critical rhetoric demands that critics doing such work abandon critical perspectives "that place them above the world looking down" and adopt a critical sensibility that places them inside the "complexities and contradictions of the communities with whom they work and play."[60] As we address in the following chapters, the choice to work with and within local communities elevates the importance of the ethical, political, and moral considerations faced by the participatory rhetorical critic.

The Audience

The critical turn in rhetorical studies also challenges traditional assumptions about the nature and function of the audience by recognizing the active role it plays in the construction of rhetorical texts. Indeed, for McGee and McKerrow, the audience, or consumer of discourse, assumes a primary role in the task of constructing a rhetorical text by selecting fragments of meaning for a composite text that surpasses (and exposes) the limitations of the discourse of a single rhetor or rhetorical act.[61] The influence of this theoretical maneuver is evident in many of the shifts we describe above. Embedded in vernacular and counterpublic theories of texts and rhetors is the recognition that no single text can capture the meaning or map the contours of power in a particular situation. This maneuver acknowledges that, within these contexts, rhetorical meanings and rhetorical force/influence are exerted through the totality of rhetorical experiences that form vernacular communities and (counter) public spheres. Such recognition further emphasizes the active role of the audience in rhetorical practice.

In other words, if no rhetorical text can be invested with the same sort of significance it enjoyed prior to the critical turn, the negotiations of local communities that construct shared meanings by identifying significant fragments of discourse becomes an important focus of study. Previously held commitments to the stability of texts become challenged in light of audiences that may derive different meanings from texts as they are constructed.[62] That is, critics must take up an interest in how audiences act, how they construct meaning among themselves using the rhetorical resources to which they have or are denied access, and how those endeavors expand, extend, or sustain the rhetorical agency of audiences. One way that critics have accomplished this is by becoming part of the audience to directly observe rhetorical performances and the reaction to them by other audience members. When critics embody the dual role of researcher and audience member, they become decentered in making critical judgments as they gain firsthand knowledge of audiences' engagement with rhetorical practices, elevating the voices of others into the critical project. On the one hand, the critical turn eschews the notion of audience as the passive consumers of rhetorical texts in favor of an active role for the audience in the construction of meaning and the influence of power. On the other hand, critical rhetoric also recognizes the audience as part of the political stakes involved in the construction of rhetorical fragments (texts) by empowered rhetoricians. While it may be true that "no single finished text could possibly comprehend all perspectives on even a single human problem," it remains to be said that each text engages in a struggle over what the audience is or is not, as well as who counts as an appropriate or legitimate audience for that text and, by extension, a legitimate member of the rhetorical community that it envisions.[63]

Nonetheless, if the question of the audience is a political one insofar as it is constructed in and through discourse that names a *people*, then it is also a question of what audiences are excluded from particular texts, of who occupies the space of *non-people*, and of who provides the foil against which *the people* are named.[64] Certainly, neither inclusion nor exclusion is free from the influence of power; the act of constituting an audience simultaneously creates what that audience is not and, to be sure, draws boundaries that includes some and necessarily excludes others. However, in this operation, which Maurice Charland describes as constitutive rhetoric, both the included and excluded enjoy recognition as such.[65] Wander, on the other hand, explores the space of nonrecognition by encouraging critics to identify the "third persona" present in discourse. For Wander, the third persona is neither the rhetor (the "I" of discourse) nor the audience (the "you" of discourse), constructed or otherwise. Rather, it is the "it" that is objectified and alienated both in language and in the actual, material conditions that enable rhetorical subjects to speak for and about themselves. As he notes, "the third persona . . . refers to being negated," including a "negation [that] extends beyond the 'text' to include the ability to produce texts, to engage in discourse, to be heard in the public space."[66] As a consequence, Wander further nuances an understanding of audience as contingent, active, and politicized that is embedded in rhetoric's critical turn.

Rhetorical criticism necessarily must not only adopt techniques that recognize and account for the terrain of political struggle summarized in the term *audience*, but that also enable critics to glimpse the ways in which individuals and communities struggle to navigate questions of inclusion, exclusion, and recognition in the rhetorical practices to which they are subjected and in which they participate. Critics engaging in participatory critical rhetoric attempt to glimpse the audiences' experiences, evaluations, and judgments of rhetoric through observation and inquiry, offering audience members the chance to elaborate on the ways rhetors speak to, with, and about them. In chapter 5, we address this challenge in more detail as we meditate on the complex relationships that develop (and disintegrate) between critics and participants of rhetorical inquiry, explaining how, by joining audiences and by asking them about the effect of rhetorical performances, critics gain new perspectives and further develop their critical judgment.

KEY ASSUMPTIONS OF PARTICIPATORY CRITICAL RHETORIC

It is against this theoretical backdrop in rhetorical studies that we develop our theorization of participatory critical rhetoric. While we avoid advocating for a prescriptive technique, method, or set of procedures, we do contend that a few assumptions traverse the broad range of ways in which rhetorical scholars can engage with participatory critical rhetoric. In this section, we briefly address each of these assumptions.

Key Assumption 1: Texts are Embedded in Social Practices, Performances, and Contexts

Participatory critical rhetoric builds from the theoretical work that has deconstructed the notion of a stable text that records and makes available rhetorical practices to the expert critic after the fact. Instead, participatory critical rhetoric embraces the fragmentation of discourse and uses the insight gained from embodied participation in emplaced rhetoric to draw together meaningful fragments into a text suitable for criticism. This heightened commitment to contextually- and locally-informed rhetorical sensibilities as a guide for assembling a sketch of discourses that exert rhetorical force in local contexts emerges from the recognition by participatory critical rhetoricians that texts are embedded in social practices, performances, and material contexts. In other words, the *text* is a segmented concept that includes a composition of various fragments—fragments that are often illusively corporeal, spatial, experiential, and affective. While components of fieldwork generate *texts* in the form of fieldnotes and other documents, these are merely partial understandings of the complex nature of a social and rhetorical scene.

To understand rhetoric as a practice or part of a social practice is to recognize a double sense of the notion of practice. This means recognizing rhetorical action as fluid; productive of ideology, identity, and meaning; ordinary and taken for granted; and intertwined with materiality insofar as it is an embodied enactment.[67] It also encourages rhetoricians to see rhetoric in terms of *doing*; that is, rhetoric is engaged in by individuals and communities seeking to *do something* within the contexts they engage. Following Norman Fairclough, recognizing rhetoric as a part of social practice acknowledges that it is always constrained by the context from which it emerges, but that it is also constantly steeped with the potential to transform social structures, ideologies, and identities.[68]

Additionally, recognizing that texts are embedded in social practice requires the participatory critical rhetorician to make choices about how to textualize the *in situ*, embodied, emplaced, ephemeral rhetorical practices one encounters in the vernacular and counterpublic communities, as well as everyday spaces where participatory critical rhetorical research unfolds. To textualize a practice, Foucault reminds critics that they must account for those places where "what is said and what is done, rules imposed and reasons given, the planned and the taken for granted meet and interconnect."[69] The participatory critical rhetorician looks for these interconnections and encounters between contexts and rhetorical action by making use of participant observation, interviewing, focus groups, membership in the community, and other means available to gain a close-up view of how communities negotiate these intersections.

Finally, the scope of artifacts, utterances, and other rhetorical traces that inform the criticism of participatory critical rhetorical research expand beyond those used in traditional after-the-fact rhetorical criticism. Participatory critical rhetoric recognizes that in addition to analysis of verbal discourse "material culture is thus necessary for most social constructs. An adequate study of social interaction . . . depends on the incorporation of more material evidence," such as the sensuous, affective, embodied, and emplaced aspects of interaction.[70] To be clear, our conceptualization of rhetoric's materiality, following Blair, recognizes the materiality of rhetoric as operating on two intersecting planes.[71] In the first sense, we refer to rhetoric's materiality to highlight that, while a symbolic practice, rhetoric has material consequences that are infused with power.[72] That is to say, it can produce community where one fails to exist prior to its rhetorical enactment, it defines how we interact with spaces in ways that make them function differently, and it produces actions and judgments that have consequence in the world. In the second sense, we refer to the fact of rhetoric's materiality in and of itself. That is, symbolic, discursive consequences cannot be divorced from the material scene of their enactment (i.e., a protest speech is not simply a text, but rather a gathering of bodies in physical space, time and set of material conditions), the mode of their representation (i.e., the meaning of a museum or memorial is not just found in the argument it makes, but also in the physical form through which that argument is experienced), and the means of their delivery (i.e., the nondiscursive dimensions of rhetorical enactment that influence its force and effect but that can never be captured in the textual trace that is left behind, the something more that being there accesses in ways that cannot be grasped otherwise).

In my return to the Phoenix area, I quickly took up a new participatory project. Continuing my interest in health advocacy, I teamed up with a local birthing center to study the promotion of natural childbirth. The natural birth movement is invested in changing the attitudes toward and language about birth from being an overly medicalized phenomenon to something that was well within a woman's ability. Doctors are replaced with midwives, fathers are included in the delivery, and drugs are avoided unless absolutely necessary. The birthing center facility provides women the opportunity to labor in relative comfort and have a water birth, if desired. My project included focus groups, observational work, and interviews with expecting women about why they are interested in natural birth. As advocates, the owners of the center were allied with midwives and doulas across the valley, even those who performed homebirths, which didn't directly support the birthing center.

Toward the beginning of my work with the center, I participated in a protest outside of the Arizona Department of Health Services about proposed legislation that would restrict the types of medical activities a midwife could perform during a homebirth. While not affecting the birthing center directly, the legislation would have been a significant blow to the natural birth movement as a whole. The protest was scheduled in late May, when the Phoenix heat was beginning to rise into the triple digits. My family joined the protesting mothers, fathers, midwives, and doulas outside of the government building under the limited shade at the Downtown Phoenix government building. My two sons, aged six-months and two-years-old at the time and both born in birthing centers, were among many other children who were a part of the protest activities.

The scene was a familiar one, insofar as it included typical rhythmic chanting found at many protests; but it also included a line of protesting children, holding signs that although they couldn't read, embodied and enacted the protest. In between juice boxes and adjacent to bubble machines, these children held signs that said, "My Mom birthed me slowly! Did she fail? No way!" "There's no place like home—4 birth!" and "Home Made, Home Birthed, Home Grown." Certainly, the ethics of children holding signs is questionable, given their relative inability to fully comprehend the act of protest; yet, they perfectly embodied the concerns and argument of those present. By their mere existence, they gave proof to the efficacy of homebirth. Women of all kinds joined the chants in between nursing, after resting a very pregnant belly, and with babies wrapped around their bodies. The familiar lines of "My body, my choice!" filled the air, although sounding different than how they were spoken in the past. This context—this material scene—of the desert sun and children being slathered in sunscreen in between chants, was juxtaposed with the air conditioned government building and its occupants looking down on the signs and strollers. The striking distance between those inside and out gave credence to the protesters, whose bodies comprised the powerful corporeal and affective argument offered to the bureaucrats above.

—Aaron

Participatory critical rhetoricians are awash in a sea of rhetorical fragments, artifacts, conversations, interactions, spaces, embodied gestures, local culture, and other phenomena from which to identify a suitable representation of the rhetorical acts they witness. Guided by the insights gained from a close relationship to the local context in which one is embedded, as in Aaron's case, and the *reading formations* those communities use to engage in rhetorical practice,[73] participatory critical rhetoricians engage in research that recognizes the necessity of casting the net broadly for rhetorical insights. In chapter 4 specifically (and others indirectly), we flesh out efforts to theorize the relations between context and field encountered by participatory critical rhetoricians and begin to develop heuristics to guide those pursuing this type of rhetorical research.

Key Assumption 2: A Participatory Epistemology Enhances Rhetorical Theory and Criticism

Participatory critical rhetoric is guided by a participatory epistemology, which includes a range of possibilities activated in the interactions with everyday rhetors and in the material locations of rhetoric. As an epistemology, this assumption highlights the nature of knowledge as it is gained through the interactions with participants, or as Middleton, Senda-Cook, and Endres suggest, the "ways of interacting with and experiencing the rhetorics we study that [allow us to] participate in the meaning making and the material contexts of the rhetors that draw our attention."[74] Informed by ethnography and performance studies, participatory critical rhetoric takes seriously the ways in which communities of rhetors manage to advocate and speak on behalf of their cause. In other words, participatory critical rhetoric practitioners take member meanings seriously in their participation with, as well as collection and analysis of, field rhetorics. The nature of participation itself places the critic in a role that differs from traditional rhetorical criticism. Rather than a strictly textual perspective, the critic becomes implicated within the places of rhetorical invention. Epistemologically, this means that participatory rhetorical critics may be informed by a multiplicity of voices and rhetorical forms and that the knowledge gained cannot be separated from an embodied and affective experience of the emplaced rhetorical event.

As such, the participatory critical rhetorical scholar engages in a "multiperspectival epistemology" that engages all senses of the body to discover ranges of meaning and to form judgments.[75] While the critic may come into a scene with rhetorical theories and concepts in mind, a participatory epistemology is also generative in that it can foster new ways of theorizing about argument and deliberation through the direct engagement in those activities.[76] These ways of knowing, in Dwight Conquergood's words, are "grounded in active, intimate, hands-on participation and personal connection."[77] Those personal connections are established through the interactions within the material landscapes and places of rhetorical production, and they become the source of critical authority and insight for the rhetorical scholar.

Yet, in conceptualizing participation from an ethnographic perspective, the material and subject positioning of the site often guide the types of participation available for the participatory critical rhetorician. In some cases, movements can be directly experienced by joining and taking part in the protest by holding signs, engaging the public, and attending rallies. In other cases, participation may be limited to observation of activities as they occur and by inquiring into the choices made by members of an advocacy group. In still other cases, target audience members may be available for inquiry into their interpretations of and judgments about rhetorical performances. Similar to notions of membership available in many qualitative projects,[78] and the various levels of performative involvement within performance studies,[79] participation will vary. However, while the nature of the activity and people involved will determine levels of participation, participatory critical rhetoric is guided by a desire to learn the insider's perspective, to learn how and why rhetoric is performed. Chapters 3 and 5 specifically, as well as chapters 2 and 4, indirectly, explore the range of participatory possibility available to *in situ* critical rhetoricians as they navigate the opportunities and challenges opened by engagement with participants in live(d) rhetoric.

Key Assumption 3: Embodied and Emplaced Understandings of Rhetoric Reveal its Intersectionality

Finally, participatory critical rhetoric is an embodied and emplaced phenomenon informed by both the rational and affective conditions of its emergence. Rhetoric is not simply words on a page that the rhetorical critic examines to write up more words on a page (although we would not deny that writing is embodied and emplaced). Rhetoric encompasses the visual, aural, affective, aesthetic, tactile, visceral dimensions of meaning making. Viewing rhetoric as embodied and emplaced builds from a strong lineage of rhetorical scholarship that highlights the rhetoricity of bodies and places, part of which we outlined above.[80] This, in itself, does not require that the critic engage in participatory research in the field. However, participatory critical rhetoric allows for a consideration of how rhetoric is always a combination of verbal and nonverbal messages in interrelationship with bodies, places, and context.[81] Similar to Darrel Enck-Wanzer's argument for intersectional rhetoric, rhetoric is always embodied and emplaced.[82] In other words, whereas body rhetorics have importantly highlighted the ways in which a body or group of bodies can create nonverbal rhetorical or argumentative force in and of themselves,[83] participatory critical rhetoric highlights the way in which even seemingly verbal texts are actually imbricated within bodies, places, and the stakes of immanent political struggle. Although we see immense value in critical rhetorical scholarship that takes on one aspect of a rhetorical act (e.g., body rhetoric) or work that looks at a representation of an embodied and emplaced rhetorical act (e.g., a transcribed speech), we also see value in examining the multimodal nature of rhetorical acts as they happen. Participatory critical rhetoric, because it encourages the rhetorical critic to enter the field and be present in the moment of the rhetorical act, offers the critic access to live(d) rhetorics in their complex intersections between words, places, bodies, and context.

As I entered the Ground Zero Theater at the National Atomic Testing Museum (just off the Strip in Las Vegas, Nevada), I was not sure what to expect. The description outside the theater described the film as a "multisensory experience" that explains the history of Atomic Testing. I sat on a wooden bench in the small theater along with what seemed to be a family. The lights dimmed and all of a sudden, I found myself transported to the 1950s as an observer of an aboveground nuclear test. The theater shook, air shot out of vents, and the screen went white as the nuclear bomb exploded. As my eyes adjusted, the white faded into a distinct image of a mushroom cloud. As this was happening, I felt unsettled, disoriented, and a bit in awe at the simulated nuclear blast. I turned to look at the family that shared the experience with me. A young child was leaning in to her mother's embrace. At the end of the nuclear blast, the mother said to her child: "It's the closest you'll ever come to the nuclear blast." I turned back to the screen as the film transitioned from the nuclear explosion to a series of talking heads and images of the history of Atomic Testing, particularly the Nevada Test Site. On the one hand, the simulated detonation felt somewhat corny and gimmicky. Yet, on the other hand, the experience of "watching" a nuclear explosion really stuck with me as one of the more persuasive parts of the museum. Even after several field visits to the museum, it is what I remember the most, even provoking visceral bodily memories of the experience.

As I marched through the streets of downtown Salt Lake City to protest the arrest of Tim DeChristopher, a local activist turned monkey-wrencher who, when mistakenly given a bidding paddle, decided to use it to disrupt an oil and gas lease auction by bidding on and winning parcels of pristine BLM land in Southern Utah, I was struck by the ways in which our message was not just one of the words we chanted, but also of our bodies taking up the city street and sending a message of the size and strength of our collective body, of our temporary reconstruction of those streets as a place of protest, and of the disruption of normalized practices in Salt Lake City. I was able to observe how onlookers responded to our message, some with disgust in the form of rolled eyes, some with support in the form of a raised fist or a honk of their horn, and some with seeming indifference as they continued walking. I thought about the experience of being there in the protest event as opposed to watching a video of it, reading about it, or hearing about it. Of course, there were many things about this protest march that were not so different from the many other protest marches I have experienced. The point, rather, is that the experience of being a part of the protest gave me access understanding its rhetoric not only through a variety of conjoining forms but also through gauging the reactions of the people participating in and observing the protest.

The opening plenary of the nuclear science conference began with a performance of the Star Spangled Banner. Surprised by this choice, I looked around the room unsure if I should stand and hold my hand to heart. The reactions of the people around me assured me that I was not alone in my uncertainty. Although most of the audience stood, few held their hands to their hearts. This seemingly simple opening the conference's opening plenary session might be easily dismissed as irrelevant to the messages promoting nuclear technology in the plenary presentations. It might not be included in a textual transcript of the plenary session. Yet, the performance of the national anthem and the varying responses to it by the audience not only foreshadowed the tone of the plenary presentations with patriotic undertones but also signaled the multiple perspectives and judgments present in the audience.

In each of these examples, rhetoric came at me as a multi-sensory, multimodal intersectional experience. It was something that could not be contained by words alone. Nor could it be contained as a purely rational experience, but rather a merger of rationality, affect, emotion, and the sensorium. It was something that would be difficult to textualize through just words. Yet, these experiences of intersectional rhetoric in the moment offered a window into the complexity of in situ *rhetorical invention.*

—Danielle

Danielle's vignette shows the range of intersectionality present in participatory critical rhetoric, which can also include visceral and affective elements. Understanding rhetoric in this way calls for a reconsideration of traditional notions of rhetoric as rational persuasive discourse and opens the critic to experience the affective dimensions of rhetoric. Our intention is not to uphold a binary between rational and affective rhetoric but rather to highlight that rhetoric can be both.[84] While affect can mean many things from emotion to sensual experience, to an intensity of feeling, to visceral reaction to an encounter, to how things stick together, it implies the multimodality of rhetoric because it is an intangible extra-discursive sensation that is difficult to capture in text or words alone. Rather than eschewing rationality in favor of affect, an embodied and emplaced perspective on rhetoric recognizes what McKerrow describes in relation to corporeal rhetoric as the "merger of reason and emotion."[85] In chapters 2 and 4, we further develop how this type of participatory critical rhetoric might be enacted by nuancing extant understandings of context, field, and rhetoric, as well as the political stakes involved in embodied, emplaced rhetorical situations.

Taken together, these key assumptions of participatory critical rhetoric call our attention to questions related to politics, embodiment of the critic, emplaced rhetoric in the field, and engagement with participants, which structure the remaining chapters of the book. Before proceeding, we conclude this chapter by briefly highlighting some of the implications offered by a programmatic theorization of participatory critical rhetoric.

IMPLICATIONS: THE CHALLENGE(S) AND PROMISE OF PARTICIPATORY CRITICAL RHETORIC

Participatory critical rhetoric is not a critical procedure or a methodology in a strict sense that identifies for critics pre-given units of analysis, ways of manipulating texts to gain critical insight, or specific aims of critical inquiry. Rather, participatory critical rhetoric describes a wide range of approaches that share, to varying degrees, the assumptions and commitments that we describe in the previous sections. Throughout the book, we aim to underscore the relationship between critical rhetoric, the field, and participatory research. Informed by a number of theoretical and methodological perspectives, this book charts the growing connections between ethnography, performance, and rhetoric. From each, we gain new insights into the production, reception, and effect of rhetorical discourse. At its core, participatory critical rhetoric is an exercise in *rhetoric*, meaning that it is most directly understood as an investigation into rhetorical discourse. While defined in myriad ways, rhetoric in our estimation is best understood as embodied and emplaced meaning making through the advocacy of perspectives within a contested field of argumentation. This perspective on rhetoric highlights the temporal and ephemeral nature of much of rhetorical discourse, including those conversations that elide recording or some other form of textual manifestation. Moreover, rhetoric is partisan; it is contested and advocated. In an Aristotelian sense, the discipline of rhetoric inherently exists as competing perspectives of the past, present, and future. Deliberations over these competing notions provide part of the context of rhetoric. Participatory critical rhetoric aims to directly engage that context, drawing from existing rhetorical theory to best comprehend the means by which rhetors, critics, and audiences make sense of it.

Likewise, participatory critical rhetoric owes a debt to ethnography and, in particular, critical ethnography in communication. Nonetheless, while it is informed by this body of scholarship, participatory critical rhetoric also provides new avenues of exploration for ethnographers seeking to underscore the relationship between advocacy, identity, and performance. Ethnography's interpretive aim can be augmented by a rhetorical sensibility, especially one that attends to the contests over meaning that lie at the heart of the rhetorical enterprise. As constellations of meaning are articulated, challenged, and rearticulated, those engaged in participatory critical rhetoric carry with them the fundamental appreciation for language and its power in forming the discourses of hegemony and resistance. Moreover, participatory critical rhetoric enables ethnographers to participate in the advocacy of these endeavors, linking discursive possibility with embodied action. In other words, the participatory critical rhetorician can appreciate the firsthand knowledge and wisdom gained through direct experience within rhetoric.

The field of performance studies also contributes to participatory critical rhetoric by sensitizing the critic to the contingent, improvisational nature of live(d) rhetorical practice. It encourages the critic to recognize rhetoric as processual, as thought-in-action. In this respect, performance provides a critical set of tools for rhetorical critics who make the leap from stable, finished texts that represent past rhetorical actions to rhetorical practice that is unfolding in the presence of those critics and whose consequences may not be fully known at the time critics must leave the field to write up their analysis. At the same time, a rhetorical lens brings to performance a more focused approach for thinking about the strategic dimensions of embodied rhetorical performances and how they interact with the practical aims of rhetorical practice. By drawing on its initial interest in the use of discourse to strategically influence an audience, rhetorical theory adds a practical, evaluative edge to the often descriptive lens of performance studies.

Finally and most fundamentally, participatory critical rhetoric advances our understanding of rhetoric in a number of ways. Participatory critical rhetoric, at minimum, extends efforts (feminist, postcolonial, etc.) to expand the textual and theoretical archive that informs rhetorical inquiry by challenging traditional critical orientations centered on the after-the-fact verbal text. Working from this perspective, participatory critical rhetoric locates those texts that often escape the purview of the traditional critic. It is able to more fully embrace the insights of vernacular, intersectional, and sensorial discourses. Fresh perspectives, gained from insider purviews, may provide rhetorical theory new avenues for understanding the strategies and tactics of everyday rhetoric.

Participatory critical rhetoric also enhances rhetorical studies through its emphasis on reflexivity. Charles E. Morris III recognizes the need for a more robust account of rhetorical reflexivity.[86] Toward that end, participatory critical rhetoric takes seriously the role of the critic, asking fundamental questions about the epistemology and ontology of being in the field. The engaged critic calls for a new knowledge of rhetorical theorizing, one that is linked directly to the embodied and emplaced experiences of the field. The cerebral methods of textual criticism are bolstered with an account of the body in relationship to others. Rarely in traditional rhetorical scholarship do critics directly reflect upon and take stock of their relationship to participants or rhetors. Participatory critical rhetoric's commitment to direct engagement with rhetors and audiences *in situ* demands reflection on issues such as the role of the critic, the nature of relationships with participants, the way in which the critic's embodied presence affects the rhetorical field, and the ethical considerations of representation and textualization. To be sure, following Morris, these are issues that can also be addressed in non-field-based rhetorical criticism. Yet, participatory critical rhetoric, drawing from the insights of qualitative inquiry on reflexivity, offers nuance to reflexivity given the differences in the way critics are embodied and emplaced in the field in relation to participants, as we discuss further in chapters 3 and 5. Enhanced attention to rhetorical reflexivity is not limited to the research process, but should also be included in the scholarship rhetoricians produce.

Finally, participatory critical rhetoric provides an approach and orientation toward rhetoric that opens spaces for understanding embodied and emplaced rhetoric as it is produced and experienced. The body is a central site for comprehension, extending and elaborating on an intersectional rhetoric experience, as we discuss in more detail in chapter 3. The bodily experience of rhetoric cannot be separated from the time and place of its creation, meaning that participatory critical rhetoric also attunes rhetorical scholars to the emplaced nature of rhetoric, which we outline in more detail in chapter 4. Our perspective on embodied and emplaced rhetoric is not limited to field-based rhetorical practice, but also has implications for larger conversations across the field of rhetoric. Recognizing the political consequences of these implications, the next chapter advances the argument for an activist-scholar, politically and immanently engaged in the practices rhetorical criticism.

NOTES

1. Carole Blair, "Reflections on Criticism and Bodies: Parables from Public Places," *Western Journal of Communication* 65 (2001): 271–94, doi: 10.1080/10570310109374706; Greg Dickinson, "Memories for Sale: Nostalgia and the Construction of Identity in Old Pasadena," *Quarterly Journal of Speech* 83 (1997): 1–27, doi: 10.1080/00335639709384169; Greg Dickinson, "Joe's Rhetoric: Finding Authenticity at Starbucks," *Rhetoric Society Quarterly* 32 (2002): 5–27, doi: 10.1080/02773940209391238; Greg Dickinson, "The Pleasantville Effect: Nostalgia and the Visual Framing of (White) Suburbia," *Western Journal of Communication* 70 (2006): 212–33, doi: 10.1080/10570310600843504; Greg Dickinson, Brian L. Ott, and Eric Aoki, "Memory and Myth at the Buffalo Bill Museum," *Western Journal of Communication* 69 (2005): 85–108, doi: 10.1080/10570310500076684; Greg Dickinson, Brian L. Ott, and Eric Aoki, "Spaces of Remembering and Forgetting: The Reverent Eye/I at the Plains Indian Museum," *Communication and Critical/Cultural Studies* 3 (2006): 27–47, doi: 10.1080/14791420500505619; Danielle Endres and Samantha Senda-Cook, "Location Matters: The Rhetoric of Place in Protest," *Quarterly Journal of Speech* 97 (2011): 257–82, doi: 10.1080/00335630.2011.585167.

2. Kevin Michael DeLuca, "Unruly Arguments: The Body Rhetoric of Earth First!, Act Up, and Queer Nation," *Argumentation and Advocacy* 36 (1999): 9–21; Kevin Michael DeLuca and Jennifer Peeples, "From Public Sphere to Public Screen: Democracy, Activism, and the 'Violence' of Seattle," *Critical Studies in Media Communication* 19 (2002): 125–51, doi: 10.1080/07393180216559; Mindy Fenske, "Movement and Resistance: (Tattooed) Bodies and Performance," *Communication and Critical/Cultural Studies* 4 (2007): 51–73, doi: 10.1080/14791420601138302; Phaedra C. Pezzullo, "Performing Critical Interruptions: Stories, Rhetorical Invention, and the Environmental Justice Movement," *Western Journal of Communication* 65 (2001): 1–25, doi: 10.1080/10570310109374689.

3. Carole Blair, "Contemporary US Memorial Sites as Exemplars of Rhetoric's Materiality," in *Rhetorical Bodies,* eds. Jack Selzer and Sharon Crowley (Madison: University of Wisconsin Press, 1999): 16–57; Blair, "Reflections on Criticism and Bodies"; Carole Blair, Marsha S. Jeppeson, and Enrico Pucci Jr., "Public Memorializing in Postmodernity: The Vietnam Veterans Memorial as Prototype," *Quarterly Journal of Speech* 77 (1991): 263–88, doi: 10.1080/00335639109383960; Ralph Cintron, *Angels' Town:* Chero *Ways, Gang Life, and Rhetorics of the Everyday* (Boston, MA: Beacon Press, 1997); Dickinson, "Memories for Sale"; Dickinson et al., "Memory and Myth at the Buffalo Bill Museum"; Dickinson et al., "Spaces of Remembering and Forgetting"; Danielle Endres, Leah Sprain, and Tarla Rai Peterson, "The Imperative of Praxis-Based Environmental Communication Research: Suggestions from the Step It Up 2007 National Research Project," *Environmental Communication: A Journal of Nature and Culture* 2 (2008): 237–45, doi: 10.1080/17524030802141794; Danielle Endres, Leah M. Sprain, and Tarla Rai Peterson, eds., *Social Movement to Address Climate Change: Local Steps for Global Action* (Amherst, NY: Cambria Press, 2009); Marouf Hasian, and Rulon Wood, "Critical Museology, (Post) Colonial Communication, and the Gradual Mastering of Traumatic Pasts at the Royal Museum for Central Africa (RMCA)," *Western Journal of Communication* 74 (2010): 128–49, doi: 10.1080/10570311003614484; Aaron Hess, "Critical-Rhetorical Ethnography: Rethinking the Place and Process of Rhetoric," *Communication Studies* 62 (2011): 127–52, doi: 10.1080/10510974.2011.529750; Tamar Katriel, "Rhetoric in Flames: Fire Inscriptions in Israeli Youth Movement Ceremonials," *Quarterly Journal of Speech* 73 (1987): 444–59, doi: 10.1080/00335638709383818; Tamar Katriel, "'Our Future is Where our Past Is': Studying Heritage Museums as Ideological and Performative Arenas," *Communication Monographs* 60 (1993): 69–75, doi: 10.1080/03637759309376296; Samuel McCormick, "Earning One's Inheritance: Rhetorical Criticism, Everyday Talk, and the Analysis of Public Discourse," *Quarterly Journal of Speech* 89 (2003): 109–31, doi: 10.1080/00335630308176; Martin J. Medhurst, "The Contemporary Study of Public Address: Renewal, Recovery, and Reconfiguration," *Rhetoric & Public Affairs* 4 (2001): 495–511, doi: 10.1353/rap.2001.0048; Michael K. Middleton, Samantha Senda-Cook, and Danielle Endres, "Articulating Rhetorical Field Methods: Challenges and Tensions," *Western Journal of Communication* 75 (2011): 386–406, doi: 10.1080/10570314.2011.586969; Kent A. Ono and John M. Sloop, "The Critique of Vernacular Discourse," *Communication Monographs 62* (1995): 19–46, doi: 0.1080/03637759509376346; Pezzullo, "Performing Critical Interruptions"; Phaedra C. Pezzullo, "Resisting 'National Breast Cancer

Awareness Month': The Rhetoric of Counterpublics and Their Cultural Performances," *Quarterly Journal of Speech* 89 (2003): 345–65,doi: 10.1080/0033563032000160981; Phaedra C. Pezzullo, *Toxic Tourism: Rhetorics of Pollution, Travel, and Environmental Justice* (Tuscaloosa: University of Alabama Press, 2007); Peter Simonson, "The Streets of Laredo: Mercurian Rhetoric and the Obama Campaign," *Western Journal of Communication* 74 (2010): 94–126, doi: 10.1080/10570310903466045; Jennifer Stromer Galley and Edward Schiappa, "The Argumentative Burdens of Audience Conjectures: Audience Research in Popular Culture Criticism," *Communication Theory* 8 (1998): 27–62, doi: 10.1111/j.1468–2885.1998.tb00210.x; Bryan C. Taylor, "The Bodies of August: Photographic Realism and Controversy at the National Air and Space Museum," *Rhetoric & Public Affairs* 1 (1998): 331–62, doi: 10.1353/rap.2010.0070; Kenneth S. Zagacki and Victoria J. Gallagher, "Rhetoric and Materiality in the Museum Park at the North Carolina Museum of Art," *Quarterly Journal of Speech* 95 (2009): 171–91, doi: 10.1080/00335630902842087; Richard Wilkins and Karen Wolf, "The Role of Ethnography in Rhetorical Analysis: The New Rhetorical Turn," *Empedocles: European Journal for the Philosophy of Communication* 3 (2012): 7–23, doi: http://dx.doi.org/10.1386/ejpc.3.1.7_1.

4. Phillip Wander, "The Ideological Turn in Modern Criticism," *Central States Speech Journal* 34 (1983): 1–18; Raymie E. McKerrow, "Critical Rhetoric: Theory and Praxis," *Communication Monographs* 56 (1989): 91–111; Michael Calvin McGee, "Text, Context, and the Fragmentation of Contemporary Culture," *Western Journal of Speech Communication* 54 (1990): 274–89.

5. George F. McHendry Jr., Michael Middleton, Danielle Endres, Samantha Senda-Cook, and Megan O'Byrne, "Rhetorical Critic(ism)'s Body," *Southern Journal of Communication,* 79 (2014), 293–310, doi: 10.1080/1041794X.2014.906643.

6. Michael C. Leff, "Interpretation and the Art of the Rhetorical Critic," *Western Journal of Speech Communication* 44 (1980): 337–49, doi: 10.1080/10570318009374019; Michael C. Leff, "Things Made by Words: Reflections on Textual Criticism," *Quarterly Journal of Speech* 78 (1992): 223–31, doi: 10.1080/00335639209383991.

7. Herbert A. Wichelns, "The Literary Criticism of Oratory," in *Readings in Rhetorical Criticism,* ed. Carl R. Burgchardt (State College, PA: Strata, 2005), 3–27.

8. Edwin Black, *Rhetorical Criticism: A Study in Method* (Madison: University of Wisconsin Press, 1978).

9. Lloyd F. Bitzer, "The Rhetorical Situation," *Philosophy & Rhetoric* 6 (1973): 154–61.

10. Leff, "Interpretation"; Michael Leff and Andrew Sachs, "Words the Most Like Things: Iconicity and the Rhetorical Text," *Western Journal of Speech Communication* 54, (1990): 252–73, doi: 10.1080/10570319009374342.

11. McGee, "Text, Context, and the Fragmentation of Contemporary Culture," 284.

12. Ibid, 288.

13. Blair et al., "Public Memorializing in Postmodernity," 272.

14. Ono and Sloop, "Critique of Vernacular Discourse"; John M. Sloop, and Kent A. Ono, "Out-law Discourse: The Critical Politics of Material Judgment," *Philosophy & Rhetoric* 30 (1997): 50–69; Gerard A. Hauser, *Vernacular Voices:*

The Rhetoric of Publics and Public Spheres (Columbia, SC: University of South Carolina Press, 1999); Robert Glenn Howard, "The Vernacular Web of Participatory Media," *Critical Studies in Media Communication* 25 (2008): 490–513, doi: 10.1080/15295030802468065.

15. Ono and Sloop. "Critique of Vernacular Discourse," 19.

16. Ibid, 20.

17. Hauser, *Vernacular Voices.*

18. Ibid, 277.

19. Dana L. Cloud, "The Materiality of Discourse as Oxymoron: A Challenge to Critical Rhetoric," *Western Journal of Communication* 58 (1994): 141–63, doi: 10.1080/10570319409374493.

20. McGee, "Text, Context, and the Fragmentation of Contemporary Culture," 274–289; McKerrow, "Critical Rhetoric: Theory and Praxis"; Kent A. Ono and John M. Sloop, "Commitment to *Telos*: A Sustained Critical Rhetoric," *Communication Monographs* 59 (1992): 48–60, doi: 10.1080/03637759209376248.

21. Ronald Walter Greene, "Another Materialist Rhetoric," *Critical Studies in Media Communication* 15 (1998): 21–40, doi: 10.1080/15295039809367031.

22. Blair, "Contemporary US Memorial Sites."

23. Thus, the context or field, conventionally understood as distinct from the text, could become part of the artifact under analysis. For instance, Endres and Senda-Cook illuminate how spaces shape the rhetorical opportunities available for participants in social activism, while at the same time those same activists can reinvest old spaces with new meanings that complement, reinforce, and undermine their rhetorical goals. Similarly, Dickinson, as well as Stewart and Dickinson, explore rhetorical spaces, including shopping malls and coffeehouses, to illustrate how ways of interacting and navigating space (both structured and improvised), sensorial encounters (including sight, smell, and touch), and other practices of everyday life that reveal the intertwined relationships between discourse and materiality that shape the rhetorical force of interactions in those spaces. Endres and Senda-Cook, "Location Matters;" Dickinson, "Memories for Sale"; Jessie Stewart and Greg Dickinson, "Enunciating Locality in the Postmodern Suburb: FlatIron Crossing and the Colorado Lifestyle," *Western Journal of Communication* 72, (2008): 280–307, doi: 10.1080/10570310802210148

24. Raymie E. McKerrow, "Corporeality and Cultural Rhetoric: A Site for Rhetoric's Future," *Southern Communication Journal 63* (1998): 320–21, 25, doi: 10.1080/10417949809373105.

25. For example: Dwight Conquergood, "Performance Studies: Interventions and Radical Research," *The Drama Review* 46 (2002): 145–56; Pezzullo, "Resisting 'National Breast Cancer Awareness Month'"; Carole Blair and Neil Michel, "Reproducing Civil Rights Tactics: The Rhetorical Performances of the Civil Rights Memorial," *Rhetoric Society Quarterly* 30 (2000): 31–55; Frederick C. Corey, and Thomas K. Nakayama, "Sextext," *Text and Performance Quarterly* 17 (1997): 58–68, doi: 10.1080/10462939709366169; DeLuca, "Unruly Arguments"; Kelly Happe, "The Body of Race: Toward a Rhetorical Understanding of Racial Ideology," *Quarterly Journal of Speech* 99, (2013): 131–55, doi: 10.1080/00335630.2013.775700; Debra Hawhee, *Bodily Arts: Rhetoric and Athletics in Ancient Greece* (Austin: University of Texas Press, 2005); Christine Harold, "On Target: Aura, Affect, and

the Rhetoric of 'Design Democracy,'" *Public Culture* 21 (2009): 599–618, doi: 10.1215/08992363–2009-010; Brian L. Ott, "The Visceral Politics of *V for Vendetta*: On Political Affect in Cinema," *Critical Studies in Media Communication* 27 (2010): 39–54, doi: 10.1080/15295030903554359; Mary S. Strine, "Articulating Performance/Performativity: Disciplinary Tasks and the Contingencies of Practice," in *Communication: Views from the Helm for the Twenty-First Century,* ed. Judith Trent (Boston: Allyn and Bacon, 1998), 312–7.

26. Steve Whitson and John Poulakos, "Neitzsche and the Aesthetics of Rhetoric," *Quarterly Journal of Speech* 79 (1993): 382, doi: 10.1080/00335639309384025.

27. Ronald Walter Greene, "The Aesthetic Turn and the Rhetorical Perspective on Argumentation." *Argumentation and Advocacy* 35 (1998): 19.

28. DeLuca, "Unruly Arguments," 10.

29. Deluca and Peeples, "From Public Sphere to Public Screen." 19: 125–51.

30. Art Herbig and Aaron Hess, "Convergent Critical Rhetoric at the 'Rally to Restore Sanity': Exploring the Intersection of Rhetoric, Ethnography, and Documentary Production," *Communication Studies 63* (2012), 270, doi: 10.1080/10510974.2012.674617.

31. Leff, "Things Made by Words."

32. Kenneth Burke, *A Rhetoric of Motives, Vol. 1.* (Los Angeles: University of California Press, 1969); Kenneth Burke, *A Grammar of Motives*, (Los Angeles: University of California Press, 1969).

33. Ono and Sloop, "The Critique of Vernacular Discourse."

34. Edwin Black, *Rhetorical Criticism*, 35.

35. McKerrow, "Critical Rhetoric: Theory and Praxis," 101.

36. Ibid, 101.

37. Robert Asen and Daniel C. Brouwer, eds. *Counterpublics and the State.* (Albany: SUNY Press, 2001); Nancy Fraser, "Politics, Culture, and the Public Sphere: Toward a Postmodern Conception," in *Social Postmodernism: Beyond Identity Politics*, eds. Linda Nicholson and Steve Seidman (Cambridge: Press Syndicate of the University of Cambridge, 995): 287–312; Hauser, *Vernacular Voices;* Catherine R. Squires, "Rethinking the Black Public Sphere: An Alternative Vocabulary for Multiple Public Spheres," *Communication Theory* 12 (2002): 446–68, doi: 10.1111/j.1468–2885.2002.tb00278.x.

38. Fraser, "Politics, Culture, and the Public Sphere"; Rita Felski, *Beyond Feminist Aesthetics: Feminist Literature and Social Change* (Cambridge: Harvard University Press, 1989); Jane Mansbridge, "Cracking Through Hegemonic Ideology: The Logic of Formal Justice," *Social Justice Research* 18 (2005): 335–47, doi: 10./007/s11211–005-6828–0.

39. Nancy Fraser, "Rethinking the Public Sphere: A Contribution to the Critique of Actually Existing Democracy," *Social Text* 25/26 (1990): 67, doi: 10.2307/466240.

40. Asen and Brouwer, *Counterpublics and the State,* 2–3.

41. Maurice Charland, "Constitutive Rhetoric: The Case of the Peuple Quebecois," *Quarterly Journal of Speech* 73 (1987): 133–50, doi: 10.1080/00335638709383799.

42. Black, *Rhetorical Criticism,* xii–xiii.

43. McKerrow, "Critical Rhetoric: Theory and Praxis," 101; McGee, "Text, Context, and the Fragmentation of Contemporary Culture."

44. McGee, "Text, Context, and the Fragmentation of Contemporary Culture." 275.

45. McGee, "Text, Context, and the Fragmentation of Culture." 276.

46. McKerrow, "Critical Rhetoric: Theory and Praxis," 101.

47. McKerrow, "Critical Rhetoric in a Postmodern World," *Quarterly Journal of Speech* 77 (1991): 76, doi: 10.1080/00335639109383945.

48. McGee, "Text, Context, and the Fragmentation of Contemporary Culture."

49. Ibid, 288.

50. Ono and Sloop, "Commitment to *Telos,*" 50.

51. Ibid, 51.

52. McKerrow, "Critical Rhetoric: Theory and Praxis," 108.

53. Gerard A. Hauser, "Forum: The Nature and Function of Public Intellectuals," *Philosophy & Rhetoric* 39 (2006): 125.

54. Steve Fuller, "The Public Intellectual as Agent of Justice: In Search of a Regime," *Philosophy & Rhetoric* 39 (2006): 147–56, doi: 10.1353/par.2006.0013.

55. Nathan Crick, "Rhetoric, Philosophy, and the Public Intellectual," *Philosophy & Rhetoric* 39 (2006): 127–39, doi: 10.1353/par.2006.0012.

56. Steven Mailloux, "Thinking in Public with Rhetoric," *Philosophy & Rhetoric* 39 (2006): 147–56, doi: 10.1353/par.2006.0013.

57. The debate over public intellectualism is beyond the scope of this chapter. The prevailing antagonism between rhetorical reflection and political agency has led to a number of scholars espousing activist routes for their scholarship or ways in which rhetoric can be more publically minded. For a more thorough discussion, see: Scott Welsh, "Coming to Terms with the Antagonism between Rhetorical Reflection and Political Agency," *Philosophy & Rhetoric* 45 (2012), 1–23, doi: 10.5325/philrhet.45.1.0001.

58. McKerrow, "Critical Rhetoric: Theory and Praxis"; Lawrence R. Frey, W. Barnett Pearce, Mark A. Pollock, Lee Artz, and Bren A. O. Murphy, "Looking for Justice in All the Wrong Places: On a Communication Approach to Social Justice," *Communication Studies* 47 (1996): 110–127, doi: 10.1080/10510979609368467; Lawrence R. Frey, "Communication and Social Justice Research: Truth, Justice, and the Applied Communication Way," *Journal of Applied Communication Research* 26 (1998): 155–64, doi: 10.1080/00909889809365499; Stephen John Hartnett, "Communication, Social Justice, and Joyful Commitment," *Western Journal of Communication* 74 (2010): 68–93, doi: 10.1080/10570310903463778.

59. Hartnett, "Communication, Social Justice, and Joyful Commitment," 71–5.

60. Ibid, 78.

61. McGee, "Text, Context, and the Fragmentation of Contemporary Culture"; McKerrow, "Critical Rhetoric: Theory and Praxis."

62. Wayne C. Booth. *The Company We Keep: An Ethics of Fiction* (Berkeley, CA: University of California Press, 1988).

63. McGee, "Text, Context, and the Fragmentation of Contemporary Culture," 288. For instance, in theorizing constitutive rhetoric, Charland contributes to rethinking the role of the audience by objecting to Aristotelian and Burkean notions of an audience that unproblematically precedes the rhetorical act. See, for example, Charland, "Constitutive Rhetoric."

64. Wander took up this question as one of examining who and what subject positions are negated in discourse, in addition to those that are named, or constituted, in and through discourse. See Philip Wander, "The Third Persona: An Ideological Turn in Rhetorical Theory," *Central States Speech Journal* 35 (1984): 197–216, doi: 10.1080/10510978409368190.

65. Charland, "Constitutive Rhetoric."

66. Ibid, 210.

67. Samantha Senda-Cook, "Rugged Practices: Embodying Authenticity in Outdoor Recreation," *Quarterly Journal of Speech* 98 (2012): 132, doi: 10.1080/00335630.2012.663500.

68. Norman Fairclough, "Critical Discourse Analysis as a Method in Social Scientific Research" in *Methods of Critical Discourse Analysis*, eds. Ruth Wodak and Michael Meyer (Thousand Oaks, CA: Sage Publications, 2001): 121–38.

69. Michel Foucault, "Questions of Method," in *The Foucault Effect: Studies in Governmentality,* eds. Graham Burchell, Colin Gordon, and Peter Miller (Chicago: University of Chicago Press, 1991): 73–86.

70. Ian Hodder, "The Interpretation of Documents and Culture," in *Collecting and Interpreting Qualitative Materials*, eds. Norman K. Denzin and Yvonna S. Lincoln (Thousand Oaks, CA: Sage Publications, 1998): 114.

71. Blair, "Contemporary US Memorial Sites as Exemplars of Rhetoric's Materiality."

72. McKerrow, "Critical Rhetoric: Theory and Praxis."

73. Bennett, Tony. *Critical Trajectories* (Malden, MA: Blackwell Publishing Ltd, 2007).

74. Middleton et al., "Articulating Rhetorical Field Methods," 393.

75. Norman K. Denzin, *Interpretive Ethnography: Ethnographic Practices for the 21st Century* (Thousand Oaks, CA; Sage Publications, 1997), 36.

76. Kathy Charmaz, *Constructing Grounded Theory: A Practical Guide through Qualitative Analysis* (Thousand Oaks, CA: Sage Publications, 2006).

77. Dwight Conquergood, "Performance Studies: Interventions and Radical Research," 146.

78. Patricia A. Adler and Peter Adler, *Membership Roles in Field Research* (Thousand Oaks, CA; Sage Publications, 1987).

79. Eric E. Peterson and Kristin M. Langellier, "The Politics of Personal Narrative Methodology," *Text and Performance Quarterly* 17 (1997): 135–52, doi: 10.1080/10462939709366178.

80. Blair, "Reflections on Criticism and Bodies"; Greg Dickinson, Carole Blair, and Brian L. Ott, eds. *Places of Public Memory: The Rhetoric of Museums and Memorials*. 1st ed. (Tuscaloosa, University Alabama Press, 2010); Endres and Senda-Cook, "Location Matters"; Dickinson, "Memories for Sale"; Stewart and Dickinson, "Enunciating Locality"; Andrew F. Wood, *City Ubiquitous: Place, Communication, and the Rise of Omnitopia* (Cresskill, NJ: Hampton Press, 2009); Sonja Modesti, "Home Sweet Home: Tattoo Parlors as Postmodern Spaces of Agency," *Western Journal of Communication* 72, (2008): 197–212, doi: 10.1080/10570310802210106; Isaac West, "PISSAR's Critically Queer and Disabled Politics," *Communication*

and Critical/Cultural Studies 7 (2010): 156–75, doi: 10.1080/14791421003759174; Zagacki and Gallagher, "Rhetoric and Materiality"; DeLuca, "Unruly Arguments"; Greg Dickinson, "Joe's Rhetoric"; Jack Selzer and Sharon Crowley, eds. *Rhetorical Bodies*, (Madison: University of Wisconsin Press, 1999); Hawhee, *Bodily Arts*.

81. Endres and Senda-Cook, "Location Matters."

82. Darrel Enck-Wanzer, "Trashing the System: Social Movement, Intersectional Rhetoric, and Collective Agency in the Young Lords Organization's Garbage Offensive," *Quarterly Journal of Speech* 92 (2006): 174–201, doi: 10.1080/00335630600816920.

83. Blair, "Reflections on Criticism and Bodies"; Pezzullo, *Toxic Tourism;* McKerrow, "Critical Rhetoric: Theory and Praxis"; McGee, "Text, Context, and the Fragmentation of Contemporary Culture"; DeLuca, "Unruly Arguments."

84. Theories of affect are making their way into rhetorical studies. Some examples of initial essays bringing in affect include: Harold, "On Target"; Ott, "The Visceral Politics of *V for Vendetta*"; Jeff Pruchnic and Kim Lacey, "The Future of Forgetting: Rhetoric, Memory, Affect," *Rhetoric Society Quarterly* 41 (2011): 472–94, doi: 10.1080/02773945.2011.597818; Joshua Gunn, and Jenny Edbauer Rice, "About Face/Stuttering Discipline," *Communication and Critical/Cultural Studies* 6 (2009): 215–9, doi:10.1080/14791420902868029. For a more general discussion of affect theory in the humanities, see Melissa Gregg and Gregory J. Seigworth, *The Affect Theory Reader* (Durham, NC: Duke University Press, 2010).

85. McKerrow, "Corporeality and Cultural Rhetoric," 322.

86. Charles E. Morris III, "Performing/Rhetorical Studies: Differential Belonging across Intradisciplinary Borders," *Text and Performance Quarterly* 34 (2014): 104–7, doi: 10.1080/10462937.2013.849813.

Chapter 2

The Politics of Participatory Critical Rhetoric

A few months into my episodic fieldwork studying the efforts of SafeGround Sacramento, I arrived at the homeless service center that the group used as their organizing base. When I arrived at "Fellowship Park" (a small green space adjacent to the homeless services center where both members of SafeGround and other homeless persons gathered each day), the members of SafeGround were busily at work getting ready for the day's events. Later that afternoon, there would be a protest march from the park to city hall about twelve blocks away. Once there, members of SafeGround would give protest speeches, listen to the thoughts of supporters, religious leaders, and politicians, and work to recruit support from the broader community. The members of SafeGround were also energized by the news that one of their members, a twenty-something homeless woman named "Jackie," had received information that she would soon have access to temporary housing. She was in attendance that day, celebrating with and supporting her homeless allies as they prepared for the events that would occupy their afternoon.

On the edge of the park, a set of mobile buildings that were normally used for providing services to the homeless community (both SafeGround members and others) had been temporarily taken over by SafeGround members to organize for the protest. When I walked inside, "Jackie" and others were crafting protest signs out of bright, neon poster board, talking about their protest plans, and discussing "Jackie's" opportunities now that she had access to (short-term) housing. It didn't take long before I was recruited to help with the posters, coloring in the provocative demands and protest slogans that "Jackie" artfully traced onto each poster.

A few hours later, the posters were being distributed and SafeGround members, as well as other homeless activists, were lining up to begin the march. My SafeGround friends quickly placed a protest sign in my hand

and asked me to join in with their protest. As we walked toward city hall, the conversations that moved seamlessly between talk of political organizing and more mundane interpersonal relationship building continued between SafeGround members new and old, as well as those members of the larger homeless community who had joined them. A few hours later, with the protest march completed and the protest rally concluded, the SafeGround members who had started their day in the mobile buildings gathered at the home of a lawyer and activist with whom they regularly collaborated to celebrate the day's events. Having been invited to join them, I continued to participate in the conversations about politics and life that had percolated throughout the group all day, and that continued until well past midnight. Finally, we dispersed, planning to gather the next day to discuss future efforts the group would make. As I went home, I replayed the day's events in my mind, tired from the activities and recognizing that few fieldnotes had been taken that day. My experience that day with SafeGround has remained with me for the several years since my fieldwork with the group of activists has concluded. While not an especially unique day in the life of a community of protestors and activists, the activities of SafeGround, as well my participation as a researcher at those events, reflect the political realities that confront the critic who chooses to enter the field and that exceed those faced by critical rhetoricians whose attention is primarily focused on already documented rhetorical texts.

—Michael

When critics take to the field, they encounter firsthand the mundane conversations that, through their ability to build "*communitas*," are remarkably powerful rhetorical moments (often, more so than the more commonly analyzed rhetorical forms, e.g., protest speeches).[1] Like Michael's experience, critics who enter the field, especially those who participate with communities of political advocates, find themselves faced with the competing demands of, on the one hand, a participant confronted with immanent opportunities to take part in and support the political efforts that attracted their interest in the first place; and, on the other hand, an observer whose vocation is producing careful notes that can be later analyzed for the rhetorical and political lessons to be learned from the events they witness in the field. These tensions highlight the reality that rhetoricians' increasing interest in participatory modes of rhetorical criticism ensures that these political choices become all the more important to our scholarship. Participatory critical rhetoric enters this conversation by figuring the political entanglements between critics, audiences, and spaces of rhetorical practice as a central challenge that confronts rhetorical critics choosing to enter the field. However, what is, in one sense, a challenge offers, from a different perspective, an opportunity to expand and refine the critical rhetorical sensibilities that inform participatory critical rhetoric.

Participatory critical rhetoric, drawing from other politically-motivated approaches to rhetorical criticism, insists that criticism can never be neutral,[2] that criticism ought to engage in a "search for alternatives" to "powerful vested interests . . . that threaten life on the planet,"[3] and that criticism should serve a demystifying and emancipatory purpose by both unmasking how the discourse of power sustains inequality and by fostering "the self-clarification . . . of those oppositional social movements with which it has a partisan though not uncritical identification."[4] Participatory critical rhetoric mobilizes these commitments while placing them within the lived experiences and material constraints of *in situ* rhetorical practice.

In this chapter, we develop a critical framework that supports the negotiation of political commitments within participatory critical rhetoric. We argue that participatory critical rhetoric builds on critical rhetoric and ideological criticism by expanding its focus beyond (fragmented) textual discourses of power; that it places the critic within rhetorical scenes where immanent political and rhetorical efforts can be enacted by the critic; and that it, thereby, refigures the role of the critic toward that of an activist-scholar. We conclude by considering how refiguring the political commitments of critical rhetoric in relation to a participatory approach to criticism can expand the possibilities for critics to engage in activist research, as well as sharpen the critical judgment of critics in relation to the rhetorical contexts they examine.

PARTICIPATORY CRITICAL RHETORIC AND THE POLITICS OF CRITICISM

Participatory critical rhetoric expands the critical opportunities opened by the critical turn in rhetorical studies by theorizing a politicized rhetorical perspective that accounts for the differences in the critical focus, the political methodology, and the political identity of rhetorical critics who shift their attention to embodied, emplaced rhetorical practices. In this section, we develop a working definition of participatory critical rhetoric's approach to each, share some of our own experiences with these challenges from the field, and consider implications of these shifts in the theorizing of critical rhetorical practice. In doing so, we address participatory critical rhetoric's shift in focus toward *minor rhetorics*, the opportunity presented by *in situ* criticism to enable a turn to immanent politics generated by this shift in focus, and the refiguring of the role of the rhetorical critic from that of a critical scholar to an activist-scholar enabled by this change in critical orientation.[5] Our aim is not to circumscribe the political commitments of participatory critical rhetoric to just these three theoretical or methodological planes. Rather, ours is an attempt to draw attention to what we contend is, or ought to be, at the core of a shift to *in situ* rhetorical criticism while recognizing that the particular encounters between critics and their experiences in the field will necessitate supplements to these considerations, as well as theorizing that extends the arguments we outline here.

Participatory Critical Rhetoric and the Critique of Minor Rhetorics

Participatory critical rhetoric positions rhetorical scholars to more directly address the politics embedded in the varying levels of textocentrism—a privileging of the already documented (written) text—that inform the critical efforts of rhetorical theorists.[6] While participatory critical rhetoric shares the impulse of critical rhetoric and contemporary rhetorical criticism to rethink the object of rhetorical criticism and what constitutes a text suitable for analysis,[7] it also pushes this further by spotlighting how the enduring textual focus, albeit a focus on textual fragments, that dominates the practice of rhetorical criticism is not without political consequences for those communities where knowledge is produced in ways that exceed, or evade, textualization. As with Michael's experiences with SafeGround and its protest organizers, participatory critical rhetoric places the critic in rhetorical fields where they encounter a range of rhetorical practices, artifacts, performances, places, and other rhetorical phenomena that resist the forms of textualization familiar (and comfortable) for many critical rhetoricians. However, rather than simply conceptualizing this as a refiguring of rhetoric's object of analysis, we contend that participatory critical rhetoric highlights the political edge of these choices by providing an opportunity to examine rhetorical phenomena and fields of argument in ways that open critics' analyses to a broader range of rhetorical practices and (often unheard) voices.[8]

Central to this theoretical commitment of participatory critical rhetoric is the recognition of at least two political consequences of textocentrism. First, as Dwight Conquergood notes, the problem with textocentrism is not texts, it is that texts "are valorized to the exclusion of other media, other modes of knowing."[9] Phaedra Pezzullo, and Kent Ono and John Sloop, contend that textocentrism enacts a de facto choice to write out of history the rhetorical practices, acts of resistance, and moments of inventiveness that are embedded in the rhetorical lives of communities whose interactions are defined by talk on the corner, community-based media, counterpublic performances, and other vernacular exchanges, as well as those rhetorical events that fail to generate the immediate import to warrant transcribing their happenings.[10] As we discuss in chapter 5, one of the primary contributions made to rhetorical theory and criticism by the turn to participatory modes of rhetorical inquiry is that it creates opportunities for rhetorical theorizing to be informed by the multiperspectival forms of judgment that emerge from interaction in and with the community one is researching.

Second, an awareness of the risks of textocentric approaches to rhetorical criticism helps critics develop more nuanced theorizing and criticism in support of the emancipatory aims that guide their research. Remaining wedded to a textocentric critical perspective (however expanded) ensures that critical rhetoricians limit their opportunities to gain insights into the non-textual terrain of struggle that animates the experiences of many marginalized rhetorical communities. Conquergood explains the implication of this argument by highlighting the ethnocentrism of a textocentric model of critical practice. He argues that, "for many people throughout the world, . . . particularly subaltern groups, texts are often inaccessible, or threatening, charged with the regulatory powers of the state" and that "only middle-class academics could blithely assume that all the [rhetorical] world is a text [or collection of textual fragments] because reading and writing are central to their everyday lives and occupational security."[11] In other words, textocentrism cuts both ways: it both blinds the critic to the panoply of intersectional rhetorical activities in the communities they examine *and* it discourages critics from considering other ways knowing, other forms of media, which might better illuminate the rhetorical practices they critique for their academic audiences. In this section, we consider the politics embedded in selection of rhetorical artifacts from the field by identifying minor rhetorics as a way of defining the object of analysis for participatory critical rhetoric. A focus on minor rhetorics, we argue, is responsive to the political implications of how we frame the rhetorical practices we choose to examine. By focusing on minor rhetorics, participatory critical rhetoric provides a critical approach that can enable critics to identify marginalized rhetorical practices, critical logics, and forms of judgment that exceed the already documented (often written) rhetorical practices that are the traditional focus of our discipline, and can offer the critic a glimpse of alternative forms of rhetorical productivity with the potential to "transform cultural logics as a whole."[12]

Gilles Deleuze and Felix Guattari's distinction between *major(ity)* and *minor(ity)* politics and, by extension, rhetorics provides a useful schematic for highlighting the critical potential embedded in this shift in focus available to participatory critical rhetorical scholars.[13] For Deleuze and Guattari, *major(ity)* and *minor(ity)* do not refer to a numerical advantage in the traditional usage of majority and minority. Rather, the terms refer to those forms of politics (or rhetoric) that conform to a particular (usually dominant) standard set of cultural logics that ensure their legitimacy (*majority*) and those that do not and, therefore, reveal potential "becomings," that is, rhetorical and political opportunities, foreclosed by dominant cultural logics (*minority*).[14]

In this respect, they parallel the distinction between *civic* and *outlaw* discourses theorized by Sloop and Ono.[15] Distinguishing between majority and minority rhetorics focuses attention on the embodied performances, affective interchanges, and other practices of local communities of rhetorical practice that challenge political logics, shape identities, and build (the possibility for new forms of) community. In other words, "the 'minorization' of politics [or rhetoric]" focuses the critic's attention on rhetorical and political practices insofar as they demonstrate "seeds or crystals of becoming whose value is to trigger uncontrollable movements within the mean or the majority."[16] That is, to claim that participatory critical rhetoric provides a methodological opportunity to focus on minor rhetorics is to argue that it offers a critical orientation that encourages critics to engage local communities and their rhetorical practices with deliberate attention to those rhetorical efforts whose (embodied, fragmented, ephemeral) form fails to rise to the standard of typical texts suitable for criticism, and especially those practices whose substance challenges dominant cultural logics. For instance, during Michael's fieldwork experiences, the backstage interactions between SafeGround protestors as they prepared for and reflected on their protest march and rally demonstrate both the sorts of rhetorical productivity that resist textualization, as well as exemplify the sites of minor rhetorics that can inform participatory critical rhetorical inquiry. In this regard, then, participatory critical rhetoric provides the critic with an opportunity to simultaneously access these sorts of practices and—because of the dialogic, embodied, and emplaced dimensions of participatory rhetorical criticism—better apprehend and explain the import of those practices. As a consequence, it provides a valuable supplement to the enduring commitment to texts and textual fragments that grounds the majority of critical rhetorical scholarship. Simultaneously, we argue that scholars who adopt participatory critical rhetoric approaches recognize that they can productively rethink the preference toward already documented texts that informs scholarly production. Such a rethinking clears the space for critical interventions by scholars that can productively range from performance ethnography to documentary production to other embodied, aesthetic means by which the critic can articulate the lessons learned from their engagement with their rhetorical community of study.[17]

One of the most powerful implications of the recognition of the critical import of minor rhetorics is the new spaces for criticism such a shift reveals. As Samantha discovered, important rhetorical insights can be gained in the everyday experiences we share in our communities (often those communities we take for granted or do not envision as a site of research).

When I first moved to Omaha, I started volunteering because I wanted to support causes that I care about, learn more about local politics, and make friends. For me, fighting for a multi-modal approach to transportation has the potential to empower people living in poverty, contribute solutions to ever-increasing environmental problems, and advance feminist agendas. With this in mind, I have gotten involved with a few bike advocacy and education organizations; one of them is housed in my neighborhood, Gifford Park. A few years ago, I was thinking about Gifford Park visually and experientially. On the surface, this neighborhood can seem desolate. Many buildings have been abandoned and empty lots accumulate trash. I have witnessed police raids and been told stories about violence and danger. But this neighborhood is changing. The organization with which I volunteer, the Community Bike Project Omaha (CBPO), gave away over 150 bikes last year to children and adults who could not afford to buy a refurbished bike, many of whom live in or within a few miles of Gifford Park. By getting involved with this organization and talking with friends who volunteer with the Gifford Park Community Garden and Big Muddy Urban Farm, I have learned about efforts to materially change the neighborhood.

I did not join these organizations with a research project in mind. And, indeed, I do not plan to "leave the field" after I have published an essay about the rhetorical strategies some community members are using to transform Gifford Park. However, after four years of participating in the burgeoning local food and multi-modal transportation movements in Omaha, I now have a rich understanding of not only current relationships and politics, but also what has happened in decades past and what people hope for the future. By accessing these minor rhetorics I understand some of the intricacies of the neighborhood. For instance, three men own several buildings and lots that they rent to organizations like the CBPO, the Community Garden, and Big Muddy Urban Farm for a dollar/year because, as best as I can tell even with my honed skepticism and probing questions, they have altruistic goals for the neighborhood and the people who live there. They want to see these places become important members of the community in their own right. I also know that we have businesses run by a diverse group of people: a Latino family runs a small grocery store, a white man runs a Mexican restaurant, a white woman runs a homeopathic wellness center, a Middle Eastern family runs a gas station, and a Moroccan man runs a restaurant. I have a hunch that one man, who owns two central but unused buildings in Gifford Park, will probably never sell them because his family has owned one of the buildings since the early 1900s. Although I did not set out to acquire informants and win-over gatekeepers, I have gained an intimate knowledge of this community, which gives me an advantage as a researcher.

I was worried when I started interviewing people for a project, that some would be angry or feel betrayed. But I was met with curiosity about the project and a desire to help. In fact, a few people even approached me when they learned about the project, asking to be included in the interviews. Additionally, I have shared research findings with community members through informal conversations and a formal presentation, which creates a sense of openness and accountability. Through my embeddedness and relationships, I have developed a deeper knowledge of this neighborhood and the material, visual, and experiential rhetorics that govern the logic of movement through this place. Participatory critical rhetoric has, in this circumstance, allowed me to turn what might have been a simple observation about the changing nature of the neighborhood and the potential material, rhetorical reasons for that into a site of knowledge production. By valuing and attending to the rhetoric I experience often, walking through my neighborhood and volunteering, I have gained insight into patterns of behavior that reveal rhetorical constructions.

—Samantha

Experiences like Samantha's, as well as the growing focus on minor rhetoric by other rhetorical critics, suggest a range of political implications for rhetorical criticism. That is, our argument is not that one must necessarily engage in participatory critical rhetoric to critically examine minor rhetorics, but that participatory critical rhetoric provides greater access to these discourses. Insofar as we contend that the choice about what rhetorical practices we examine is a political one embedded in the practice of rhetorical criticism, our argument is that participatory critical rhetoric provides access to a set of (minor) rhetorical practices that both expand our discipline's focus beyond the traditional documented text and that offers the possibility of sharpening the political edge of rhetorical scholarship.

One way this is accomplished is by shifting critical focus toward the prefigurative politics that are embedded in minor rhetorics. Prefigurative politics describe the sorts of minor political and rhetorical interventions that form the substance of participatory critical rhetorical analysis and that are the foil to strategic politics. "Strategic politics" refer to "building [an] organization" in order to "achieve power" necessary to effect economic, political, or social change at the level of institutional shifts; on the other hand, "prefigurative politics represent critiques of existing social orders and realities, and attempt to create new forms of social interaction and alternative realities."[18] They are politics "put into practice in the collective actions and everyday interactions of social movement actors."[19] For example, the local strategies of agitation developed by homeless advocates in Sacramento investigated by Middleton reveal a political community developing a set of political affiliations and structures of governance, as well as rearticulated homeless identities, that enact the types of relationships between homeless and housed individuals, and homeless individuals and representatives of state institutions (e.g., police, social workers, etc.), for which the members of the homeless social movement in Sacramento are organizing.[20] What makes these efforts unique and highlights the potential of prefigurative politics as a conceptual frame is that the homeless activists are establishing these relationships, structures of governance, and articulations of homeless identity without the immediate support of or formalization of their efforts by state institutions. In fact, they often do so in spite of institutional work aimed at limiting their political actions. That is, homeless advocates are establishing forms of community-making that operate in parallel to state efforts to manage homelessness, efforts toward which homeless advocates are often opposed.

In this regard, participatory critical rhetoric is a necessary extension of rhetoric's ideological and critical turns if minor rhetorics are to be included within the scope of critical rhetorical scholarship because many, if not most, minor rhetorics can only be accessed through fieldwork and direct participation. Participatory critical rhetoric places rhetoricians alongside these acts of rhetorical resistance in ways that both let critics gain insights into how such efforts are experienced by their audiences, as well as to gain insights into how members of rhetorical communities inventing such rhetorics structure their rhetorical strategies.[21] For instance, by working closely with (often) unknown rhetorical communities and political movements, participatory critical rhetorical scholars are able to glimpse the enactment of prefigurative politics in the communities they examine. This focus supplements the impulse of critical rhetoric to demystify oppressive power relations and upend practices of domination by enabling critics to grasp the *in situ* rhetorical practices of resistance as developed in local communities.

Second, a focus on minor rhetorics sharpens critical focus on the import of immaterial, affective rhetoric that participatory critical rhetoricians encounter while in the field, like those encounters between members of SafeGround where stories of the shared experience of homelessness were exchanged as they prepared for their protest marches. As George McHendry et al. argue, affective, immaterial rhetoric describes rhetorics that "do not necessarily exert influence, leave traces, or function to constitute an (oppositional) identity in the way that rhetorical critics traditionally think of such processes."[22] Instead, they "are the rhetorical practices of which those later material rhetorical texts are expressions."[23] In other words, affective, immaterial rhetoric is not the naming of a community of resistance. Instead, it names the intimate, immanent interactions (e.g., organizing and sharing life stories before a protest march) where communities establish trust, share the willingness to be affected, and wherein the possibility for recognition of collective identity is nascent, but unnamed. Participatory critical rhetoric locates critics within the rhetorical milieu where such rhetorics circulate. As such, participatory critical rhetoricians are positioned to both make sense of the rhetorical import of such practices and begin to articulate why such rhetorical practices cannot be dismissed as merely phatic communication. Although rhetorical practices may fail to share the same formal characteristics that are present in more traditional rhetorics that operate constitutively or within a logic of influence (reason and argument) rather than affect, they contribute to the rhetorical milieu and deserve critical attention.

Participatory Critical Rhetoric and the Enactment of Immanent Politics

Participatory critical rhetoric approaches *in situ* rhetorical criticism as a political undertaking in two respects: first, it recognizes the political implications of the selection of research sites a scholar chooses to examine and, second, it considers the consequences regarding what rhetorical practices are brought back from the field for examination and use in efforts to shape future rhetorical practice.[24] However, participatory critical rhetoric also expands and redefines the commitments to emancipatory politics and praxis it shares with critical rhetoric, as well as efforts by scholars to focus their attention on *in situ* rhetorics, by embracing the potential to engage in an immanent politics of criticism.

Central to this theoretical shift by participatory critical rhetoric is recognizing a limitation to the contemporary practice of critical rhetoric.[25] In his development of critical rhetoric, Raymie McKerrow contends that the "ultimate test" of critical rhetoric is whether it "serve[s] to identify the possibilities for *future action*" [emphasis added] for participants in a particular rhetorical context.[26] Participatory critical rhetoric brings into focus the reality that an orientation toward theorizing *future* critical rhetorical practice can prevent critical rhetoric scholars, as Maurice Charland notes, from activating, assisting, or even reaching efforts at social agitation or change on which they focus in the moments where they encounter those practices.[27] In other words, because critical rhetoric is concerned with offering counsel about future action, the politics of the immediate rhetorical situation can be deferred. The critic is charged not with intervening in the immediate circumstance, but instead with locating insights that can be utilized to inform a future rhetorical situation or that can be used to engage in future action.

Participatory critical rhetoric enables a critical praxis that creates opportunities for and affirms the value of immanent politics.[28] In this respect, if Ono and Sloop critique the tendency toward critical paralysis present in critical rhetoric and argue for a critical commitment when one "puts pen to paper," then participatory critical rhetoric suggests that critical rhetoric can be pushed further by critics making the same immanent political and critical choices when their bodies are present in the field of rhetorical practice.[29] For instance, the critic in the field confronts the opportunity to join with and adopt the political commitments of the communities in which they conduct their research (by, for example, joining protest marches, helping prepare for protest, etc.), as well as to challenge those commitments as they participate in the field. These opportunities often present themselves as and morph between several participatory roles, including critic, advocate, and ally (and sometimes all three at once). Navigating these roles presents a challenge to the critic in the field as they work to understand the rhetorical practices of the communities they engage, as well as how their involvement with them makes claims on our their political and ethical commitments.[30] One way these challenges can be navigated is through a turn to immanent politics.

Attention to immanence, immanent participation, and immanent politics by participatory critical rhetoricians challenges how critics relate to the specific community they research and the rhetorical practices of that community (i.e., the object of analysis). This prompts participatory rhetorical critics to reimagine the political horizon of their rhetorical inquiry. McHendry et al. argue that reimagining the relationship between the critic and the community they research can foster the possibility for immanent participation. Immanent participation, they argue, "encourages a willingness to be affected in a serious way by the local and singular struggles of grassroots rhetorical communities" as a way to sensitize critics to the "active politics of the sites they (temporarily) inhabit."[31] Said differently, immanence positions critics "in terms of relations 'in'" a community, whereas a future-oriented *telos* understands critics (and their work) in relation "to" a community.[32] Immanent participation challenges participatory rhetorical critics to focus on the immediate social relations in which they are present when in the field of rhetorical practice. It opposes transcendence, which holds that "there is a true path toward which to aspire" that cannot be revealed in the immediate rhetorical context that occupies critics, and that "requires accepting unequal power relations for the time being," so that critics can use their relations to a community to mine discursive fragments that may inform future rhetorical practices.[33] Immanent participation follows Stephen Hartnett's lead,[34] asking critics to privilege their relationship with the members of the communities they research in the locations they research and on an equal plane with their relationship to a community of critics or an imagined, future political community to whom they will provide counsel.

Refiguring the relationship between critics and the rhetorical field they (temporarily) inhabit through immanent participation further shapes participatory critical rhetoric as a politically engaged mode of critical inquiry. Specifically, it positions critics to participate in immanent politics. Once critics limit their desire to find a transcendent truth to guide future politics, it positions them to shift their focus from politics deferred toward an immanent politics that challenges the critic to adopt a participatory role in the field they inhabit and to search for emancipatory opportunities availed by their presence in the field. This can include choosing to offer expertise to the rhetorical community hosting the critic's research, lending one's body to support those of other protestors from whom a researcher is collecting rhetorical insight, or any of a range of other options for participation by the critic. Often, these contributions are rather banal, including passing out fliers, setting up tables, scheduling meetings, making PowerPoint slides, and providing transportation, for example. While they can be dismissed as relatively unimportant, it is our argument that through these forms of participation and others, participatory rhetorical critics are able to embed themselves in what Raymond Williams refers to as the "whole way of life" that defines a (rhetorical) culture.[35] Importantly, each of these opportunities to participate with and in the community one researches reflects what McHendry et al. describe as "doing rhetoric," as opposed to merely observing or analyzing the rhetoric of others. They note, "Doing rhetoric means that the critic is engaged in rhetorical action . . . [as] opposed to observing rhetoric for future potential to affect change through action-deferred . . . . Critics who do rhetoric . . . open a space for understanding rhetoric at the level of its practice in the community they are researching and inhabiting."[36] Of course, some of these options are also available to practitioners of critical rhetoric who choose not to enter the field. However, our argument is that critics who choose to enter the field are in a better position to shift from offering *advice to* a community where the stakes of participation are relatively low (after all, critics can escape the consequences of their participation to the safety of their office) to *participating in* a community where the critic shares similar, if not the same, stakes in the consequences of the rhetorical practices engaged in by the community they examine. The participatory critical rhetoric approach often sees these two forms of engagement, the political and the critical, as always intertwined, rather than compartmentalized, endeavors.

The opportunities to engage in immanent politics for the researcher in the field are both abundant in their existence and unpredictable in their frequency. However, in addition to supplementing the horizon of action-deferred politics with immanent practice, participating in immanent politics is often the only way the politically-motivated participatory critical rhetorician can be sure that their engagement will offer a meaningful contribution, in the future or otherwise. Danielle's experiences during her research about the "Atomic West" forced her to directly confront the challenges (and pleasures) of integrating rhetorical scholarship and immanent participation in the communities she studied.

For me, there are always moments in the course of fieldwork when I know that I have to temporarily abandon my researcher role and actively participate in something going on in the field. In the moment, it seems to me like the right thing or even the only thing to do. Several years back, I attended an activist gathering by the Nevada Test Site (now called the Nevada National Security Site)—the most heavily nuclear-bombed location in the world—as a part of my ongoing research about nuclear colonialism in the American West. The climax of the gathering came on the last day with a Mother's Day march to the gate of the test site, followed by a planned act of civil disobedience for those who chose to enter the test site and get arrested for trespassing on federal land. Western Shoshone representatives issued passports for participants to hand over to NTS security officers when crossing into the test site, in recognition that the test site is on land claimed by the Western Shoshone under the 1863 Ruby Valley Treaty of Peace and Friendship. Mass trespassing and arrests on the Nevada Test Site had been going since the early 1980s, a typical part of protests and activist gatherings at the Test Site. In some ways, this had become a ritualistic form of civil disobedience that came with little physical or permanent risk to the transgressor. From what I heard during the civil disobedience training the day before, the most likely event was to be held in a chain link detention pen on the other side of the boundary for a while and then released. It was also unlikely that the charges would actually be processed, go through a court proceeding, or result in a permanent arrest record. Previous protests, especially in the 1980s and 1990s (before the Comprehensive Test Ban Treaty stopped nuclear testing at the site) had more severe outcomes (e.g., a jail stay, a permanent record), and while the officers always had the option of these more severe outcomes, it was unlikely given its taking place in 2007 and the small size of the protest. Within this context and as a part of my commitment to the cause, I decided that being involved in this act of civil disobedience, crossing the boundary into the Test Site and presenting a Western Shoshone passport, was something that I had to do. I wanted to show my support; I wanted to lend my body to the group to bolster its force; I wanted to advocate with the movement.

On the day of the protest, I started out assuming my usual role as researcher and archivist (making audio recordings of the protest to share with the organization later). I walked along with the protest, but avoided too much chanting or talking to help preserve the quality of the audio archive. I stayed close to the speakers and the center of the protest, and merely holding recording equipment helped make that possible. As the group approached the gate to the test site, we stopped and the people who planned to take part in the planned arrest prepared to cross the boundary. I turned off my recorder when the speeches were done, handed it to someone for safe keeping, and walked into the test site. A few people next to me laid down and had to be carried by NTS officers as they made their bodies limp. I chose to keep walking along with some others and was led into the female detention pen. It was an odd site. The gate to the test site is miles away from any buildings, structures, or ground zero craters on the test site and these are not visible in the horizon. What is visible beyond the gate is simply a road into the desert and the chain link fenced detention pens on the left side of the road. In that moment I became one of many female bodies being held within this chain link fence. I temporarily shed my researcher and archivist roles, and took on the role of a participant and advocate with the movement. This was an important move for me, not so much in terms of credibility with the community (though I cannot deny that it had an affect on how the community saw me), but in terms of solidifying my own commitment and taking this small action to demonstrate my belief that the test site is an unlawful use of Western Shoshone land. This moment of immanent politics felt more important in the moment than what I could do with my writing in the future. I could write about the Western Shoshone's objection to nuclear testing on their sacred land, I could unpack the rhetorical dynamics of the protest (which were actually quite ordinary in terms of protest rhetoric), or I could be part of the rhetorical protest body in that moment. However small, participating in this collective act of civil disobedience allowed me to be a part of the movement, be a part of the body rhetoric, and perform my own politics in that moment. Had I waited to perform some sort of future critical action, it would have delayed this commitment that felt so important to me in the moment. Further, given that I have not yet published on this particular event, I have yet to make an after-the-fact political contribution though my analysis and writing. Despite intent to do something in the future, future actions and future interventions are always uncertain. Given this uncertainty, immanent participation can take on additional importance as perhaps the only chance to contribute to the political aims of the movement.

—Danielle

Based on our collective experiences struggling with how to adopt an orientation of immanent participation and to engage our own work with the immanent political struggles of the communities we research, we have grappled with some implications of immanent politics for scholars interested in theorizing the political and methodological dimensions of rhetorical theory and criticism. First, immanent politics addresses the challenges embedded in what we see as rhetoric's bias toward politics deferred. As Dilip Gaonkar notes, McKerrow's effort to discuss the critique of domination and the critique of freedom in his original formulation does not offer a set of organized principles "for the conduct of practical criticism."[37] Rather, he argues that it offers a densely loaded set of theoretical resources out of which critics can develop a procedure for pursuing its emancipatory political aims. Our argument is that participatory critical rhetoric, by encouraging critics to engage in immanent participation and politics, can supplement and revitalize the political consequence of critical rhetorical scholarship, as well as some previous efforts to theorize field-based rhetorical methods, by privileging the politics encountered by the critic *in situ* rather than a future political struggle to which they will offer counsel. At the same time, it also begins to augment the role of the critic from just an expert who evaluates and critiques the rhetoric of others to one who also participates in and reflects alongside their fellow community members. In chapters 3 and 5, we articulate the significance of this shift as we turn our attention to how a move toward participatory critical rhetoric reconfigures how we conceptualize critics in relation to both rhetors and rhetorics in the field.

Second, an approach to participatory critical rhetoric, as well as rhetorical criticism more broadly, that engages with immanent politics can shift the horizon of rhetoric's political focus. A perspective informed by immanence recognizes that "though any species, thing, system, or civilization may last for a long time, nothing lasts forever. Each . . . oscillates between periods of relative arrest and those of heightened imbalance and change, followed again by new stabilizations."[38] Recognizing this, immanent politics, and the criticism it informs, assumes neither that critical rhetoric's emancipatory goals can be fully realized nor that the politics of an immediate rhetorical context will usefully inform future actions during another period of political oscillation and stabilization. Rather, it looks for the ways in which critics can meaningfully be affected by and participate in the moment in the rhetorical field they occupy. McHendry et al. summarize this, noting that, immanent politics "refuse to limit the consequence of one's critical commitments in the field to only bringing back rhetorical traces that can help us direct 'future action;' it asks what can be done in the immanent moments of (co)participation in the field and demands that such moments (and the choices they entail) equally influence our critical findings."[39] Making this shift, as we discuss in the next section, can radically alter not only our scholarship, but how we conceive of our identity as critical rhetorical scholars.

Participatory Critical Rhetoric and Activist Scholarship

Participatory critical rhetoric provides a context in which rhetorical critics can rethink the political identity of the rhetorical scholar. More specifically, whereas critical rhetoric's twin commitments to the critique of freedom and the critique of domination risk, as Ono and Sloop note, leaving critical rhetorical scholars paralyzed in regard to participating in the political praxis of the communities they examine or issuing critical judgments about the discursive formations they demystify,[40] participatory critical rhetoric provides a means, through a sensitivity to immanent action and a recognition of the import of minor rhetorics, by which critical scholars can actively and materially engage in the political milieu on which they focus their research.

Participatory critical rhetoric accomplishes this by embracing a perspective on critical praxis that is informed by the knowledge and critical judgments of the communities in which scholars conduct their research. In place of disembodied texts or documented textual fragments, participatory critical rhetoric gives critics a way to understand that those texts are the products of emplaced rhetorical *bodies* and to access the embodied and emplaced instantiation of rhetorical invention that produced them. By doing so, participatory critical rhetoric recognizes the rhetor's role in the production and circulation of rhetoric, enabling critics to ground their critical judgment in an assumption that the individual rhetors and localized rhetorical communities they examine are differently "thinking, theorizing, [and] culture-processing human beings."[41] As such, participatory critical rhetoric helps reveal alternative foundations for critical judgment, as well as rhetorical and political tactics, that often "fly under the radar" when criticism focuses on documented textual artifacts alone.[42] In this respect, participatory critical rhetoricians enact the challenge Hartnett outlines, which states that rhetorical critics ought to replace "third-person perspective studies" with "first-person perspective studies" that enable critics to account for and "navigate the complexities and contradictions of the communities with whom they work and play" that are often unseen in the traditional rhetorical texts focused on by rhetorical critics.[43]

Of course, like a focus on minor rhetorics, one need not necessarily engage in participatory critical rhetoric, or fieldwork of any sort, to do the work of an activist-scholar. For instance, in recent years, several collective volumes have taken up and provided examples of how communication scholars generally, and rhetorical scholars specifically, can connect their work with a recognition that rhetoricians "may find [them]selves on the front line of defending democracy in [a] highly charged and inhospitable culture of fear."[44] In this section, we consider what is entailed by the move toward activist scholarship, as well as how participatory critical rhetoric provides a productive, but not exclusive, means by which rhetorical scholars might interweave their scholarly endeavors with their political commitments.

The growing debate about the political responsibilities of the critic and the call to rethink communication scholars, and especially rhetorical critics, as activist scholars grow out of recognition of the political potential of rhetorical criticism as an intellectual undertaking that requires a significant shift in the way rhetorical scholars think about how they approach their research.

As David Coogan and John Ackerman argue, part of the growing focus on the political implications of rhetorical scholarship, is a shared desire among rhetoricians who value the emancipatory aims of rhetoric's critical and ideological turns to "reject the idea that public life is dead, that it has been stripped of agitation, assembly, and deliberation, and that it is devoid of political discourse beyond shouts of anger."[45] Instead, they argue that the growing risk of these troubling realities should serve as a call to action among rhetorical scholars to recognize that "rhetorical practice is all the more relevant in comprehending how this moment came to pass," and how best to respond.[46] Paired with the recognition that there is still a place for rhetoric and rhetorical criticism to inform public life and salvage democratic engagement, scholars have increasingly acknowledged that politically meaningful work must necessarily work to expand the limited boundaries of productivity valued by the academy. As Cloud observes, while "I still write, teach, publish, and serve in my academic life," "these activities . . . cannot make a new world . . . [,] putting ideas into action is the only conceivable thing to do."[47]

The perhaps premature claims about the limited value of academic productivity aside, if one accepts these the argument that rhetorical practice is more important now than ever and that, to be effective politically, rhetorical critics cannot limit their work to only (traditional) scholarly forms of productivity, then it requires a concomitant shift in how rhetoricians approach their research. As Coogan and Ackerman state, "we have a choice to make as critics: we can limit our analyses to the attributes of the circumstances before us," or "we can learn from those circumstances how to look at the world differently."[48] Participatory critical rhetoric, we argue, provides a means of doing the latter and strengthening the political consequences of the work done by rhetorical critics. While it is not the only path, we believe that it offers a useful one for critics aiming to align their research with a set of political commitments that exceed the requirements of the academy in favor of contributing to a broader political community.

In one respect, participatory critical rhetoric provides a way of restoring the political consequence of academic productivity. By wedding our critical endeavors that are directed to academic audiences with embedded, emplaced work in existing rhetorical communities, the bifurcation of academic productivity and political activism articulated by Cloud begins to dissolve. Data collection can occur alongside political engagement, rhetorical analysis can correspond with participation in the formation of protest events and other political actions, and theorizing critical praxis can occur alongside experimenting with possible interventions with the communities joined by rhetorical critics. In each instance, the community of political struggle about which participatory rhetorical critics write ceases to be out there engaging in some future rhetorical action and the possibility of productively blurring the boundaries between scholar and activist is thrown open.

Like moments that invite immanent participation and that signal presence of minor rhetorics, opportunities to connect critical work with political commitments are abundant in field research. However, as Aaron discovered, it is also important that the activist-scholar be prepared to accept that such a fusion of commitments is not always exciting, despite their importance to the causes one examines in the course of their research.

You wouldn't think that there could ever be a boring day at a rave. Nearly by definition, raves are supposed to be chemically accented experiences in pleasure and sensory stimulation. Still, for DanceSafe advocates who go to raves nearly every weekend, sometimes raves can be "quiet." The cops didn't show up and bust the event; ambulances weren't called to cart an overdosed teen off into the night. Things can be "normal"—as normal as hundreds of intoxicated ecstasy eaters can be, I suppose.

As a researcher in the scene, I was frequently attuned to these moments where my data collection could be inflected with narratives of extreme acts of DanceSafe bravery, deep deliberations regarding legality of drugs, or sensual stories about hallucinogens. These critical incidents sparked my interest in the work. But they didn't happen every day. Mostly, DanceSafe was there to answer questions about drugs and interactions between drugs, provide information for treatment centers, and occasionally help out someone who was in serious need of medical attention. Being a participant meant that I experienced all of the elements of the group, even the most mundane moments of scouting for a place to set up camp, hauling tables and chairs into the desert, and clipping pamphlets down so they wouldn't blow away in the wind. These moments barely made my fieldnotes, but they certainly made a difference in the overall cause. Sometimes, participation in an organization like DanceSafe means completing the drudgery of the campaign. This level of participation may not feel like much, but can really help.

As time progressed, even the more interesting interactions became less and less interesting from a researcher perspective. This could be a sign of saturation in data collection, but was better understood as becoming more and more involved within the immanent political needs of the organization. After one particular rave, I recall meeting up with my dissertation advisor and chatting about the night. It was full of interactions with ravers asking the typical questions about drug use and abuse, but nothing stood out. My fieldnotes felt sparse and ordinary, especially when juxtaposed with stories of tripping out on ayahuasca. Talking about the night, my advisor commented that, at the very least, I was still doing work—good work—for the cause.

It's true. I may not have anything profound to recount for that one night, but the tables still got set up, the pamphlets didn't blow away in the wind, drug education was still passed on, and donations were collected to continue the fight.

—Aaron

Our experiences, and others' accounts of their efforts in their own scholarship, of navigating the political entanglements of critical participatory research reveal a growing interest by rhetorical scholars to make connections between their academic endeavors and their political allegiances, as well as the challenges entailed by those (sometimes) competing interests. Participatory critical rhetoric does not provide the only means of navigating these challenges or, in some cases, the best critical orientation. However, we do contend that participatory critical rhetoric offers unique opportunities for critics working to integrate an identity as an activist with their identity as a scholar, as well as providing a space to theorize these questions in relation to other efforts pursued by scholars adopting different critical orientations.

One means by which participatory critical rhetoric fuses the practice of rhetorical criticism with activism is via the opportunities for *witnessing* by rhetorical critics, which we take up in greater detail in chapter 3. By witnessing, we use the term in the double sense highlighted by John Durham Peters, wherein witnessing describes both the act of observation and recording, as well as the act of *bearing witness* and participating in building, circulating, and advocating for a political community or a rhetorical practice.[49] In the first sense, archiving mundane rhetorics that fail to gain the status of objectified text contributes to gaining more developed insights into the processes that guide the development of oppositional political collectivities.[50] Second, witnessing provides a means through which the boundaries that bifurcate research and research subject can be eroded. As Peters explains, witnessing is a "means by which experience is supplied to others who lack access to the original" experience.[51] Against the power relations that hold in place particular identities and representations, witnessing enables participatory critical rhetoricians to blur the lines between becoming informed about a rhetorical community, while, at the same time, "it reorients our conception of what citizens can do."[52] Lastly, witnessing is also a critical concept for identifying the interconnections between the embodied and discursive dimensions of local rhetorical practices. Because "one can witness with the eyes, the voice, or the body," acts of witnessing by participatory critical rhetoricians perform a two fold critical function: on the one hand, they enact a rhetorical strategy in which "information and participation are one."[53] By sharing experiences from the field, participatory critical rhetoricians can invite outsiders (allies and potential researchers) into the rhetorical communities with whom they work. On the other hand, these acts of witnessing make moral claims on their audiences.[54] These claims become the foundation of collective identifications and acts of solidarity by positioning critics to make meaningful contributions to the communities with which they interact because, through witnessing and other critical strategies, it enables critics to develop strong relationships and intense understandings of the rhetorical practices and political stakes at play in the community one researches.[55] Additionally, witnessing provides an opportunity to develop *phronesis* that can be used to both better support the community through volunteer efforts and to offer expert feedback for activist communities who seek the input of researchers with whom they work.[56] More importantly, as we discuss in chapter 5, by embedding the critic in the community from where such rhetorics emerge, participatory critical rhetoric helps the critic navigate the ethical entanglements involved in the choice to join the political struggles of communities we interact with as researchers.

PARTICIPATORY CRITICAL RHETORIC AND PRODUCTIVE CRITICISM

Our aim in this chapter has been to highlight some of the political commitments that inform participatory critical rhetoric, both as we theorize it and as it has been practiced in some rhetorical scholarship that engages with field-based rhetorical inquiry. Ours is not an attempt to create a recipe or set of steps for the practice of participatory critical rhetoric, but rather to argue for an orientation to participatory critical rhetoric in relation to some of the critical questions and challenges it raises. In this chapter, we tried to keep that focus on the political commitments of participatory critical rhetoric. In other chapters, we address some ways that scholars can orient to the question of text, field, participants, and other factors that are made relevant by the rhetorician's choice to enter the field.

It is worth noting, however, that our argument is not that participatory critical rhetoric is the only, or always the best, means of engaging in politically-motivated rhetorical scholarship; nor do we argue that scholars who are engaging in more common, textually-oriented forms of critical scholarship cannot have commitments sensitized to the same concepts and issues we raised in this chapter. Instead, our argument is two fold. First, participatory critical rhetoric offers some unique opportunities and challenges as regards the intersection between rhetorical scholarship and political engagement. We think the concepts introduced in this chapter provide a good starting point for thinking about those challenges and opportunities. Second, given the proliferation of field-based rhetorical studies, we argue that outlining an approach, participatory critical research in this case, and arguing for the unique possibilities and contributions it can make can help push forward efforts to theorize participatory critical rhetoric, create dialogue across field-based rhetorical approaches, and sharpen the critical insights developed by scholars operating from a variety of methodological perspectives on rhetorical analysis.

Nonetheless, it is also important to acknowledge that, while we generally characterize participatory critical rhetoric in terms of research focused on marginalized communities, social justice-oriented rhetorical practices, and emancipatory political aims, participatory critical rhetoric does not require that one's scholarship necessarily align with her or his personal political commitments. Rather, we contend that the concepts we introduce in this chapter could as easily inform research that focuses on communities with whom one disagrees or about whom one has serious reservations. Indeed, if the goal of rhetorical scholarship following the critical turn is emancipatory politics, part of that project is understanding the efforts by communities of resistance. But, an equally important part of engaging in those politics is understanding the rhetorical logics of communities that sustain inequality. For example, one can learn how to engage in more effective environmental activism by learning about the rhetorical practices of communities with little regard for the environment, by building affective bonds through immanent participation, by locating minor rhetorics within those communities that could possibly reveal the potential for cooperation that is not present in majority rhetorics as they are currently practiced, and that can enable critics to move from analysis of those communities for their shortcomings toward analysis that identifies potential for effective rhetorical interventions. In other words, while participatory critical rhetoric often engages with communities working against dominant institutions and ideological interests, that is neither a necessary condition of its practice, nor is it reflective of the range of contexts in which participatory critical rhetoric can offer generative insights. Following Robert Ivie, we contend that, in this respect, participatory critical rhetoric enables rhetoricians to engage in "productive criticism," which requires critics to retool their approach to criticism by trading the "reconstruction of rhetorical reality" for a desire to "invent realistic alternatives" to those realities.[57] In other words, productive criticism encourages critics to examine local instances of rhetorical practice by unpacking their strategic and tactical choices as new rhetorical frames and conceptual vocabularies, whether those are vocabularies of domination or grammars of resistance. In the next chapter, we argue that participatory critical rhetoricians embody different roles and must consider the forms their bodies take in the field as they attempt to enact these political commitments.

NOTES

1. Victor Turner, *From Ritual to Theater: The Human Seriousness of Play* (New York: PAJ Publications, 1982): 44.

2. For the first iteration of this debate, see the debate between Karlyn Kohrs Campbell and Forbes Hill. Forbes Hill, "Conventional Wisdom—Traditional Form—the President's Message of November 3, 1969," *Quarterly Journal of Speech* 58 (1972): 373–86, doi:10.1016; Karlyn Kohrs Campbell, "Response to Forbes Hill," *Central States Speech Journal* 34 (1983): 126–27, doi: 10.1080/10510978309368130.

3. Phillip Wander, "The Ideological Turn in Modern Criticism," *Central States Speech Journal* 34 (1983): 18, doi: 10.1080/10510978309368110.

4. Raymie E. McKerrow, "Critical Rhetoric: Theory and Praxis," *Communication Monographs* 56 (1989): 91–93, doi: 10.1080/03637758909390253.

5. Gilles Deleuze and Felix Guattari, *Essays Critical and Clinical* (London: Verso, 1998).

6. Dwight Conquergood, "Performance Studies: Interventions and Radical Research," *TDR/The Drama Review* 46 (2002): 151, doi:10.1162/105420402320980550.

7. Michael Calvin McGee, "Text, Context, and the Fragmentation of Contemporary Culture," *Western Journal of Speech Communication* 54 (1990): 274–89, doi: 10.1080/10570319009374343; McKerrow, "Critical Rhetoric: Theory and Praxis."

8. While our critique and the approach to criticism we develop in this chapter builds on Conquergood's critique of textocentrism in communication research, we, agreeing with Conquergood, are not suggesting that texts are unvaluable. Rather, we aim to highlight that participatory critical rhetoric creates the opportunity to include the often excluded extratextual rhetorical practices of local communities with our critical efforts and (as we discuss in later chapters) sometimes demands that critics' scholarly productivity traverse the boundaries of traditional academic forms, producing less textocentric critical projects that reveal and illuminate the rhetorical practices of those communities. Rather, in turning to a discussion of the implications of textocentrism, we are aiming to critique the dominance of an already documented textual focus among critical rhetoricians at the expense of other forms of rhetorical activity.

9. Dwight Conquergood, "Performance Studies." 151.

10. Kent A. Ono and John M. Sloop, "The Critique of Vernacular Discourse," *Communication Monographs* 62 (1995): 19–46, doi: 10.1080/03637759209376248; Phaedra C. Pezzullo, "Resisting 'National Breast Cancer Awareness Month': The Rhetoric of Counterpublics and their Cultural Performances," *Quarterly Journal of Speech* 89 (2003): 345–65, doi: 10.1080/0033563032000160981.

11. Conquergood, "Performance Studies," 147.

12. John M. Sloop and Kent A. Ono, "Out-law Discourse: The Critical Politics of Material Judgment," *Philosophy & Rhetoric* 30 (1997): 65, doi: 10.1080/14791420.2015.1071309.

13. Deleuze and Guattari, *Essays Critical and Clinical.*

14. Ibid, 291.

15. Sloop and Ono, "Outlaw Discourse."

16. Daniel. W. Smith, "'A Life of Pure Immanence': Gilles Deleuze, "'Critique et Clinique' Project," in *Essays Critical and Clinical,* eds. Gilles Deleuze and Felix Guattari (Minneapolis: University of Minnesota Press, 1997): xlii–xliii.

17. Art Herbig and Aaron Hess, "Convergent Critical Rhetoric at the 'Rally to Restore Sanity': Exploring the Intersection of Rhetoric, Ethnography, and Documentary Production," *Communication Studies* 63 (2012): 269–89, doi: 10.1080/10510974.2012.674617; Art Herbig, Aaron Hess, and Alix Watson, *Never Forget: Public Memory & 9/11*, Motion Picture directed by Art Herbig (2014; USA, Living Text Productions), Digital Video. Dwight Conquergood, "Rethinking Ethnography: Towards a Critical Cultural Politics," *Communication Monographs* 58 (1991): 179–94, doi: 10.1080/03637759109376222; Dwight Conquergood, "Performing as a Moral Act: Ethical Dimensions of the Ethnography of Performance," *Text and Performance Quarterly* 5 (1985): 1–13, doi: 10.1080/10462938509391578.

18. Timothy Ingalsbee, "Earth First! Activism: Ecological Postmodern Praxis in Radical Environmentalist Identities," *Sociological Perspectives* 39 (1996): 266, doi: 10.2307/1389312.

19. Ibid., 266.

20. Michael K. Middleton, "Housing, Not Handcuffs: Homeless Misrecognition and 'SafeGround Sacramento's' Homeless Activism," *Communication, Culture & Critique* 7 (2014): 320–37, doi: 10.1111/cccr.12055; Michael K. Middleton, "'Safe-Ground Sacramento' and Rhetorics of Substantive Citizenship," *Western Journal of Communication* 78 (2014): 119–33, doi: 10.1080/10570314.2013.835064.

21. Smith, "'A Life of Pure Immanence,'" xlii-xliii.

22. George F. McHendry Jr., Michael K. Middleton, Danielle Endres, Samantha Senda-Cook, and Megan O'Byrne, "Rhetorical Critic(ism)'s Body: Affect and Fieldwork on a Plane of Immanence," *Southern Communication Journal* 79 (2014): 305, doi: 10.1080/1041794X.2014.906643.

23. Ibid, 305.

24. Michael K. Middleton, Samantha Senda-Cook, and Danielle Endres, "Articulating Rhetorical Field Methods: Challenges and Tensions," *Western Journal of Communication* 75 (2011): 390, doi: 10.1080/10570314.2011.586969.

25. McKerrow, "Critical Rhetoric: Theory and Praxis"; A. Susan Owen and Peter Ehrenhaus, "Animating a Critical Rhetoric: On the Feeding Habits of American Empire," *Western Journal of Communication* 57 (1993): 169–77, doi: 10.1080/10570319309374440; Dilip Parameshwar Gaonkar, "Performing with Fragments: Reflections on Critical Rhetoric," in *Argument and the Postmodern Challenge: Proceedings of the eighth SCA/AFA Conference on Argumentation*, ed. Raymie. E. McKerrow (Annandale, VA: SCA, 1993): 149–55; Maurice Charland, "Finding a Horizon and *Telos*: The Challenge to Critical Rhetoric," *Quarterly Journal of Speech* 77 (1991): 71–74, doi: 10.1080/00335639109383944; Kent A.Ono and John M. Sloop, "Commitment to *Telos*—A Sustained Critical Rhetoric," *Communication Monographs* 59 (1992): 48–60, doi: 10.1080/03637759209376248; Raymie E. McKerrow and Jeffrey St. John, "Critical Rhetoric and Continual Critique," in *The Art of Rhetorical Criticism*, ed. Jim A. Kuypers (Boston: Allyn & Bacon, 2005): 345–66; Raymie E. McKerrow, "Critical Rhetoric and the Possibility of the

Subject," in *The Critical Turn: Rhetoric and Philosophy in Postmodern Discourse*, eds. Ian Angus and L. Langsdorf (Carbondale: Southern Illinois Press, 1993): 51–67; Raymie E. McKerrow, "Critical Rhetoric in a Postmodern World," *Quarterly Journal of Speech* 77 (1991): 75–78, doi: 10.1080/00335639109383945; Robert Hariman, "Critical Rhetoric and Postmodern Theory," *Quarterly Journal of Speech* 77 (1991): 67–70, doi: 10.1080/00335639109383943.

26. McKerrow, "Critical Rhetoric: Theory and Praxis," 91–92.

27. Charland, "Finding a Horizon and *Telos*." See also, McHendry et al., "Rhetorical Critic(ism)'s Body."

28. Because of its commitment to *in situ* research practices, participatory critical rhetoric highlights McHendry et al.'s contention that, "occupying . . . the space of live rhetorical action creates the space for students of rhetoric to make good on the [unfulfilled] impulse of critical rhetorical studies to envision themselves as . . . potential actors in emancipatory practice, not simply critics of interventions already performed." See McHendry et al., "Rhetorical Critic(ism)'s Body," 295.

29. Ono, and Sloop, "Commitment to *Telos,*" 53.

30. However, that is not to say that critics in the field alone possess the authority or opportunity to practice immanent politics. Indeed, as Campbell notes, critics of more traditional rhetorical discourse (and with more traditional aims) could still choose to take action in relation to a community or topic they explore through already archived rhetorical artifacts by engaging in "social criticism" alongside more traditional forms of "academic," rhetorical criticism. The difference we contend is that participatory critical rhetoric asks critics to navigate these opportunities in the moment without the opportunity to make choices with the benefit of the distance and time (and, sometimes, increased safety) offered by working only with after-the-fact rhetorical discourse. See Karlyn Kohrs Campbell, "Criticism: Ephemeral and Enduring," *The Speech Teacher* 23 (1974): 9–14, doi: 10.1080/03634527409378050. See also, Valerie R. Renegar, "Critical/Cultural Scholarship and the Responsibility for Building Theory: Enduring Criticism Revisited," *Western Journal of Communication* 77 (2013): 509–13, doi: 10.1080/10570314.2013.804194.

31. McHendry et al., "Rhetorical Critic(ism)'s Body," 305; see also Jamie Merchant, "Immanence, Governmentality, Critique: Toward a Recovery of Totality in Rhetorical Theory," *Philosophy & Rhetoric* 47 (2014): 227–50.

32. James Williams, "Immanence," in *The Deleuze Dictionary*, ed. Adrian Parr (New York: Columbia University Press, 2010): 126.

33. McHendry et al., "Rhetorical Critic(ism)'s Body," 297.

34. Stephen John Hartnett, "Communication, Social Justice, and Joyful Commitment," *Western Journal of Communication* 74 (2010): 68–93, doi: 10.1080/105703109034.

35. Raymond Williams, "Culture is Ordinary," in *Cultural Theory: An Anthology*, eds. Imre Szeman and Timothy Kaposy (Oxford: Wiley-Blackwell, 2011): 54.

36. McHendry et al., "Rhetorical Critic(ism)'s Body," 298.

37. Gaonkar, "Performing with Fragments," 151.

38. William E. Connolly, *A World of Becoming* (Durham: Duke University Press, 2011): 44.

39. McHendry et al., "Rhetorical Critic(ism)'s Body," 298.

40. Ono and Sloop, "Commitment to a Telos."

41. E. Patrick Johnson, *Appropriating Blackness: Performance and the Politics of Authenticity* (Durham: Duke University Press, 2003): 10.
42. Ibid.
43. Hartnett, "Communication, Social Justice, and Joyful Commitment," 78.
44. M. J. Braun, "Against Decorous Civility: Acting as if you Live in a Democracy," in *Activism and Rhetoric: Theories and Contexts for Political Engagement*, eds., Seth Kahn and JongHwa Lee (London: Routledge, 2011): 140. See also: John M. Ackerman, and David J. Coogan, eds. *The Public Work of Rhetoric: Citizen-Scholars and Civic Engagement* (Columbia, SC: University of South Carolina Press, 2010).
45. Ackerman and Coogan, eds., *The Public Work of Rhetoric,* 10.
46. Ibid, 11.
47. Dana L. Cloud, "The Only Conceivable Thing to Do: Reflections on Academics and Activism," in *Activism and Rhetoric: Theories and Contexts for Political Engagement*, eds., Seth Kahn and JongHwa Lee (London: Routledge, 2011): 22.
48. Ackerman, and Coogan, eds., *The Public Work of Rhetoric*, 10–11.
49. John Durham Peters, *Courting the Abyss: Free Speech and the Liberal Tradition* (Chicago: University of Chicago Press, 2005). See also, Hartnett, "Communication, Social Justice, and Joyful Commitment."
50. Ono and Sloop, "The Critique of Vernacular Discourse;" Pezzullo, "Resisting 'National Breast Cancer Awareness Month.'"
51. Peters, *Courting the Abyss,* 250.
52. Ibid, 249.
53. Ibid, 249.
54. Ibid, 244–265; see also Della Pollock, "Memory, Remembering, and Histories of Change: A Performance Praxis," in *The Sage Handbook of Performance Studies,* eds., D. Soyini Madison and Judith Hamera (Thousand Oaks, CA: Sage Publications, 2006): 87–105.
55. Phaedra C. Pezzullo, *Toxic Tourism: Rhetorics of Pollution, Travel, and Environmental Justice* (Tuscaloosa: University of Alabama Press, 2009): 145–47.
56. While similar examples appear in more traditional, textually-oriented rhetorical scholarship, we argue that participatory critical rhetoric provides a unique means of accessing these sorts of relationships with rhetorical communities and, as a consequence, uniquely enable the critic to engage in political collaboration.
57. Robert L. Ivie, "Productive Criticism," *Quarterly Journal of Speech* 81 (1995): 2, doi: 10.1080/00335639509384093.

Chapter 3

An Embodied Critical Presence

After a conversation with a park ranger and a short shuttle ride, beyond the well-used horse trails and the places where I could still hear the faded remnants of conversations, I walked through a forest of small trees. When I emerged in a clearing full of rocks that ranged from pebble- to house-sized, I felt alone. This was not the first time in Zion Canyon I had the dual pleasure/fear experience of silence and solitude. Without signs telling me where to go or a description of a trail that gave its name and length, I had to consider the time of day, the terrain, and my body's capabilities. I followed an increasingly faint trail and then bushwhacked through scrubby, tough bushes to the base of an unnamed (as far as I knew) canyon wall. With no obvious next step, I sat down and had lunch.

A few weeks into my fieldwork at Zion National Park, I thought I had hiked every trail in Zion Canyon, the main part of the park. Studying the map, though, I noticed an unnamed trail winding away from a small shuttle stop. I asked a ranger about it, and she said that it was the trail that people took for horse rides, which made it unpleasant for hiking. However, off of that trail was a social trail—an animal path, really—that lead to a largely ignored nook of the canyon, which is where I was having lunch, thinking about conducting fieldwork for a communication research project with no clear human communication in sight.

Then, as they do, my thoughts turned to worries. First, they were about the future of the project: Would I complete it? What would I say about these experiences? How would I write about approaches and artifacts that did not fit neatly into what I knew about rhetorical criticism? But, then, they became focused on the present: What if I hurt myself descending through these thick bushes, which had evolved to protect themselves? How would anyone find me back here? How long before anyone even noticed I was missing? A couple of sighs and a few moments concocting half-baked escape plans, and I was back to worrying about my dissertation, like any other graduate student.

Putting worried thoughts into activity, I pulled out my notebook and pen and started taking fieldnotes about the experience of hiking a horse trail, a social trail, and no trail at all. Thinking about how maps control information, I made notes about strategies and tactics and institutional and individual power. I reflected about how easily the ranger provided me with this information, and I questioned if she would be that forthcoming with everyone or if it was something about the way I looked that made her trust me. At the time, she told me the trail was more of an animal path and that this was a slide area, meaning that any tracks I made would be erased with the next slide. But, she must have also trusted my ability to avoid getting lost or hurt on my own. During this reflection, I also took stock of my own body: I was hot but not tired, neither thirsty nor hungry, a little scratched but not hurt, and, after a lingering a little longer, ready to move on.

I hiked back to the shuttle stop, letting the now-familiar conversations and behaviors wash over me. Because every visitor (with very few exceptions) must ride the shuttle in the peak months, I became accustomed to observing vastly different behaviors. Some people carried with them the practice of being quiet in nature and, thus, remained quiet on the shuttle. Some speculated about gear while others, mostly to the chagrin of their parents, whined about discomforts. On other trails, I watched people disobey warnings and commonsense, feeding squirrels, drinking too little water, and once, amazingly, trying to fly a kite off of a 1,000-foot cliff. While these experiences contrasted sharply with the times I spent alone, both provided insights that I combined and nurtured into theories about how rhetoric worked in outdoor recreation.

—Samantha

In participatory critical rhetoric, critics' bodies can add to and alter how they interpret rhetoric because when they are present at moments of rhetorical invention, critics can gather information formerly unavailable to them. For example, hiking trails in a national park, as Samantha discovered, provided a sense of how other people used the park and how different trails felt from one another and at different times of day. As the vignettes in this chapter show, embodying the practices of rhetorical criticism as rhetoric unfolds has advantages. Analyzing the transcripts from a city council meeting would not offer the opportunity to talk with those who spoke up for the rights of people experiencing homelessness, as Michael did. These conversations might even challenge how a researcher interprets the transcript of the meeting. Listening to a news report of a protest rally does not give critics a sense of the affective responses they might have had if they were present, as Danielle was, singing along with other participants. And, critiquing pamphlets would not encourage critics to consider their own credibility, as Aaron did, while in the presence of other people, who might make judgments based on the critic's clothing and body. Some of the main advantages of participatory critical rhetoric are made available primarily because critics' bodies are present as rhetoric unfolds. Critics observing images, and even videos, of how people use and manipulate their bodies to rhetorical ends lack the ability to look around and notice how others are employing their bodies and what constraints exist in the form of material structures or other conditions; they also lack the ability to experience the other senses that cannot be captured in photos or videos. Participatory critical rhetoric requires critics to embody roles beyond that of the traditional critic.

Embodying varying participatory roles while engaging with *in situ* rhetorical acts is not uncommon in participatory critical rhetoric. Arguably, all rhetorical critics experience a variety of roles in their work. However, participatory critical rhetoricians experience multiple roles simultaneously because critics' bodies are present in the field as opposed to conventional forms of criticism, which are separated in time and space from the creation of rhetoric. Being in the field involves an embedded challenge to engage participatory roles beyond critic, such as advocate, observer, participant, witness, opponent, or companion. These roles are also available in many kinds of rhetorical criticism, but participatory critical rhetoric closes the distance between the critic and the rhetorical event, introducing a host of ethical, political, and practical questions. Participatory roles are those that rhetorical critics embody in the process of fieldwork for a variety of purposes. Participatory critical rhetoricians interact with other bodies as they construct rhetoric—an interaction that can influence rhetorical invention, data collection, and interpretation that guides subsequent criticism of those rhetorics. When in the field, critics cannot exist outside of the unfolding events and therefore must embody some additional role(s) beyond critic, even if it is only observer. Critics' presence in the field means that their bodies become a more obvious part of the critical process, impacting the roles in which they engage. While criticism is always an embodied phenomenon, when engaging in participatory critical rhetoric, critics' bodies can be used to gather data unavailable through conventional rhetorical criticism, can become part of a field of affect, and, sometimes, can be a hindrance while in the field.

We argue that participatory critical rhetoric invites critics to reconsider what embodiment means in rhetorical criticism and introduces new ways of conceptualizing critics' bodies and the participatory roles available to critics. Participatory critical rhetoric extends body studies in rhetorical criticism to include more than the representations of rhetors' bodies, which can produce different ways of thinking about bodies in rhetoric. Then, we focus attention on critics' bodies, which are integral in participatory critical rhetoric, and offer three interpretations of critics' bodies when they enter the spaces of rhetorical practice and participate in the creation of rhetoric. We conclude by explaining how participatory critical rhetoric expands our understanding of participatory roles and rhetorical reflexivity, contributing to a growing movement to conceive of rhetoric and the process of criticism materially.

STUDYING BODIES IN RHETORICAL CRITICISM

Participatory critical rhetoric extends body studies in rhetorical criticism by privileging material bodies rather than representations of bodies and by including attention to critics', audience members', and participants' bodies in addition to those of rhetors. Instead of approaching the analysis of bodies from the perspective of conventional critics,[1] who may seek out images, news reports, or written materials that refer to the body, participatory critical rhetoric takes an interest in materiality (and material bodies). Recall that in chapter 1, we argue that materiality has several definitions ranging from economic structures to physical features.[2] We build on Carole Blair's understanding of the materiality of rhetoric not only in terms of codified laws that might result from rhetoric and implied cultural norms, but also in terms of rhetoric's place in and consequences for the material world.[3] We follow a number of rhetoricians who have started their projects with the assumption that rhetoric has physical qualities such as weight and depth that can interact with the bodies of audiences, rhetors, participants, and critics.[4] The experience of *in situ* rhetoric is a symbolic and material phenomenon that is embodied and emplaced within a temporally bound moment. While we see the embodied and emplaced aspects of rhetoric as intersecting in particular cases, we treat them separately for the purpose of clarifying each on its own terms. Chapter 4 examines emplaced rhetoric and criticism to understand how space and place interact with rhetorical invention.

From Representations of Bodies to Material Bodies

Participatory critical rhetoric gives critics the chance to be at the site of materializing rhetoric, and, as a result, they can experience the spontaneous and strategic (inter)actions of material bodies as rhetoric unfolds. By contrast, conventional, documented text-based rhetoricians often approach the role of the body through representations of bodies. Attempting to push forward both rhetorical and social movement theory, rhetorical critics have turned to theorizing rhetoric in relation to the body, which has fueled theorization about disciplinary diversification, political struggle, the merging of material and symbolic forms, the risks that activists take, and the importance of visual rhetoric to bodies.[5] We agree that studying the embodied dimensions of rhetoric has usefully extended rhetorical theory, but we supplement this perspective by arguing that material bodies themselves experienced *in situ* have qualitatively different characteristics than analyzing representations of bodies.

Although rhetorical scholars consider how the body can be deployed rhetorically to orchestrate meaningful social change and how it participates in the advocacy of complex arguments, they mostly study representations of bodies or remain vague on the exact object of analysis.[6] By contrast, participatory critical rhetoric allows critics to access to the *in situ* material body itself to provide opportunities to parse delicate yet meaningful distinctions between bodies in theory and bodies *per se*. For example, Samantha's vignette at the beginning of the chapter reveals how being at a national park and hiking the trails that other visitors hiked allowed her to make connections between the representation of trails on maps, visitors' uses of those trails, and the enactment of identity among members of the outdoor recreation subculture.[7] We agree with scholars who study representations of bodies—bodies function rhetorically both in their construction and deployment—and we extend that idea to assess physical bodies *in situ*. Bodies are necessarily both material and symbolic. They occupy physical space and interact with other bodies and material objects while conveying meaning and building cultures and identities. Embodied rhetoric and criticism attends to the ways that the body itself—that of participants, audiences, rhetors, and critics—communicates. As Debra Hawhee explains, "rhetoric isn't just a cerebral, conscious process, . . . it's messy, unpredictable, and . . . at some level at least, the body is involved."[8] Participatory critical rhetoric follows Darrel Enck-Wanzer's urging for scholars to "see beyond how <bodies plus words> function, and begin seeing how <bodies-words-images> intersect to form (an)other rhetoric of resistance that is qualitatively different than a critic might have assumed."[9] Finally, participatory critical rhetoric attends to how distinct, rhetorical elements (e.g., bodies, aspects of the natural world, and human-made structures) comingle and develop from material and symbolic forms.[10] This extension from representations to material bodies acknowledges the additional information available when critics are physically present as rhetoric happens.

One of the reasons that live(d) rhetorics differ from the artifacts they leave behind is the presence of other intersectional material elements of *in situ* rhetorics: bodies, structures, signs, spoken words, and atmospheric conditions. Blair claims that much of the work of the rhetorical critic deals in reproductions removed from their initial instantiation in a particular time and place.[11] Although going to the field and being physically present can still be a form of representation, "the materiality of the experience also differentiates it from the act of seeing reproductions."[12] In other words, critics experience and access something qualitatively different when they go into the field. Instead of being able to access only representations of bodies, participatory critical rhetoricians can see otherwise unrecorded movements, uncaptured decisions, and undocumented interactions. This site of research opens opportunities to see forms of rhetorical action that are not always textualized in after-the-fact reproductions: feeling the effects of weather or the close proximity of other bodies on the rhetorical act, gaging immediate audience responses and reactions to the rhetorical message, participating with and contributing to rhetorical invention in the moment, and grappling with the role of the critic when a layer of distance is removed by being there and engaging in the process of fieldwork.[13]

Of course, fieldnotes and other documents created by the critic are still representations of the embodied rhetorical practices under study, but these representations are a result of critics' direct experiences as opposed to mediated and documented texts that were experienced and represented by someone else. We are acutely aware that participatory critical rhetoric's focus on *in situ* rhetoric may be read as over-privileging physical presence and romanticizing the notion of direct experience and participation over seemingly inferior forms of documented and mediated texts. While participatory critical rhetoric does involve fieldwork and a direct engagement with *in situ* rhetoric, it does not deny the value of analysis of more traditional mediated and documented rhetorical artifacts. Rather, our goal is to extend opportunities to put different forms of rhetoric, which remain unavailable to textually-oriented critics, in context and conversation with one another. And, in doing so, critics can access the insights that are made available by shifting from textocentric models of rhetorical criticism, which we discuss in chapter 2, toward intersectional and multifaceted rhetorical events. More than simply focusing on material bodies instead of representations of bodies, participatory critical rhetoric shines a light on critics', audience members', and participants' bodies in addition to bodies of rhetors or bodies deployed by rhetors.

From Rhetors' Bodies to Many Bodies

Analyses of the body in rhetoric focus almost exclusively on the bodies of rhetors or how rhetors deploy bodies to their own ends rather than including attention to the bodies of critics, audiences, or participants. Participatory critical rhetoric deepens the way critics think about the material body as rhetoric by attending to not only rhetors' bodies but also audiences' and participants' bodies. Participatory roles such as participant, observer, advocate, witness, opponent, or companion give critics multiple perspectives about unfolding rhetoric. Additionally, participatory critical rhetoric turns a critical lens on critics' bodies, conceptualizing them in a number of different ways, as we articulate in the next section. It also highlights audience and participant bodies and the potential impact they have on critics, which we address in chapter 5. In short, participatory critical rhetoric gives critics the ability to choose what aspects of the situation would be advantageous to document and analyze. By being present, participatory critical rhetoricians can see a variety of people choosing to use their bodies in different (or similar) ways and thus produce a rich understanding of the body rhetoric of one or more people simultaneously.

The dominant critical practice in rhetorical studies of the body, however, primarily analyzes how rhetors use their bodies or evoke bodies of others to serve their purposes. When news media or rhetors themselves document rhetoric, they do not typically include equal attention to audiences or the physical situation. Therefore, employing artifacts created by someone other than the researcher puts boundaries on the claims critics can make. Nevertheless, rhetoricians have made progress, demonstrating how rhetors use other people's bodies verbally and visually to reinforce and challenge social norms about gender, war, disease, ability, and sexuality.[14] Scholars also analyze documentation of rhetors employing their own bodies to do the rhetorical work of protesting living conditions, oppressive rule, harmful environmental practices, corporate dominance, and hidden identities.[15] When scholars only account for rhetors, though, they miss interpretations, improvised changes, acts of cocreation, and responses to performances. We do not argue that participatory critical rhetoric allows critics to see and document every aspect of a rhetorical situation; critics will necessarily see, hear, and feel some things and not others. Rather, we contend that participatory critical rhetoric emphasizes the importance of accessing these bodily comportments, which may reveal fissures between the interpretations of critics, rhetors, and audience members, all participants during *in situ* rhetorical invention. It further builds on theories of rhetoric as fragmented, acknowledging rhetoric's polysemic and coproduced nature.

This research about embodied rhetoric has laid important foundations for participatory critical rhetoric but also has particular limitations. Participatory critical rhetoric, by including attention to bodies *per se* and bodies of critics and participants, alleviates some of these constraints. We contend that critics' presence at the site of rhetoric changes the quality of rhetorical criticism, making different pieces of discourse available for analysis, creating opportunities to see bodies in motion, and putting different people's bodies in conversation with one another. For example, in Samantha's vignette, she references the conversation she had with a park ranger and her surprise at the ease with which the ranger revealed information about a trail not included on the standard park service map. Even at the time, she reflected on her own subject position implied by her body, wondering if her age, race, sex, clothing, and equipment allowed her to be read in favorable ways in this situation. Additionally, in person critics can see the dynamic body, engaging in movement and learned behaviors. Critics simply have to turn their heads to see others' responses in the moment and open themselves to the experience in order to feel the presence of others. Additionally, although rhetoricians have embraced analysis of rhetors' bodies, critics' own bodies have been left out of the conversation. In the next section, we argue that by reconceptualizing the body of the critic as an actor in the field, critics can embrace and embody participatory roles in ways that expand what insights are available through conventional rhetorical criticism.

CRITICAL EMBODIMENT

When engaging in participatory critical rhetoric, critics' bodies become part of the site of rhetoric and this repositioning can open opportunities to embody additional roles beyond that of critic. In conventional rhetorical criticism, critics have different possible roles to play as well, such as inventor, observer, advocate, or opponent.[16] Although critics may not be observing *in situ*, they follow argument production, distribution, death, and resurgence, and they track the tropes of historical and contemporary political movements, carefully collecting and parsing examples of rhetorical phenomena. Combined with a critical perspective, they also become advocates and opponents, identifying and critiquing rhetors who perpetuate oppressive power structures, as well as amplifying commonly dismissed voices.

However, conceptualizing rhetoric as embodied and emplaced means that critics must also recognize and theoretically interrogate their own bodies. We contend that engaging in fieldwork, particularly from a participatory critical rhetoric perspective, demands that critics challenge themselves to consider the uses of their own bodies and the consequences of their own research practices, to engage in what Dwight Conquergood calls, "rhetorical reflexivity."[17] Charles E. Morris III defines rhetorical reflexivity as, "an unceasing process of self-engagement, deeply reading one's multiple cultural, political, ideological *situatedness* and its implications, privileges, relations to others, and effects. . . ."[18] Doing so not only acknowledges critics' (always already) presence in their research but also grapples with the role that their own bodies play when engaging in participatory critical rhetoric. Engaging in rhetorical reflexivity means that critics are conscious of the roles they play as well as the impact they have on the critical process and remain willing to account for themselves. Participatory critical rhetoric encourages reflexivity, which we thread through this section and extend in the last section of this chapter. Here, we offer three ways of thinking about researchers' bodies, as: critical bodies, affective bodies, and risky bodies. These ways of thinking overlap, problematize, and reinforce one another, both introducing new and reaffirming old rhetorical theories about bodies.

Critical Bodies

Critics, whatever other roles they may embody, work toward gathering data and analyzing it so that they may better understand rhetoric's cultural construction. To that end, their bodies become research instruments, and this is particularly salient in the field. Edwin Black argues that the act of rhetorical criticism is strongly influenced by a critic's personal orientation; "in critical inquiry, the critic is the sole instrument of observation."[19] If we accept that rhetoricians themselves embody the role of critical instrument, then we must investigate the critic as well as the artifact.[20] Participatory critical rhetoric positions not only the minds of critics but also their bodies in the field as critical instruments. When critics start with the understanding of their bodies as material—physical beings with rhetorical consequence—they make available additional rhetorical data, including data of their own experiences and sensations. This section investigates the role of critics' bodies in participatory critical rhetoric and encourages critics to provide self-accounts in their essays to make clear the uses to which they put their bodies. The following vignette demonstrates how critics can use their bodies as rhetorical instruments in the field.

When I arrived on the scene where the members of SafeGround Sacramento were waging their struggle against the conditions of homelessness in their community, I was sure that there would be much to learn about rhetoric, advocacy, homelessness, and other issues that informed my interests at the time. Like anyone embarking on a new critical project, I had familiarized myself with literature about homelessness, read ethnographies about other homeless communities, and had scoured news accounts of the work being done by the homeless persons in Sacramento. Over time, however, as I made return trips to Sacramento, I began to realize how little my homework had prepared me for understanding what rhetorical advocacy meant in the context of a community of people for whom every day was a struggle.

Intellectually, I knew that mainstream homeless services were flawed and that they often failed to serve the needs of homeless communities despite their intentions to do so. However, it was not until I began spending time with the community that I actually grasped both the barriers to their goals as a movement and the scope of what their advocacy meant. Time spent walking the streets, lounging in the homeless park at a local service center that was their base of operations, setting up nightly encampments, and planning protests began to help make these challenges clear. Accomplishing any of these tasks were made doubly hard because, in each instance, taking the time to engage in these tasks meant that my homeless companions often sacrificed access to services that were only available to those homeless individuals who were willing to sacrifice large portions of each day to standing in line for services that would eventually be provided. What started as an intellectual understanding of the challenges my homeless interlocutors faced quickly became a set of challenges that I began to understand from the perspective of the physical toll it took on my companions. Eat or protest, sleep in a bed or organize for meeting of homeless activists and allies from the surrounding community of "normies" (their word for individuals with homes).

As I witnessed and sometimes shared in these experiences, the significance of their advocacy, which at first blush seemed so modest, became apparent. The ability to enjoy a few hours without fearing the pursuit of law enforcement of various types attempting to enforce anti-camping laws, vagrancy statutes, etc. meant the difference between having the time to begin thinking about long-term solutions to their individual struggles with homelessness and not. Similarly, once I was invited to join in with my new companions as they prepared for protest, I began to understand the ways their struggles intersected with their understanding of their own identity. As we made posters with protest slogans, like "housing not handcuffs," activists from the homeless community shared with me both their aspirations and their struggles. The protests they staged, which they often knew would have little immediate effect, made apparent to me how these efforts were about reclaiming an identity that allowed them to view themselves as persons of worth in their community. Furthermore, through these, they resisted the attempts, which circulated in the mainstream discourse of local media and in the everyday talk of many in the broader community who detested their presence in California's capital city, to make them invisible, dangerous, or worse. As they marched in protest after these preparations, I witnessed and shared in the value they found in their resistance and in the immense struggle that my homeless companions, often deprived of adequate sleep, food, medical care, and more, waged. Their efforts made apparent that the measure of their rhetorical success was not to be found in securing more resources, changing local laws, or other typical goals of a social movement (although, those were important to them). Instead their measure of success lay in their ability, through their protest, to construct something different, something more than was implied by their constant mis-recognition as diseased, deviant, or disorderly in local media and political discourse.

Witnessing these strategies and talking with the members of the community about their participation, I found myself returning to my training and reflecting on Brian Ott's observation that all too often rhetorical critics, from their relatively insulated position in the academy, find it all too easy to dismiss many oppositional rhetorical practices as "not progressive enough."[21] *By placing my body alongside the homeless community from whom I learned, sampling the challenges of their daily life by spending time in the encampments, organizing for the interventions, and interviewing members of the community, the truth of his claim evolved from an intellectual assumption to an embodied truth; one that I both felt during my time in the field and one that I witnessed in the experiences of my new community of interlocutors. By situating my critical judgment within these embodied experiences and in relation to the realities of the community with whom I participated, the relevance of traditional metrics of success for social movements moved to the margins and the importance of small acts, sometimes with and sometimes without material consequences, became more important. By bracketing my own critical assumptions and letting them be guided by the insights of the community I inhabited, a new metric of rhetorical success emerged. Now, as I observe their struggle from afar against the same conditions and laws that were present when I arrived on the scene, my experiences in the field remind me that what might look like a Sisyphean task without much to show for the effort is, for its participants, in reality a daily enactment of the claim that the individuals engaged in it are something more than homeless (and all that that label entails) and, as a consequence, is a daily exercise in reclaiming and reaffirming an identity that supports their efforts to both resolve their individual struggle with homelessness and resist the political and economic efforts that further marginalize them.*

—Michael

Witnessing rhetoric as it emerges means that participatory critical rhetoric necessitates a form of critical presence that impacts not only our understanding of rhetorical theory but also rhetoric itself. Arguing that "being there" creates a different perspective because of the information available, Blair foregrounds the importance of the materiality of rhetoric.[22] She links this to feelings, both physical and emotional, that become part of the experience during fieldwork. Similarly, Conquergood "privileges the body as a site of knowing."[23] To go into the field and disregard meaningful elements of the rhetorical scene (e.g., emotions, smells) because they are outside the conventional parameters of rhetorical criticism would be a mistake; it would be to deny critics' physicality. Contending that the information we receive at the site of rhetoric changes when we experience it firsthand, Phaedra Pezzullo grounds her argument for being there in the concept of presence.[24] She concedes that presence can be rhetorically constructed without physically being there. However, we argue that the information made available when bodies are present as rhetoric unfolds around (and with) them is qualitatively different from that shared through texts and mediation. For example, Michael's vignette reveals the difference between the information available about Safe-Ground Sacramento through traditional channels and that accessed through participation with the group. In joining this community of homeless rights advocates through fieldwork, Michael developed a sense of not only the political motivations of the group but also the personal motivations of individuals. By embodying participatory roles, critics can gain perspectives and interpretation not available through other channels.

Being present at the site of rhetorical invention and gathering information with multiple senses at once empowers the critic to take back control of documents that remain after a rhetorical moment and prompts questions about critics' power in those situations. Michel Foucault invites us to consider the role that power has on the body and how biopower (i.e., the power of docile bodies moving in predictable, controllable ways) enables some forms of rule to remain in power.[25] In this context, it is important to consider the role that critics' bodies play in perpetuating some forms of power. Critics engage in embodied rhetorical criticism whether they employ participatory critical rhetoric or not. On the one hand, embodied critics are embedded and emplaced in the rhetorical situation, where they can construct an analyzable artifact from the material discourse encircling them rather than constructing it from fragments of documents others have created later, which could be a way to gain additional power and shape interpretations.[26] On the other hand, positioning critics' bodies in proximity to other bodies and within a field of affect, which we discuss in the next section, provides a chance for critics to share their power and decenter themselves. By standing alongside people experiencing homelessness, Michael considered his own privilege in terms of his life as a "normie" (the label used by SafeGround activists to describe many housed persons) and his role as a critic, documenting conversations for analysis.

As such, fieldwork gives access to additional pieces of information that influence how critics create artifacts from fragments. Pierre Mayol emphasizes how the body can function as a research instrument by locating critical awareness within itself. He states, "The body is truly a *learned memory* that records the signs of recognition."[27] Being in the field will be recorded onto critics' bodies and into their minds. Samantha experienced this in the field, becoming accustomed to sounds, sights, and smells of the shuttle in Zion National Park and using that learned memory to determine patterns and extraordinary events. In using various senses to collect information, critics are shaped by and shape the world they encounter. Critics hold on to experiences and employ them to make sense of the subsequent rhetorical situations they enter. And they will use them to form and cull the discourses they encounter to produce documents, such as fieldnotes.

Critics, then, embody their roles as critic and inventor through the research process. They become part of the rhetorical situation under examination by embodying varying roles in participatory critical rhetoric. But the advantage of being there is that critics gain a sensitivity to elements that remain unspoken and unrecorded, which means that although they maintain their control over the essay they produce, they may also be decentered in the process. Conquergood encourages scholars, "To 'do ethnography *with*, not *of*' (43) a group of people because it alters the power relations of fieldwork and changes the hierarchy of observer and observed into more of a partnership."[28] Acknowledging these power relationships prompts critics to decenter themselves and consider if and why they have the ability to speak for the people who occupy the social locations they examine. Joining in the process of rhetorical production, witnessing actions and interactions, and forging relationships with participants contributes to the decentering process. A willingness to be a part of what is happening shifts critics from observers, in the detached sense, to companions and advocates standing side by side as rhetoric unfolds. They can function in these roles during rhetorically extraordinary events, such as a protest urging housing not handcuffs, as well as those ordinary moments of planning and engaging in administrative tasks. And, accounting for those embodied roles in written form further distinguishes participatory critical rhetoric from conventional rhetorical criticism.

As outlined above, most studies of rhetoric's embodied dimensions have focused on rhetors' bodies and few have included audience members' and participants' bodies, which produces analyses of embodied rhetoric that can ignore the critics' bodies.[29] Although rhetorical criticism as a discipline acknowledges, even embraces, the subjectivity of scholarship, critics nevertheless often fail to account for themselves or give much consideration to themselves in the criticisms they produce. This strategy potentially gives critics more power by concealing their involvement or impact on the rhetoric produced. This practice also contains the possibility to reproduce the politics that accompany hidden bodies or disembodied arguments and voices. As Pezzullo states, "Bodies powerfully and undeniably do inform our experiences, our beliefs, and our judgments in socially meaningful ways."[30] We extend this idea to acknowledge that bodies, functioning rhetorically, affect how critics read, process, and produce rhetorical criticism. We argue that theorizing critics' bodies is productive because, in participatory critical rhetoric, critics' bodies contribute to how participants make meaning in the moment.

The bodies that critics take to the field remain while they write essays of rhetorical criticism; accounting for those bodies increases transparency.

Some critics not only argue for this, they also engage in it through the practice of writing.[31] Through forms of self-reflection and description of their own background and experiences, some critics present their own bodies in their criticisms. For example, in his examination of political campaign rhetoric, Peter Simonson accounts for himself in his criticism by describing his approach to his project, political affiliations, feelings of anticipation, and the roles that he plays during in-the-moment rhetorical invention. He positions what he does as, "based on making contact with audiences and interlocutors outside the academy, and feeling the force of rhetoric as an embodied activity manifest in particular cultural scenes. . . Performing as a member of the campaign, I'll try to learn something of value to critics, theorists, or other observers of rhetoric."[32] Simonson conceptualizes his goals and two of his roles—both participant and researcher—while in the field through this reflexive account. While he addresses this at the beginning of his essay, Samantha Senda-Cook explains her body's "learned memory" developed while conducting research in Zion National Park in the introduction to her analysis of experiences with outdoor recreation.[33] In acknowledging the materiality of their own bodies and that of others, critics position their bodies as critical instruments with their own abilities and constraints and thus decenter themselves from the implied, unnamed center of the critical process. Engaging in such reflexivity may also reveal to the critic some lingering, unnamable elements of the research process.

Affective Bodies

Through participatory critical rhetoric, critics' bodies experience and contribute to a field of affect. Their own bodies engage in situations alongside rhetors and audience members by being physically present and potentially vulnerable. In line with McHendry et al.'s urging for rhetoricians to carefully consider their own immanent and affective bodies in the field, participatory critical rhetoric attends to affective dimensions of rhetoric.[34] Our experiences in the field demonstrate the affective potential implied by critics' involvement, vulnerability, and availability to participants, as the vignette below demonstrates. In this section, we advance current theories of rhetorical affect by linking them to bodies and relationships formed *in situ*. This vignette attempts to put into words some of those ineffable experiences that happen in the field.

When I think about the opportunities available to participatory critical rhetoricians to experience, interpret, and report on affective encounters, I think about my student Megan's work on singing in protest movements. She has focused her attention on a local climate justice movement in Salt

Lake City called Peaceful Uprising. This group formed in response to Tim DeChristopher's trial and sentencing for his act of monkey wrenching to stop the lease of wilderness lands in Southern Utah for oil and gas development. DeChristopher attended the auction, was mistakenly given a bidding paddle, and took advantage of that serendipity to disrupt the auction by outbidding and winning leases. He was arrested, went to trial, and was sentenced to federal prison time. During the trial and sentencing hearings that took place at the district court house in Salt Lake City, Peaceful Uprising planned protest events to span the duration of the trial and sentencing hearing. DeChristopher called for singing to be a key part of the protest rallies, claiming "we will be a movement when we sing like a movement."[35]

I attended some of the protest rallies with Megan, who attended them all. The first day of the trial, there was a march through downtown Salt Lake City, followed by a rally across the street from the district court house. Singing was prominent in both the march and rally. She and I both had personally affective moments during collective singing that we simultaneously experienced through a variety of participant roles. I won't speak for Megan's engagement, but I can speak for my own affective experience that day.

As we marched through the streets of Salt Lake City, we sang a variety of classic protest songs that had been modified for the case at hand. While I had been closely following the DeChristopher case and experienced feelings of injustice, rage, and fear of what further oil and gas development would do to our planet before attending this march, something different happened when I was present in the moment, singing and marching. I was a part of something bigger than me; I was aligned with people I barely knew in a collective body of movement in the streets, I believed that it was possible to do something about climate change. In some ways I have experienced this sort of reaction at other protest events, not exactly the same but similar, and that is likely one of the reasons people still engage in protest events. Yet, this encounter was also unique because of the strong emphasis on singing.

There is something about singing in a group of people that is more powerful to me than other forms of protest activity. For me, singing is a profoundly meaningful part of my life—it was something I did and continue to do with my family, something I had done at church as a child, something I had done with friends at music shows, and something that I had done at previous protests and rallies. I love to sing. My own connection with singing as both desirable and pleasurable cannot be separated from the way I reacted to the collective singing at the Peaceful Uprising march and rally. Yet, in addition to the pleasure of singing with this group of mostly strangers, I also felt a powerful sense of doing something about DeChristopher's case and climate change. I found myself crying at times, not exactly sure why in the moment and not exactly sure how I would put that into words. I moved closer to other people, perhaps desiring stronger connection to the bodies that surrounded me. Children caught my gaze and I found myself staring at them and thinking about my own kids. In retrospect, I have assigned various emotions to this encounter including hope that something can be done to address climate change, sadness for the climate crisis that we have made for my children, but even these emotions don't fully account for my experience in the occasion.

I felt present in the moment and deeply moved by this encounter and when I looked around, I could see that others were having powerful responses too. I can't say what their responses were because I did not ask, but physical signs from the bodies surrounding me not only lead me to believe that they felt the power of that encounter too, but also that we were all tied together as one body of singers. I knew that something powerful, affective, and difficult to articulate in words was happening.

Megan is in the process of writing her own experience of the collective singing into her dissertation, and is on the front line of theorizing the implications of affect for critic and participant bodies in moments of collective singing. We have had some conversations about how tricky it is to account for affect, while at the same time knowing that it is an essential part of the rhetoric of collective singing. Despite the difficultly of putting it into words, and accounting for these pre-emotional, in-between states, I always come back to the idea that we have to try to find a way to account for it in rhetorical criticism.

—Danielle

Attending to critics' bodies in the field means that critics become both vulnerable and available to participants. Accounting for these roles, however, remains elusive in part because it is difficult to put such experiences into words. Gregory J. Seigworth and Melissa Gregg write about affect as "in-between-ness," "the capacities to act and be acted upon," and as an intensity of experience.[36] And, they connect affect specifically to bodies, explaining, "affect is found in those intensities that pass body to body (human, nonhuman, part-body, and otherwise), in those resonances that circulate about, between, and sometimes stick to bodies and worlds, *and* in the very passages or variations between these intensities and resonances themselves."[37] In other words, affect does not merely refer to emotions or indeed any singular thing easily understood through language. As Brian Massumi reminds us, "An emotion is a subjective content, the sociolinguistic fixing of the quality of an experience which is from that point onward defined as personal. Emotion is qualified intensity, the conventional, consensual point of insertion of intensity into semantically and semiotically formed progressions, into narrativizable action-reaction circuits, into function and meaning."[38]

Emotions are subjectively understood through language, yet affect lacks a "cultural-theoretical vocabulary."[39] Affect moves and engages people who are copresent, experiencing rhetoric together as it unfolds and calls upon and creates shared meanings and feelings. Danielle's vignette illuminates the sense of "something bigger" that she co-constructed as she marched and sang with people she hardly knew. She was moved through this collective action but remains cautious about identifying her felt-emotions as the emotions everyone else felt.

Critics are enmeshed in fields of affect when they venture into the sites of emergent rhetorical practice, but may find it difficult to account for affect's role in persuading or constituting reality. This is partially because, as Josh Gunn and Jenny Edbauer Rice explain, "affect as such is ineffable and difficult to represent or quantify."[40] Nevertheless, when critics encounter fields, audiences, and rhetors, they have an opportunity to participate affectively, experiencing embodied and emplaced rhetorical experiences. For example, Pezzullo describes the affective impact that RavenLight made when she arrived at a Toxic Links Coalition event and another participant reached out to touch her mastectomy scar. After seeing this powerful interaction, she describes the atmosphere, "In that moment, all three of us, the woman in red who risked contact, the woman in pigtails who risked reaching out to communicate, and the observer who risked sharing that intimate exchange, felt present."[41] Similarly, Danielle describes the physical responses of those around her as evidence of powerful feelings of closeness and sadness but maintains that these words do not fully encompass the experience.

Scholars recognize that rhetoric exists beyond rationality, that audiences make decisions based on attachments and circumstances that we cannot predict, control, or even fully understand at times. When embroiled in a situation with participants, critics can begin to comprehend the role that affect plays in rhetoric as it unfolds. Although rhetorical criticism is not ruled by attention to logic, it is difficult to incorporate affect into rhetorical analyses because it often requires making claims about audience reception and interaction to which critics do not usually have access. Absent access to an audience's reactions, critics could incorporate their own affective responses to a piece of rhetoric in their criticism, but that is highly uncommon. However, by studying rhetoric *in situ*, critics can begin to unpack affective dimensions of rhetoric across a range of examples and cases, attending to the intensities produced by large crowds, volatile situations, or discomfort. In participatory critical rhetoric, critics are in a position to viscerally experience rhetoric in-the-moment and then look to audience members to see and inquire if they seem to be responding in the same way, as Danielle did at the protest. Moreover, because researchers are present at key rhetorical moments, they can witness how not only others' affective responses but also their own impact on the choices and consequences of rhetoric. Although rhetoricians who work with conventional texts can be affectively impacted through rhetoric and it can shape their criticisms, rhetoricians typically do not have the opportunity to contribute to the production of rhetoric through their responses.

Opening up to the affective encounters created *in situ* provides critics with multiple interpretations of a field of rhetoric. Although conventional rhetoricians can access multiple documents representing a particular rhetorical act, they cannot respond to and witness responses as rhetoric unfolds or take into consideration the varying pieces of rhetoric happening simultaneously. This allows for a critic to observe and experience the varied and sometimes conflicting in-the-moment affective responses to rhetoric that may not be captured through a transcript, media report, or other form of documentation. However, through participatory critical rhetoric, critics have the opportunity to check their own interpretations and feelings as they experience affect in the field, and after they leave the field if they have developed relationships through fieldwork. Therefore, the critic has multiple ways of both accessing and interpreting those ineffable experiences that are key to the material experience of rhetoric.

Participatory critical rhetoric, by acknowledging the affective responses of critics' bodies, compels critics to not only think about themselves but also to write themselves into their criticisms to provide the reader with a firm understanding of the grounds for their convictions. Even though affect may be difficult to put into words, the critic who has experienced it along with other people in an embodied and emplaced rhetorical experience is better equipped to try. Recall Pezzullo's description of her powerful encounter during the Toxic Links Coalition march as an example of how a critic might approach writing about their presence in the field. In this way, critics encourage rhetorical theory to take into account the nuance of understanding gained through affective experiences. Being in the field, being vulnerable, opens a variety of roles for critics to play simply because their bodies are exposed to significant and somewhat inexplicable fields of affect. Furthermore, critics' bodies can be at risk or even create risk when encountering others in the field.

Risky Bodies

Being present at the site of rhetorical invention means that critics must grapple with questions not usually asked of them: How do they self-present in the field? What information about themselves do they disclose? And, what do they keep to themselves? Just as scholars might read participants' bodies, when they enter the field, scholars' bodies become indicators of class, education, culture, and credibility.[42] Thinking of their bodies as material, critical, and affective changes how critics think about the process of rhetorical criticism and the possibility of risk. Stewart et al. offer "risk as a relational dynamic, operating on multiple levels, and manifesting as interrelated research considerations."[43] This definition makes clear that risk can impact researchers in a number of ways, not all of them are severe but nevertheless are part of the critical process in participatory critical rhetoric. In this section, we argue that participatory critical rhetoric increases the potential for risks for critics' bodies (and we discuss risks to participants in chapter 5). Although risks certainly are present in conventional rhetorical criticism, we think of the nature of risk as different when fieldwork is involved, as the vignette that follows illustrates.

When I made the decision to study drug culture, I expected it to be risky. What I didn't expect was that this risk had very little to do with my physical safety. After completing my IRB paperwork—the IRB, by the way, did not *express concern for my well-being before heading out into the desert to ask drug users about their use—I arrived in the rave scene a little nervous. After all, drugs are designed to alter perception and experience, to escape from reality. What might happen if I "enter" someone's drug induced reality, only to anger them? The drug of choice, methylenedioxymethamphetamine (MDMA, or ecstasy), wasn't necessarily a dangerous one. Typically, people became more emotionally attached to strangers, expressive, and energetic, wanting to dance or give each other massages while lying on the floor in a "cuddle puddle." But the fundamental origin of DanceSafe's advocacy is about the adulteration of ecstasy with other drugs. What if one of those drugs made ravers violent?*

While I suppose the potential was there, it never happened. Risk wasn't just contained in the chemically enhanced bodies of dancing ravers; it was also in my own body. And, the risk wasn't violence; it was failure. Failure to effectively perform the advocacy of the group, or failure to comprehend the nature of the scene as a researcher. My body was marked and its mere presence jeopardized both of my dual roles of researcher and advocate. As a researcher from an institution of higher education, my body at a rave could appear as a symbolic reminder of those teachers who didn't understand the stresses of being a kid these days, and of parents who punish children for academic underperformance. When soliciting interviews, I emphasized my identity as a graduate student. Identifying as a "student" doing a "student project" helped alleviate some of these concerns.

As an advocate, I was marked primarily because of my age, but also because I (frankly) didn't look the part. I began my research in my mid-twenties during graduate school, an age that often felt closer to the parents of those teens in the scene than to their own. So, in an attempt to mitigate the risk my body posed, I tried to dress in accordance of the culture, finding playful t-shirts to wear and adorning my arms with candy—beaded bracelets traded between ravers as a sign of friendship and cultural solidarity. During a rave, I would do the things that a raver or DanceSafe advocate would: listen to the music, dance when the spirit moved me, and tell stories about drugs while waiting for the sun to rise. But still, my body was suspicious.

Preparing for a rave takes time. On many Saturday nights before a rave, I would scour my closet looking for the appropriate shirt that would allow me to "pass" as a DanceSafe volunteer—and maybe even a raver. I imagine that ravers also planning on heading out into the night to meet friends and dance also take great care in their cultural costuming. Candy adorned arms, visors with embedded LED lights, and a new set of faerie wings might all accompany a raver to the desert or abandoned warehouse. DanceSafe volunteers played their part as well, wearing comfortable clothes that carried the ethos of the scene, but would also carry legitimacy in advocacy work. One night, in preparation for a rave at a local downtown venue, I dressed in my typical playful t-shirt—a white shirt with a definition of the word "truthiness" I had purchased after visiting a taping of The Colbert Report *in New York—shorts to beat the night heat, and comfortable sneakers for dancing.*

After setting up, my fellow volunteers decided to take a break and grab a bite to eat, leaving me to run the table on my own. I engaged in conversation with local ravers, many of whom I had met before, and didn't think much my body or attire. After all, I had done my preparatory embodiment work; playful t-shirt, beads, and the occasional dance. Check. About an hour later, they returned to the table. Chuckling, they remarked that I looked like a crazy Christian on an anti-drug mission. In horror, I asked what they meant. Not having seen The Colbert Report, *they said that the shirt looked like I was peddling truth to a bunch of drugged out teenagers.*

I never wore that shirt to a rave again.

—Aaron

In participatory critical rhetoric, many kinds of risk exist, as Aaron's vignette demonstrates. While he was concerned about violent drug reactions, he had learned that his own body could endanger his credibility—and the credibility of the advocacy group—at his research site. Through physical presence and embodiment of different roles, critics activate issues of politics and power, which carry risks of access and discipline that implicate researchers' bodies. By behaving in some ways and not others, bodies—those of critics, audiences, and rhetors—have the power to subtly reinstantiate or challenge cultural norms.[44] While researchers may be accustomed to being judged by their academic credentials, their bodies are also open for evaluation when they are in the field. On the one hand, if their bodies do not align with what is expected of a researcher, then that could pose risks to the project. Bodies that do not conform to expectations of what a researcher looks like (e.g., disabled, obese, brown, female) risk negative judgment by participants. On the other hand, some researchers might align too well with what is expected of an academic (e.g., white, male), engendering distrust among participants. In Aaron's case, his age distinguished him from participants and his attire backfired. Critics cannot escape their bodies and the way people read them in the field when engaging in embodied field research.

Physical risk sometimes also presents a concern. Samantha's vignette at the beginning of the chapter shows her awareness of the potential physical risks that hiking alone in an out-of-the-way part of Zion Canyon might hold. Despite (or perhaps because of) of her outdoor recreation safety knowledge, she felt vulnerability warring with delight at her solitary hiking experience. In other situations, though, it could be risky for women or transgendered people to do certain types of research because their bodies could be interpreted as weaknesses or targets for violence, which would not be a risk associated with conventional rhetorical criticism.

Additionally, if critics expose their bodies to pollutants or protest situations, they could be damaged. Danielle, for example, through her field research with activists at the Nevada Test Site (now Nevada National Security Site) where over 1000 nuclear bombs were detonated, has potentially exposed her body to higher than background levels of radioactivity. While these levels are safe according to acceptable risk calculations, field researchers engaged with other environmental justice issues may be exposed to similar or worse toxic exposures, particularly if they also live in the sites of exposure. Pezzullo states, "I want to reassert the importance of a fully embodied communication perspective, one that enables us to consider the additional risks of 'facing death if need be,' of placing our bodies, our health, our sanity, and our hearts at sites that we might otherwise avoid."[45] In this way, risk contributes to a different sort of embodiment for participatory critical rhetoricians because their bodies are exposed in ways that would not be possible in conventional rhetorical criticism. This exposure may be temporary and never match that of a person who lives with(in) a site of exposure, but it can both put the critic's body at risk and give the critic a better sense of empathy with those for whom such exposure is a norm.

Their bodily presence and their willingness to risk their bodies enables critics to not just observe what happens but also to serve as witnesses. While an observer status can imply a level of distance or removal from the scene, a witness is someone who is present at the scene and makes his or her presence known. For example, if police or protestors saw person with recording equipment, that could influence whether or not they responded to a situation with violence. In this way, risk becomes a more serious concern for critics' bodies. This participation in the field means that rhetorical critics become a part of the field; they embody a rhetorical position at the site of rhetoric that has implications for the unfolding rhetoric in the field. The presence of a witness, in this case the researcher, impacts how people create rhetoric spontaneously, the choices that they make, and the consequences with which they live. Therefore, critics may not even be aware of the risks made possible through their physical presence or absence.

In their interactions with participants, critics can pose a risk to rhetors, participants, and audience members, and researchers risk emotional entanglement. By exposing formerly hidden parts of participants' identity or by lacking adequate knowledge to participate ethically and responsibly in a rapidly changing scene of rhetorical interaction, critics themselves can be a risk to participants. For example, Aaron Hess explains his own misgivings at providing information about drugs without having a complete knowledge at the beginning of his fieldwork.[46]

After recognizing critics' vulnerability in the field, it is important to consider the ways that it impacts them emotionally as people. In this vein, Blair insists that rhetorical critics' bodies are part of the process and that when they enter the field, they will likely have "specific, personal critical encounters."[47] Such encounters can leave them enthusiastic, upset, depressed, angry, or embarrassed. Sarah Tracy explains the possibility of encountering the risk of feeling humiliated while engaging in fieldwork. She states, "Indeed, embarrassment, objection, and snubbing are not situations to be avoided or simply endured but, instead, are opportunities to connect with our participants, engage in potentially transformative conversations, and access tacit and unarticulated data."[48] Giving these moments and other potentially risky situations researchers encounter the same consideration critics afford the analysis itself provides insight into the situation as well as the critical process.

Through reflexivity, critics can make themselves aware of the risks to which they expose themselves and others through their presence in the field. Part of this might involve providing background about how they gather artifacts, what role they played in organizations, how many interviews they conducted, and how they produced transcripts and fieldnotes. By accounting for these research practices, critics acknowledge the possibility of meaning making, advocacy, and resistance through their participation in the site of rhetorical production. Then, they can build on those reflections about their research decisions to thoroughly assess their involvement and risks as spontaneously occurring rhetoric unfolds. Critics' bodies function to enable and constrain participation from rhetors and audience members, and participatory critical rhetoric invites critics to face their bodies and their decisions in the field and then account for those in the essays they produce.

When critics' bodies participate in the field with rhetorical practitioners, the different ways of understanding them become important sites of rhetorical theorizing. Simultaneously, researchers' bodies are, depending on the rhetorical scene, critical, affective, and risky. This largely ignored factor in rhetorical criticism becomes an integral part of the research process in participatory critical rhetoric. Considering bodies of rhetoricians as part of the rhetorical process encourages critics to reexamine participatory roles such as witness, opponent, observer, advocate, participant, and companion available to them.

IMPLICATIONS FOR ROLES AND REFLEXIVITY

Attending to materiality and bodily rhetoric is not new for rhetorical criticism. Yet, it has led researchers to engage in critical processes that take them to the site of rhetoric, which has implications for both the roles they can embody and the responsibility they carry for reflexivity. Critics can conceive of their bodies in different ways, as serving multiple functions even simultaneously. Venturing into the field reinforces those diverse ways of seeing and understanding critics' bodies, and this critical practice makes participatory roles available to critics in ways distinct from conventional rhetorical criticism. The four vignettes offer examples of how critics embody multiple participatory roles while in the field.

All the tales, except for Samantha's, showed the potential for scholars to be advocates: for the rights of homeless individuals, for the protection of the environment, and for the safety of recreational drug users. In Michael's and Danielle's cases, participation necessitated advocacy because, in Michael's case, gaining access to a community of homeless rights advocates would be difficult without earning trust. And, in Danielle's case, marching along with the protestors would be read as advocacy regardless of Danielle's commitments. In that case, to participate was to advocate. By contrast, in Aaron's case, he chose to enter the rave scene through an advocacy organization, which meant that to participate with them at raves, he needed to advocate with them. But, he could have participated in the rave without advocating for safety. In these cases, the critics aligned with the missions of the participants, which can open up space for another role-companion. Michael and Aaron developed close relationships during their fieldwork, which comes through in the tales of their experiences. Conversely, Danielle discusses the feeling of closeness she experienced with strangers in a protest rally but not the establishment of close relationships. Although Samantha did not develop close relationships at Zion National Park, she has in other fieldwork she has conducted. Nevertheless, the vignettes in this chapter demonstrate how easily a critic can become participant, advocate, and companion through fieldwork.

The advocate and companion roles can make it more difficult to embody the role of critic when critics disagree with participants.

Therefore, we recognize that scholars may not align completely with rhetors, participants, and organizations, which creates the opportunity for critics to become opponents. When traditional critics oppose the positions of rhetors, it does not typically jeopardize their research or manifest ethical dilemmas. However, when faced with opponents *in situ*, researchers could be at risk academically, physically, and emotionally. We delve into the possibility of conducting research in an organization with which a critic is ideologically opposed in the conclusion. Yet, we recognize that there are degrees of opposition. In Samantha's research at Zion National Park, she felt conflicted sometimes, not aligning completely with participants all the time. As her vignette points out, she encountered many participants with whom she disagreed about the purposes of national parks and the importance of Leave No Trace policies, for example. In these cases, although she was not fully opposed to rhetors and participants, she felt like an opponent at times and chose to negotiate most of those moments by keeping silent. Researchers do not need to express their feelings for their perception of their roles to change, which becomes most apparent in the distinction between observer and witness.

The differences between observer and witness reside almost entirely in the critic's mind. At a large-scale event, scholars could move in a moment between observer and witness, given the right combination of actions, bodies, identities, circumstances, and frame of mind. A witness differs externally by their willingness to confirm, rather than deny or ignore, what they saw or heard; an observer makes no such promise. Although the vignettes in this chapter do not state explicitly that Samantha, Michael, Danielle, and Aaron think of themselves as witnesses, participatory critical rhetoric implies as much. Because we theoretically ground participatory critical rhetoric in the critical tradition, it would be appropriate for researchers to muster their courage in the face injustices and act as witnesses. Moreover, we invite scholars to consider how some of the roles not previously considered could be extended into conventional rhetorical criticism. Although some of these roles do not depend on critics' presence at research sites, the interactions engendered through embodiment alter critics' capacity to act in different roles, which demands reflection.

Embodiment, such as it is in participatory critical rhetoric, implies the ethical need for a different kind of reflexivity, one that acknowledges researchers' bodies as material and part of the critical process, and thus decenters them. Reflexivity to this degree encourages critics to acknowledge and understand their vulnerability, emotional attachments, and political commitments in addition to their past experiences and characteristics of their bodies. In addition to Morris's definition of reflexivity above, we draw from critical qualitative research that explores how researcher roles vary depending on the nature of access to a particular scene and the degree to which the researcher can be an active participant within the cultural activities under investigation as well as the reflection they should continuously perform.[49] Reflexivity, in participatory critical rhetoric, does not differ significantly from how it is performed in critical qualitative methods and performance studies. Accounting for one's self in essays at the end of a project is a good option, but we argue that reflexivity should be an ongoing part of research.

In this vein of rhetorical criticism, critics account for themselves in ways that most other rhetoricians (even those who subscribe to critical projects) do not because they are there, mentally and materially, shaping rhetoric as it happens, observing participants as they choose one path over another. Peter McLaren echoes this position when he writes, "field-workers engage not just in the analysis of field sites but in their active production."[50] Rhetoricians, by being immanently present as we discuss in chapter 2, witness both the reflex-like, unexamined practices that construct everyday cultural values and they observe the calculated, strategic use of communication that battles, harms, protects, and builds coalitions for themselves and others.

In chapter 2, we explore some of the political considerations for engaging in participatory critical rhetoric. There, we argued that participatory critical rhetoric's political consequence is centered in its refiguring of when/how politics is engaged by the critic, the political choices embedded in text selection, and the identity of the critic as an activist. By bringing up these considerations, we foreground politics in rhetorical criticism and orient other aspects of the critical process—embodiment, the field, and participants—around that concern. Similarly, politics guides our impulse toward and need for reflexivity before, during, and after criticism. Critical scholars in particular are concerned about the impacts that their research will have on populations outside the academy. And, critical scholars also turn a critical lens on themselves, using reflexivity to examine their own roles and relationships in the research process.

Speculating about the consequences of their research projects drives critical scholars. In articulating how critical scholarship can reproduce dominant ideologies, for example, Helene Shugart argues that the forms our scholarly essays take and the demands of publishing reproduce oppressive systems and, thus, even critical scholarship, which seeks to emancipate, participates in systems of oppression.[51] This kind of question—that is, what are the consequences of our discipline?—is not uncommon in rhetorical criticism. But focusing reflexive practices on the self is uncommon. Rhetorical critics also need to be aware of the power implications of their own reflexivity. "Reflexivity involves the recognition that an account of reality does not simply mirror reality but, rather, creates or constitutes as real in the first place whatever it describes."[52] Keeping this in mind, participatory critical rhetoric, then, contributes to theory for text-based rhetorical critics as well as field-based critics. It encourages reflexivity on an individual level, in addition to a disciplinary level, and prods critics to be as analytical about themselves as they would be of rhetors (and audiences).

Participatory critical rhetoric gives researchers an opportunity to examine physical bodies *in situ*, opening the body to a variety of critical senses, affective dimensions, and risky situations. All of these forms of embodiment deserve reflexivity because when critics engage in self-reflection and informed decision making, they can exercise awareness of the provenance of their interpretations, acknowledging the multiple perspectives offered by participants in the field. Furthermore, attending to critics' bodies recognizes the always already embodied and emplaced nature of rhetoric. In the next chapter, we unpack the notion of rhetoric as emplaced, theorizing different interpretations of the field.

NOTES

1. Daniel C. Brouwer, "Counterpublicity and Corporeality in HIV/AIDS Zines," *Critical Studies in Media Communication* 22, (2005): 351–71, doi: 10.1080/07393180500342860; Kevin Michael DeLuca, "Unruly Arguments: The Body Rhetoric of Earth First!, Act Up, and Queer Nation," *Argumentation and Advocacy* 36 (1999): 9–21; Abby M. Dubisar, "Embodying and Disabling Antiwar Activism: Disrupting YouTube's 'Mother's Day for Peace,'" *Rhetoric Review* 34 (2015): 56–73, doi: 10.1080/07350198.2015.976305; Darrel Enck-Wanzer, "Race, Coloniality, and Geo-Body Politics: *The Garden* as Latin@ Vernacular Discourse," *Environmental Communication: A Journal of Nature and Culture* 5 (2011): 363–71, doi: 10.1080/17524032.2011.593535; Leland M. Griffin, "The Rhetorical Structure of the 'New Left' Movement: Part I," *Quarterly Journal of Speech* 50 (1964): 113–35, doi: 10.1080/00335636409382652; Raymie E. McKerrow, "Corporeality and Cultural Rhetoric: A Site for Rhetoric's Future," *Southern Communication Journal* 63 (1998): 315–28, doi: 10.1080/10417949809373105; Erin Rand, "An Appetite for Activism: The Lesbian Avengers and the Queer Politics of Visibility," *Women's Studies in Communication* 36 (2013): 121–41, doi: 10.1080/07491409.2013.794754.

2. Dana L. Cloud, "The Materiality of Discourse as Oxymoron: A Challenge to Critical Rhetoric," *Western Journal of Communication* 58 (1994): 141–63, doi: 10.1080/10570319409374493; Ronald Walter Greene, "Another Materialist Rhetoric," *Critical Studies in Media Communication* 15 (1998): 21–40, doi: 10.1080/15295039809367031; Barbara A. Biesecker and John Louis Lucaites, *Rhetoric, Materiality, & Politics* (New York: Peter Lang, 2009);

3. Carole Blair, "Reflections on Criticism and Bodies: Parables from Public Places," *Western Journal of Communication* 65 (2001): 271–94, doi: 10.1080/10570310109374706; Carole Blair, "Contemporary US Memorial Sites as Exemplars of Rhetoric's Materiality," in *Rhetorical Bodies,* eds. Jack Selzer and Sharon Crowley (Madison: University of Wisconsin Press, 1999): 16–57; Carole Blair, Marsha S. Jeppeson, and Enrico Pucci Jr., "Public Memorializing in Postmodernity: The Vietnam Veterans Memorial as Prototype," *Quarterly Journal of Speech* 77 (1991): 263–88, doi: 10.1080/00335639109383960.

4. Greg Dickinson, "Memories for Sale: Nostalgia and the Construction of Identity in Old Pasadena," *Quarterly Journal of Speech* 83 (1997): 1–27, doi: 10.1080/00335639709384169; Greg Dickinson, "Joe's Rhetoric: Finding Authenticity at Starbucks," *Rhetoric Society Quarterly* 32 (2002): 5–27, doi: 10.1080/02773940209391238; Danielle Endres and Samantha Senda-Cook, "Location Matters: The Rhetoric of Place in Protest," *Quarterly Journal of Speech* 97 (2011): 257–82, doi: 10.1080/00335630.2011.585167; Phaedra C. Pezzullo, "Resisting 'National Breast Cancer Awareness Month': The Rhetoric of Counterpublics and Their Cultural Performances," *Quarterly Journal of Speech* 89 (2003): 345–65, doi:10.1080/0033563032000160981; Phaedra C. Pezzullo, "Performing Critical Interruptions: Stories, Rhetorical Invention, and the Environmental Justice Movement," *Western Journal of Communication* 65 (2001): 1–25, doi:10.1080/10570310109374689; Phaedra C. Pezzullo,. "Touring 'Cancer Alley,' Louisiana: Performances of Community and Memory for Environmental Justice," *Text and Performance Quarterly* 23 (2003): 226–52, doi:10.1080/10462930310001635295; Phaedra C. Pezzullo, "Tourists and/as Disasters: Rebuilding, Remembering, and Responsibility in New Orleans," *Tourist Studies* 9 (2009): 23–41, doi: 10.1177/1468797609360591; Samantha Senda-Cook, "Materializing Tensions: How Maps and Trails Mediate Nature," *Environmental Communication: A Journal of Nature and Culture* 7 (2013), 355–71, doi: 10.1080/17524032.2013.792854; Samantha Senda-Cook, "Rugged Practices: Embodying Authenticity in Outdoor Recreation," *Quarterly Journal of Speech* 98 (2012), 129–52, doi: 10.1080/00335630.2012.663500.

5. Brouwer, "Counterpublicity"; DeLuca, "Unruly Arguments"; Dubisar, "Embodying and Disabling Antiwar Activism"; Enck-Wanzer, "Race, Coloniality, and Geo-Body Politics"; Griffin, "The Rhetorical Structure of the 'New Left'"; McKerrow, "Corporeality and Cultural Rhetoric"; Rand, "An Appetite for Activism."

6. Paul Achter, "Unruly Bodies: The Rhetorical Domestication of Twenty-First-Century Veterans of War," *Quarterly Journal of Speech* 96, (2010): 46–68, doi: 10.1080/00335630903512697; Brouwer, "Counterpublicity"; Michael L. Butterworth, "'Katie was Not Only a Girl, She was Terrible': Katie Hnida, Body Rhetoric, and Football at the University of Colorado," *Communication Studies* 59 (2008): 259–73, doi: 10.1080/10510970802257705; DeLuca, "Unruly Arguments"; Dubisar, "Embodying and Disabling Antiwar Activism"; Enck-Wanzer, "Race, Coloniality, and Geo-Body Politics"; Stephen John Hartnett, "'Tibet is Burning': Competing Rhetorics of Liberation, Occupation, Resistance, and Paralysis on the Roof of the World," *Quarterly Journal of Speech* 99 (2013): 283–316, doi: 10.1080/00335630.2013.806819; Jordynn Jack, "Acts of Institution: Embodying Feminist Rhetorical Methodologies in Space

and Time," *Rhetoric Review* 28, (2009): 285–303, doi: 10.1080/07350190902958909; Rand, "An Appetite for Activism"; Ross Singer, "Anti-Corporate Argument and the Spectacle of the Grotesque Rhetorical Body in *Super Size Me*," *Critical Studies in Media Communication* 28 (2011): 135–152, doi: 10.1080/15295036.2011.553724.

7. Senda-Cook "Rugged Practices: Embodying Authenticity in Outdoor Recreation," *Quarterly Journal of Speech* 98 (2012), 129–52, doi: 10.1080/00335630.2012.663500.

8. Debra Hawhee, "Rhetorics, Bodies, and Everyday Life," *Rhetoric Society Quarterly* 36 (2006): 157, doi: 10.1080/02773940600605487. Indeed, body rhetoric has been a concern since ancient times. Hawhee claims, "that rhetoric, from its inception, was and is a bodily art" (155). Only relatively recently have rhetoricians accepted the mind/body split and excluded the body as part of rhetoric. Additionally, when Mendelson argues about embodied rhetoric, he is referring to Cicero, the Romans, and the Sophists (Michael Mendelson, "The Rhetoric of Embodiment," *Rhetoric Society Quarterly* 28, (1998): 29–50, doi: 10.1080/02773949809391129.). The grounds for contemporary movements to attend to bodies are embedded in the foundations of rhetoric.

9. Darrel Enck-Wanzer, "Trashing the System: Social Movement, Intersectional Rhetoric, and Collective Agency in the Young Lords Organization's Garbage Offensive," *Quarterly Journal of Speech* 92, (2006): 181, doi: 10.1080/00335630600816920. Because Enck-Wanzer still focuses on representations we extend his conception of intersectional rhetoric to look at in situ studies.

10. Celeste Condit, "Contemporary Rhetorical Criticism: Diverse Bodies Learning New Languages," *Rhetorical Review* 25, (2006): 368–72; Robert Cox, "Nature's 'Crisis Disciplines': Does Environmental Communication have an Ethical Duty?," *Environmental Communication: A Journal of Nature and Culture* 1, (2007): 5–20, doi: 10.1080/17524030701333948; Raymie E. McKerrow, "Critical Rhetoric: Theory and Praxis," *Communication Monographs* 56 (1989): 91–111, doi: 10.1080/03637758909390253; Richard Rogers, "Overcoming the Objectification of Nature in Constitutive Theories: Toward a Transhuman, Materialist Theory of Communication," *Western Journal of Communication* 62, no. 3 (1998): 244–72, doi: 10.1080/10570319809374610; Michael Salvador and Tracylee Clarke, "The Weyekin Principle: Toward an Embodied Critical Rhetoric," *Environmental Communication* 5 (2011): 243–60, doi: 10.1080/17524032.2011.586713.

11. Blair, "Reflections on Criticism and Bodies". This is also reminiscent of Walter Benjamin's arguments about the important differences between originals and reproductions. He states, "Even the most perfect reproduction of a work of art is lacking in one element: its presence in time and space, its unique existence at the place where it happens to be." Walter Benjamin, "The Work of Art in the Age of Mechanical Reproduction," in *Illuminations: Essays and Reflections*, ed. Hannah Arendt, trans. Harry Zohn (New York: Schocken Books, 1969), 220.

12. Blair, "Reflections on Criticism and Bodies," 275.

13. Ibid.

14. Paul Achter, "Unruly Bodies"; Brouwer, "Counterpublicity"; Butterworth, "'Katie was Not Only a Girl, She was Terrible'"; Dubisar, "Embodying and Disabling Antiwar Activism"; Kelly E. Happe, "The Body of Race: Toward a

Rhetorical Understanding of Racial Ideology," *Quarterly Journal of Speech* 99, no. 2 (2013): 131–55, doi: 10.1080/00335630.2013.775700; Jack, "Acts of Institution".

15. DeLuca, "Unruly Arguments"; Enck-Wanzer, "Race, Coloniality, and Geo-Body Politics"; Enck-Wanzer, "Trashing the System"; Darrel Enck-Wanzer, "Decolonizing Imaginaries: Rethinking 'the People' in the Young Lords' Church Offensive," *Quarterly Journal of Speech* 98, (2012): 1–23, doi: 10.1080/00335630.2011.638656; Hartnett, "'Tibet is Burning'"; Singer, "Anti-Corporate Argument"; Rand, "An Appetite for Activism." 122–3. Although it is not always directly related to arguments made with the body, rhetorical enactment refers to rhetors embodying conditions, ideologies, or identities, for example. See, for example, Karlyn Kohrs Campbell and Kathleen Hall Jamieson, "Form and Genre in Rhetorical Criticism: An Introduction," in *Form and Genre: Shaping Rhetorical Action*, ed. by Karlyn Kohrs Campbell and Kathleen Hall Jamieson (Falls Church, VA: Speech Communication Association, 1978): 9–32. See also Carrie Crenshaw, "Resisting Whiteness' Rhetorical Silence," *Western Journal of Communication* 61, (1997): 253–78, doi: 10.1080/10570319709374577; Christopher Darr, "Civility as Rhetorical Enactment: The John Ashcroft 'Debates' and Burke's Theory of Form," *Southern Communication Journal* 70 (2005): 316–28, doi: 10.1080/10417940509373337.

16. Peter Andersen, "Beyond Criticism: The Activist Turn in the Ideological Debate," *Western Journal of Communication* 57, 247–256, doi: 10.1080/10570319309374447; Barbara Biesecker, "Michel Foucault and the Question of Rhetoric," *Philosophy & Rhetoric* 25, (1992): 351–364; Celeste Michelle Condit, "The Critic as Empath: Moving Away from Totalizing Theory," *Western Journal of Communication* 57, (1993): 178–90, doi: 10.1080/10570319309374441; Michael Calvin McGee, "Text, Context, and the Fragmentation of Contemporary Culture," *Western Journal of Speech Communication* 54 (1990): 274–89, doi: 10.1080/10570319009374343; James F. Klumpp and Thomas A. Hollihan, "Rhetorical Criticism as Moral Action," *Quarterly Journal of Speech* 75, (1989): 84–96, doi: 10.1080/00335638909383863; Michael C. Leff, "Interpretation and the Art of the Rhetorical Critic," *Western Journal of Speech Communication* 44, (1980): 337–349, doi: 10.1080/10570318009374019; Barbara Warnick, "Leff in Context: What is the Critic's Role?," *Quarterly Journal of Speech* 78, (1992): 232–7, doi: 10.1080/00335639209383992.

17. Dwight Conquergood, "Rethinking Ethnography: Towards a Critical Cultural Politics," *Communication Monographs* 58 (1991): 179–94, doi: 10.1080/03637759109376222. Conquergood uses the term "rhetorical reflexivity" to encourage ethnographers to adopt a rhetorical perspective when they analyze their own involvement in their research project. We advocate for rhetorical critics to bring the same perspectives and tools they would use to analyze their artifacts to reflect on their commitments (academic, political, and personal), bodies, and agendas when in the field. In this way, reflexivity becomes rhetorical.

18. Charles E. Morris III, "Performing/Rhetorical Studies: Differential Belonging across Intradisciplinary Borders," *Text and Performance Quarterly* 34, (2014): 105, doi: 10.1080/10462937.2013.849813. Emphasis in original.

19. Edwin Black, *Rhetorical Criticism: A Study in Method* (Madison: The University of Wisconsin Press, 1978), xi.

20. Ibid.

21. Brian Ott, "(Re)Locating Pleasure in Media Studies: Toward an Erotics of Reading," *Communication and Critical/Cultural Studies* 1, (2004): 195, doi: 10.1080/14791420410001685386.

22. Blair, "Reflections on Criticism and Bodies."

23. Conquergood, "Rethinking Ethnography," 180.

24. Michel Foucault, The History of Sexuality: An Introduction, Volume 1 New York: Vintage Books, 1978).

25. Phaedra Pezzullo, *Toxic Tourism: Rhetorics of Pollution, Travel, and Environmental Justice* (Tuscaloosa: The University of Alabama Press, 2007).

26. Lloyd F. Bitzer, "The Rhetorical Situation," *Philosophy & Rhetoric* 1, (1968): 1–14; McGee, "Text, Context, and the Fragmentation of Contemporary Culture."

27. Pierre Mayol, "Living," *The Practice of Everyday Life: Volume 2: Living & Cooking*, ed. Luce Giard, trans. Timothy J. Tomasik (Minneapolis: University of Minnesota Press, 1998), 22, emphasis in original.

28. Dwight Conquergood, "Book Reviews: Ethnography, Rhetoric, and Performance," *Quarterly Journal of Speech*, 78 (1992): 87, doi: 10.1080/00335639209383982.

29. See, for example: Pezzullo, *Toxic Tourism;* Senda-Cook, "Rugged Practices"; Peter Simonson, "The Streets of Laredo: Mercurian Rhetoric and the Obama Campaign," *Western Journal of Communication* 74, (2010): 94–126, doi: 10.1080/10570310903466045.

30. Pezzullo, *Toxic Tourism,* 11. Here, Pezzullo writes about Western culture's tendency to split mind and body, privileging the mind and marginalizing the body as sites of knowledge. She is challenging this convention by including sensorial data, collected through fieldwork, in her analyses.

31. Although she does not address her body specifically, Phaedra Pezzullo opens a chapter in *Toxic Tourism* with a short description of her experience with this topic. She writes, "After I began my research on toxic tours, one of my cousins was diagnosed with cancer. Her doctor told her that she was 'the healthiest person with cancer' that he had ever met. It wasn't much consolation. She was thirty-two. She also was pregnant. Within two years, she gave birth to a healthy baby girl, and she died" (Ibid, 106). Foregrounding this kind of personal reflection and connection gives context and texture to her criticism.

32. Simonson, "The Streets of Laredo," 95.

33. Senda-Cook, "Rugged Practices."

34. George F. McHendry, Jr., Michael K. Middleton, Danielle Endres, Samantha Senda-Cook, and Megan O'Byrne, "Rhetorical Critic(ism)'s Body: Affect and Fieldwork on a Plane of Immanance," *Southern Communication Journal* 79, (2014): 293–310, doi: 10.1080/1041794X.2014.906643.

35. Tim DeChristopher as quoted by Melanie Jae Martin, "Newly Released Tim DeChristopher Finds a Movement Transformed by His Courage," *Yes. Magazine*, April 22, 2013, accessed http://www.yesmagazine.org/planet/tim-dechristopher-peaceful-uprising-movement-transformed-courage on March 2, 2015.

36. Gregory J. Seigworth and Melissa Gregg, "An Inventory of Shimmers," in *The Affect Theory Reader* Melissa Gregg and Gregory J. Seigworth, ed. (Durham: Duke University Press, 2010), 1.

37. Ibid, 1.

38. Brian Massumi, "The Autonomy of Affect," *Cultural Critique* 31 (1995), 88.

39. Ibid, 88.

40. Joshua Gunn and Jenny Edbauer Rice, "About Face/Stuttering Discipline," *Communication and Critical/Cultural Studies* 6, no. 2 (2009): 216, doi: 10.1080/14791420902868029.

41. Pezzullo, "Resisting 'National Breast Cancer Awareness Month,'" 356.

42. Mindy Fenske, "Movement and Resistance: (Tattooed) Bodies and Performance," *Communication and Critical/Cultural Studies* 4 (2007): 51–73, doi: 10.1080/14791420601138302.

43. Karen, A. Stewart, Aaron Hess, Sarah J. Tracy, and H. L. Goodall, Jr., "Risky Research: Investigating the 'Perils' of Ethnography," in Norman K. Denzin and Michael D. Giardina, ed. *Qualitative Inquiry and Social Justice: Toward a Politics of Hope* (Walnut Creek, CA: Left Coast Press, 2009), 199.

44. Butterworth, "'Katie was Not Only a Girl, She was Terrible'"; Michel Foucault, *The History of Sexuality: Volume 1: An Introduction*, trans. by Robert Hurley (New York: Vintage Books, 1978); McKerrow, "Corporeality and Cultural Rhetoric."

45. Pezzullo, *Toxic Tourism*,147.

46. Stewart et al., "Risky Research."

47. Blair, "Reflections on Criticism and Bodies," 272.

48. Sarah J. Tracy, "Fieldwork Horse-Assery: Making the Most of Feeling Humiliated, Rebuffed, and Offended During Participant Observation Research," *Management Communication Quarterly* 28 (2014): 458–65, doi: 10.1177/0893318914536965.

49. Patricia A. Adler and Peter Adler, *Membership roles in field research* (Beverly Hills, CA: Sage Publications, 1987); Robert M. Emerson, Rachel I. Fretz, and Linda L. Shaw, *Writing Ethnographic Fieldnotes*, 2nd ed. (Chicago: University of Chicago Press, 2011); Thomas R. Lindlof and Bryan C. Taylor, *Qualitative Communication Research Methods*, 3rd ed. (Los Angeles: Sage Publications, Inc., 2011); James P. Spradley, *Participant Observation* (New York: Holt, Rinehart, Winston, 1980).

50. Peter McLaren, "Field Relations and the Discourse of the Other: Collaboration in Our Own Ruin," in *Experiencing Fieldwork*, eds. W. B. Shaffir and R. A. Stebbins (Newbury Park, CA: Sage, 1991), 150, emphasis in original.

51. Helene Shugart, "An Appropriating Aesthetic: Reproducing Power in the Discourse of Critical Scholarship," *Communication Theory* 13 (2003): 275–303, doi: 0.1111/j.1468-2885.2003.tb00293.x.

52. Emerson, Fretz, and Shaw, *Writing Ethnographic Fieldnotes,* 245.

Chapter 4

From Context to Field in Participatory Critical Rhetoric

At a climate change rally in Salt Lake City, Utah, there was a palpable disjuncture between the stated purpose of the event and the more nebulous and messy "feel" of being at the event. The rally was designed to support a national "Step It Up" campaign to cut carbon dioxide emissions eighty percent by 2050. Documented textual accounts of the event (both prior to and following) emphasized the central message about cutting carbon dioxide emissions to prevent these emissions from further contributing to the greenhouse effect and global warming. Yet, the layout of the space, the people gathered, and the verbal and non-verbal messages at the event communicated something different: a summer music festival. This festival-like atmosphere competed with the stated purpose of the event as a protest rally. Being at the event itself not only defied the documented messages about the event but also offered a more nuanced picture of the competing and sometimes contradictory rhetorics circulating in that particular place. When my research team and I asked participants about the event, we found that participants also resonated with the festival-like feel of the rally. Indeed, while I encountered participants ready to protest and spread the message about cutting carbon dioxide emissions, I encountered many more participants who called the event a summer concert and did not know that it was about climate change. In short, my interpretation of the rhetoric of the climate change rally was greatly influenced by the embodied and emplaced material experience of being present at the event. Gathering, participating with, and analyzing these rhetorics offered a more nuanced picture of the rhetorical dynamics and consequences of this rally than did the documented accounts from the Step It Up website or newspaper reports that reinforced the stated purpose.

—Danielle

This vignette demonstrates the importance of both context and field for *in situ* rhetorical analysis. This encounter with the Step It Up rally reveals that experiencing rhetoric as it unfolds in the field gives critics better access to an immediate context that can be different from the context surrounding a documented, reproduced, and mediated text. It is not the case that the mediated accounts of the rally have no context nor value for rhetorical inquiry (indeed, media accounts that stayed on message may have been more useful to the larger movement than the actual rally). All rhetorical texts interrelate with context. All texts, whether created and experienced by critics through field-based presence or documented and reproduced by rhetors or other observers (e.g., media practitioners), have rhetorical significance. However, experiencing the rally as it happened along with participants not only engages a different set of texts and contexts, but also draws attention to the role of *the field* in rhetorical performances, and more broadly to the practice of rhetorical criticism. In this chapter, we argue that the field is not simply a different context for rhetoric; the field is a participant in rhetorical invention that takes on a range of meanings from site of research to context to community of meaning to rhetorical actor.

Grounding our examination of the rhetorical dynamics of the field is a commitment to seeing rhetoric as a fundamentally emplaced (and embodied, as we discuss in chapter 3) phenomenon. All rhetorical acts are embedded within particular places and spatial practices. Just as rhetoric cannot be separated from bodies, rhetoric always happens in a place and that place influences the rhetorics that circulate with(in) it. The Step It Up rally happened at a particular location—the Salt Lake City and County building and grounds. That place and the way it was (re)created in the rally brought with it a range of meaning—such as that the location had previously been primarily used for summer concerts and festivals—that influenced and participated with the rhetorical invention that happened there.[1] More than the idea that rhetoric happens in place, place and space participate in all rhetorical acts. If participatory critical rhetoricians are to take seriously the materiality of rhetoric and the material experiences of rhetoric,[2] as we articulate in chapter 1, then they must also take seriously the places and spatial practices that are fundamental to the ways people experience the world,[3] as well as rhetoric's part in that world. This view of rhetoric as emplaced encourages a new spatial architecture for the practice of rhetorical criticism. In short, place and space matter in the invention, dissemination, circulation, and criticism of rhetoric.

Participatory critical rhetoric is an important (though not the only) way to access and engage with the emplaced dynamics of rhetoric. It does so, in part, with its injunction for rhetorical critics to enter the field. Yet, amid the growth of rhetorical field methods, critical-rhetorical ethnography, and other approaches to field-based rhetorical criticism that we detail in the introduction and chapter 1, there has been a palpable lack of discussion of the concept of the field and its relation to emplaced rhetoric. While the field may appear to be a simple concept that implies a different site, away from the office, in which research takes place, we argue that it actually entails much more. A sustained meditation on the role of the field in participatory critical rhetoric reveals not only the complexity of engaging in field-based rhetorical criticism but also provides a useful lens through which to better understand emplaced rhetoric and its implications for rhetorical theory and criticism more broadly. Our meditation examines four intersecting vectors of the field: (1) field as place of research; (2) field as context; (3) field as community of meaning; and (4) field as rhetorical text. Through each of these vectors we clarify not only how participatory critical rhetoricians can access emplaced rhetoric but also how engaging with, attuning to, and evaluating emplaced rhetoric in the field enhances a critic's understanding of the complex and intersectional material experience of rhetoric.

We begin by articulating emplaced rhetoric. Building from the concepts of space and place and how they have been taken up in rhetorical theory and criticism, we define emplaced rhetoric and highlight its significance to participatory critical rhetoric. Then we turn to our meditation on the four vectors of the field. We conclude the chapter by showing how the intersections between emplaced rhetoric, the field, and participatory rhetorical criticism have implications for broader conversations in rhetorical theory and criticism about space and place, intersectional rhetoric, and the material experience of rhetoric.

EMPLACED RHETORIC

To view rhetoric as an inherently emplaced phenomenon is to recognize that rhetoric is always an embodied experience in relation to place and space. Rhetorical performances are always emplaced. While rhetorical scholarship and qualitative research have made important strides in examining body rhetoric and argumentation and the role of the researcher's body in research practices, there is still work to be done to better examine the emplaced nature of rhetoric and the intersections of the embodied and emplaced dimensions of rhetorical action.[4] With an understanding that place and space are crucial to the way bodies interact with their environments, embodied rhetoric is also emplaced rhetoric. While few rhetorical scholars would disagree that rhetoric is embodied, rhetoricians have not yet come to an understanding of rhetoric as emplaced, even though rhetoric always participates with space and place such that, as Danielle Endres and Samantha Senda-Cook note, place is "more than just backdrop" for rhetoric.[5] In this sense, emplaced rhetoric is not just about the rhetoricity of places, but is more so about recognizing the ways in which rhetoric is always experienced by bodies through place and space. As Thomas Rickert notes, rhetoric is “made utterly distinctive by the manner in which it is inhabited at any given time and place.”[6] Before further unpacking the concept of emplaced rhetoric, we begin with a discussion of space and place.

Defining Place/Space

The relationship between space and place is the subject of debate within an interdisciplinary conversation, but it can be generally argued that space is more abstract than place.[7] Endres and Senda-Cook note, “Place refers to particular locations (e.g., a city, a particular shopping mall, or a park) that are semi-bounded, a combination of material and symbolic qualities, and embodied” whereas “Space refers to a more general notion of how society and social practices are regulated (and sometimes disciplined) by spatial thinking (e.g., capitalist mode of production or gendered notions of public and private space).”[8] Instead of seeing place and space as competing and distinct phenomena, they are mutually constitutive.[9] Place/space, then, is an interrelationship between sets of spatial norms and particularized performances in places. Even though it is impossible to dissect space and place, we term *rhetoric* as an emplaced activity as opposed to a spatial activity to emphasize the embodied, material experience of rhetoric as always happening with a place (that is always already interrelated with space).[10]

This idea of “happening with a place” is not meant to connote that place is static.[11] On the contrary, place is always in process.[12] Doreen Massey, in breaking down a dichotomy between time and space, highlights time-space as a way of thinking about the processual and dynamic nature of place/space.[13] Even if a particular place may be seemingly stable—such as the architectural infrastructure of city—that place is more aptly seen as a performance wherein bodies, built environment, natural environment, and discourses interact.[14] Place appears to be stable, in part, because its performance is constantly reinforced and reinscribed through normative and habitual practices.[15] Tim Cresswell argues “Place is produced by practice that adheres to (ideological) beliefs about what is the appropriate thing to do. But place reproduces the beliefs that produce it in a way that makes them appear natural, self-evident, and common sense.”[16] Yet, despite this appearance of common sense, the processual character of place/space means that these normative performances and practices can be disrupted. Danielle Endres, Samantha Senda-Cook, and Brian Cozen argue that “place, even if it has a relatively stable normalized meaning, is always in process and therefore always subject to alternative arguments.”[17] In other words, understanding place as always in process reveals how place/space can be sites of contestation, open to transgression and challenge.[18] This also reveals the importance of rhetoric and argumentation to the social construction of place/space. Emplaced rhetoric, therefore, does not imply that rhetoric happens *in* a static place, but rather implies that rhetoric happens *with(in)* a dynamic, embodied, processual, and performative place.

Shifting Focus to Emplaced Rhetoric

Our conception of rhetoric as emplaced builds from the spatial turn in rhetorical studies. Increasingly, rhetorical critics have turned to analysis of the rhetoricity of space and place with artifacts ranging from museums and memorials to shopping malls to protest events to bathrooms to roadways to cities.[19] These analyses share the assumption that space and place have rhetorical influence and consequence,[20] or that cultural places/spaces can impact the types of decorum that are afforded to the *kairos* of rhetoric.[21] This rich body of work has already advanced the argument that space and place are rhetorical and argumentative, thus further expanding the notion of what counts as a text and troubling a neat distinction between text, situation, and context. While varying definitions of space and place within rhetorical scholarship might influence how one conceptualizes the rhetoric of space and place, critical attention to spatial rhetorics is most often attuned to the ways in which physical material structures (e.g., a monument) or semi-bounded places (e.g., a shopping mall or city) are co-constituted with human meanings to have rhetorical consequence. Emplaced rhetoric builds from this corpus because it takes seriously the rhetoricity of place/space as an underlying assumption.

The concept of emplaced rhetoric expands upon this previous research by focusing not only on the rhetorical features of one discrete place, but instead focusing on place/space as a co-participant in all rhetorical acts. While others have invoked the term *emplaced* in relation to rhetoric, little work has been done to fully explore the concept, especially in regard to the participatory turn in critical rhetoric.[22] To see place as a participant includes but also goes beyond the argument that places/spaces are rhetorical. Participation with place/space happens on a least three levels. First, rhetorical invention always happens within place/space as a process (even if documented texts elide this fundamental situatedness in place/space or if place/space is filtered through textualization). In the case of Step It Up, the place was the Salt Lake City and County building and grounds, a semi-bounded place that is tied up with sets of spatial practices. Second, the rhetoricity of place/space participates with rhetorical invention. Place and spatial practices are a significant form of immediate context as well as situation that participates with the rhetoric created therein. The City and County building and grounds served as a material/symbolic context for the rhetorical invention of the Step It Up Rally and shaped both the invention and reception of the rhetorical force of the rally. Third, place/space is one intersectional rhetorical form that contributes to the whole of rhetorical experience. In addition to being part of the immediate context of rhetoric, the City and County building and surroundings—the building, the grassy adjacent grounds, its situation within a set of spatial norms, the particular setup for the rally, and the embodiment of the place on that day—was also a form of rhetoric that interacted with the other rhetorical forms (verbal, musical, embodied, etc.) that intersected in the rally. In emphasizing the participatory qualities of place/space, emplaced rhetoric views rhetoric as a symbolic/material experience of intersecting physical structures, configurations of bodies in place, environment, sensorial phenomenon, performances and practices. These qualities of rhetoric as emplaced are an essential part of rhetoric and its power-laden consequences.[23] To further unpack how emplaced rhetoric changes thinking about the relationship between rhetoric and place/space, we offer some assumptions that guide our understanding of emplaced rhetoric.

First, emplaced rhetoric assumes the intersectionality of rhetoric—that place/space is one of many modalities at play in the construction of all rhetorical acts. As we argue in chapter 1, we view rhetoric as an intersectional experience, meaning it is always made up of a variety of forms coming together and experienced through a merging of the senses. Verbal rhetoric is only one of the many forms that collide in an embodied and emplaced rhetorical experience that includes various other forms such as visual, sonic, affective, tactile, embodied, mediated, and spatial. Attention to only one form of rhetoric, as is often the case in analysis of an after-the-fact documented text, elides the emplaced nature of rhetoric. While previous rhetorical studies of place/space attend to the rhetorical influence of places, most do not engage with place/space within an intersectional rhetoric.[24] Emplaced rhetoric sees place in conversation with other rhetorical forms in an always already emplaced rhetorical act.

Second, emplaced rhetoric assumes that place/space is made, maintained, challenged, and performed through a co-relationship between bodies and environment.[25] "Place, then, needs to be understood as an embodied relationship with the world. Places are constructed by people doing things and in this sense are never finished, but are constantly being performed."[26] Even when people are not physically present in a place, we cannot separate the place from the bodies that produce it. As such, emplaced rhetoric automatically implies embodied rhetoric and the two cannot be separated.[27] Despite this, while some contemporary research on the rhetoric of place/space acknowledges the role of bodies,[28] the concept of emplaced rhetoric nuances an understanding of how bodies co-perform and co-participate with place/space. Expanding upon Greg Dickinson's argument for a "tripartite relationship among bodies, subjectivities and spaces such that each is interdependent on the others," we argue that all rhetoric is both embodied and emplaced.[29] Sarah Pink's conception of emplaced ethnography operates on a similar plane by focusing on "how both ethnographers and participants in ethnographic research are emplaced in social, sensory, and material contexts, characterized *[sic]* by, and productive of, particular power configurations that they experience through their whole bodies."[30] Pink's notion of emplaced ethnography views place as a set of contextual factors that influence participants, which we argued above is just one way of thinking about the relationship between place and rhetoric. Rather, our argument assumes that place/space is more than just context; it is simultaneously setting, context, and text. Place/space is a rhetorical form and participant in intersectional rhetoric that is always interanimated by bodies.

Third, emplaced rhetoric emphasizes the material experience of rhetoric. As we discuss in the previous chapter, filtering rhetoric through bodily experience acknowledges the materiality of rhetoric and calls the critic's attention to a variety of extradiscurive qualities. Similarly, seeing rhetoric as emplaced highlights its interrelationship with built and natural environments, not as context but as participants in rhetorical invention. Rickert's theory of ambient rhetoric highlights that viewing rhetoric as emplaced invites a recognition of its "*attunement* to the world [i.e., intimate relationship to place]."[31] Viewing rhetoric as an emplaced (and embodied) phenomenon is a way of acknowledging what has been long excluded in purely textual accounts of rhetoric: that rhetoric is just as material as it is symbolic.[32]

Fourth, given these assumptions, emplaced (and embodied) rhetoric is best accessed through participatory forms of fieldwork. We are not arguing that place/space should be the primary focus of participatory critical rhetoric. Nor are we arguing that participatory critical rhetoric is the only way to approach emplaced rhetoric. However, being in the field and experiencing rhetoric as it happens through the critic's emplaced body makes it difficult to deny the material, embodied, and emplaced experience of rhetoric. While it is possible that this can be accessed through an intersectional textual approach, such an approach is limited because an after-the-fact text is a reproduction that is removed from direct experience and immediate context, and is subject to the choices made by the person who documented the text. In the case of a newspaper account of a rhetorical event, the reporter not only makes choices about representation, but those choices reflect the newsroom as a place of creation as opposed to the place of *in situ* rhetorical invention. Indeed, as we contend in chapter 2, a textocentric approach, especially with regard to written texts, elides the complexity of emplaced and embodied experience. Emplaced participatory critical rhetoric recognizes that rhetorical critics who enter the field are not only engaging their bodies in rhetoric as it happens, but are also entering a particular place with its own rhetorical influence. The emplaced rhetorical critic is not only able to engage with minor rhetorics and immanent politics, as we discuss in chapter 2, but is also able to access all manner of nonverbal features of the process of rhetorical invention. More so, the emplaced participatory rhetorical critic also impacts the production of rhetoric in that particular time and place through a co-participation with other people and the place. The embodied and emplaced critic becomes a part of the performance of place. Participatory critical rhetoric offers ways to better assess and present place/space as a part of the intersectional material experience of rhetoric.

Before moving on, it is important to acknowledge that the notion of emplaced rhetoric might be seen as a romantic or nostalgic (re)turn to placing power and legitimacy in some form of authentic person-to-person communication that values place (as locality and uniqueness) over space (as networks and flows), actual over virtual engagement, and communion over dissemination.[33] While participatory critical rhetoric does involve fieldwork and a direct engagement with embodied and emplaced rhetoric in its immediate context, it does not deny the value of analysis of more mediated, reproduced, and disseminated rhetorical artifacts. Participatory critical rhetoric celebrates a particular way of seeing rhetorical invention wherein emplaced critics can experience the multisensory qualities of rhetoric in the moment of invention. One of the strongest justifications for the move to field-based methods in rhetorical criticism is that it gives access to different kinds of rhetorical artifacts, especially those that are likely to not be documented, may be difficult to document, and might give increased access to marginalized voices.[34] Participation and direct experience by an emplaced critic can bring these types of rhetorical phenomenon into the purview of rhetorical criticism. Field-based approaches to rhetoric (along with movements to better account for affect, intersectionality, bodies, and spaces) add complexity to the overall understanding of rhetoric by giving critics a different vantage point through which to examine the invention and consequences of rhetoric.

We also do not want to make the argument that rhetorical circulation in virtual spaces and though public screens[35] is not emplaced rhetoric. It is entirely possible that field-based rhetorical criticism can also understand the emplaced nature of rhetoric in relation to locative media and social networks that are readily available within rhetorical fields.[36] Many social movements and other vernacular discourses turn toward social media to circulate messages and publicity about their cause.[37] Participatory critical rhetoricians can thereby have firsthand experience within the emplaced rhetorical experience before it is mediated. Moreover, participatory critical rhetoricians may also examine the emplaced nature of fully virtual environments, such as massively multiplayer online games, examining the immersive nature of those digital environments.[38] The key with these approaches is starting with the assumption that these are also places/spaces and the rhetoric with(in) them is still emplaced. Not only can we examine how places/spaces are (re) mediated and removed from their immediate emplacement through social networks, we might also examine how social networks are another form of place/space.

Returning to the Step It Up example that opened this chapter, an analysis of emplaced rhetoric would begin with the assumption that the rhetorical influence and consequences of the rally cannot be separated from the place/space in which it was performed. The participating rhetors, audience, and researchers embedded their bodies within the fenced designated zone of the event—the grassy areas surrounding the City and County Building in downtown Salt Lake City. These participants co-produced the intersectional rhetoric of the rally; they cocreated a temporary performance of place along with and through verbal, visual, aural, embodied, affective, tactile, and spatial rhetorical forms. The emplaced critics at this rally were able to assess and document the visceral material experience of being at the rally, including smelling beer and pizza, hearing speakers trying to amplify above the noise of the crowd, being handed fliers and informational brochures, dancing along to the music that highlighted the event, reading the signs, seeing carnival stilt puppets walk by, feeling the heat on their backs, overhearing people react to the speakers, and experiencing how the physical setup of the event and its location in a place traditionally used for festivals contributed to a festival-like feel. Participating in the rally allowed the emplaced field researchers to experience all of the competing rhetorical forms that bombarded the senses. This embodied and emplaced experience offers a rich description of the rhetorical dynamics at play at this climate change rally, including the place in which it occurred. Not only were participants emplaced, but the place itself had rhetorical force from the way the buildings, the temporary fence, the location of the stage *vis-a-vis* the climate change informational tables, the people moving through the place, and the collective memory of other festivals in this space all contributed to the experience of the rally. For example, the temporary fence communicated that the event was also a beer garden, and the location of the climate change information tables at the periphery and the music stage at the center communicated that the event was a concert. The combination of rhetorical forms—including the rhetoric of the space itself—created competing senses of place[39] wherein the rally was experienced by some as just another summer festival and by others as a watered-down climate change protest event. The rhetorical critics who experienced this emplaced rhetoric of the Step It Up rally were then able to document it through fieldnotes and analyze the often forgotten ways in which the place/space is also a co-participant with the rhetoric.[40]

FOUR AXES OF THE FIELD IN PARTICIPATORY CRITICAL RHETORIC

Thinking about the emplaced nature of participatory critical rhetoric calls for further discussion of the field as a crucial concept, both literally and figuratively, for participatory critical rhetoric. Most simply, the participatory critical rhetoric approach assumes some form of fieldwork in which the critic directly participates with and experiences emplaced rhetorical performances. The field is simultaneously a place of research, a context, an argumentative community, and a rhetorical actor, all of which allow for access to, participation in, and analysis of emplaced rhetoric. In this section, we theorize these four intersecting vectors of the concept of the field in participatory critical rhetoric.

Place of Research

Entering the field is not a traditional move for rhetorical critics. As we discuss in chapter 1, rhetorical criticism often involves analysis of after-the-fact, reproduced, and already documented texts. Yet, increasingly critics are engaging in field-based research practices as a way to access, document, and analyze *in situ* rhetorics. Participatory critical rhetoric and other field-based approaches put critics in the position of engaging with in-the-moment emplaced rhetorical action through fieldwork.

The field is often described as a site of research.[41] We argue that, more than merely a site of research, the field should be conceived as a place of research wherein the critic is both emplaced and has access to emplaced rhetoric. Rhetorical critics enter the field when they participate with a place of rhetorical action for the purpose of better understanding the rhetorical dynamics at play in that field. In our experiences in the field, this has meant experiencing the rhetoric at a protest event, sleeping on the street, hiking trails in a national park, or dancing in the desert with drug users to see rhetorical practices in action. Given participatory critical rhetoric's embrace of emplaced rhetoric, viewing the field as a place of research opens critics to see themselves as emplaced, and to examine the rhetoric of that place/space and how it interrelates with other rhetorical forms at play in *in situ* rhetorical invention.

If rhetorical scholars take seriously the emplaced nature of rhetoric, it evinces a preference for entering and engaging with the *in situ* field. Fieldwork typically describes a variety of qualitative and ethnographic research practices that occur in a naturalistic setting and engage with normal everyday embodied and emplaced behavior.[42] According to Carol Bailey,

> Simply stated, field research is the systematic study of ordinary activities in the settings in which they occur. Its primary goal is to understand these activities

> and what they mean to those who engage in them. To gain this understanding, field researchers collect data by interacting with, listening to, and observing people during the course of their daily lives, usually in some self-contained setting, such as an elementary school classroom, a street corner, a car dealership, or a public housing community.[43]

Fieldwork can happen in a variety of locations. Anywhere that rhetoric happens is a potential site for fieldwork (assuming that the critic can make an argument for its significance). According to ethnographer David Fetterman, "Understanding the world—or some small fragment of it—requires studying it in all its wonder and complexity."[44] Studying rhetoric in the field opens the rhetorical critic to a variety of aspects of the complex invention and consequences of rhetoric. Indeed, it is one of the best ways to understand rhetoric as emplaced.

Fieldwork also allows for understanding how critics themselves become emplaced in the field. Emplacement for a critic is not just a matter of being physically present. As Harry Wolcott argues, "simply being in the field is not enough . . . the essence of fieldwork is revealed by intent rather than by location."[45] The intent that Wolcott speaks of is to produce research and share that new understanding with the world. While the critic's physical presence in the place of research, or place of rhetorical invention, is an important first step to participatory critical rhetoric, it is not sufficient. Emplaced rhetorical critics recognize and bring their own history with places/spaces to each field encounter. Understanding rhetoricians' bodies and minds as related to their sense of place helps to recognize what rhetoricians bring with them to the field that affects their interpretation. Critics are influenced by their personal history with place and spatial practices, which influences how they will encounter the place/space of the field. Further, the physical presence of a rhetorical critic in the field also participates with and potentially alters the field. Viewing critics as emplaced in the field, then, implies a form of active participation with the field that cannot be separated from the intents, interactions, and roles of embedded critics.

Once in the place of rhetorical invention, participatory rhetorical critics can choose tools that allow them to engage with the emplaced nature of rhetoric. Participant observation allows critics to account for their own interaction with the place/space. The field researcher can also draw from a variety of other participatory tools such as unstructured and structured interviews as "common techniques for supplementing observations."[46] For example, spontaneous ethnographic interviews in the field can give further insight into participant perceptions of the role of place as a participant with rhetorical invention. In another example, while follow-up interviews might be detached in place and time from the rhetorical event under investigation, they are still emplaced rhetorical encounters. The interview is a social, and we would argue rhetorical, interaction that has implications for the way critics make sense of an interview.[47] As a form of emplaced rhetorical exchange, an interview that takes place in a home versus on the side of an ongoing rally, for instance, has a different feel. As we develop more in chapter 5, interactions with participants through fieldwork invite a variety of forms of situated, or emplaced, judgment.

Moreover, emphasizing the site of fieldwork as a place encourages critics to think about both time and place/space as significant factors in doing fieldwork. Fieldwork is often judged by the level of immersion researchers attain, with the amount of time spent in the field becoming the sole or major determinant of immersion. However, relying too heavily on the amount of time spent in the field limits the concept immersion to a number of days or months that may or may not represent full engagement with the people and the place. Getting a sense of the field in terms of it as a place embedded in spatial practices, along with an appropriate level of interaction with participants (as we articulate in chapter 5), is just as important as time for determining immersion in the field.

The field, then, is a place where research happens. Drawing attention to the field as a place enhances the way critics can interpret their own emplacement in the field and the role of the field-as-place in the research process. Engaging in fieldwork and experiencing the Atomic West as a place gave Danielle the ability to think about her site of research differently, as demonstrated in the following vignette.

The Atomic West has been a research interest of mine for years, wherein I have studied the various ways in which the American West is disproportionately linked with the nuclear production process, both nuclear weapons and nuclear energy. Nuclear weapons, in particular, have a strong relationship with the American West. In the lead up to the bombings of Hiroshima and Nagasaki, many aspects of the Manhattan Project took place in the American West from Robert Oppenheimer's weapon assembly camp in Los Alamos, New Mexico to the test of the first nuclear bomb at the Trinity Site in Alamogordo, New Mexico to the testing of site for the B-29 unit that dropped the bombs on Hiroshima and Nagasaki in Wendover, Nevada. Following the bombings and the end of World War II, the Cold War ramped up between the US and USSR, sparking a nuclear arms race. Federal government land (claimed by Western Shoshone and Southern Paiute people) in Nevada, about 65 miles northwest of Las Vegas, became the site of the domestic nuclear weapons test site, where over one thousand nuclear weapons have been detonated.

While I understood this history from maps and descriptive accounts, I came to know it better when I engaged in fieldwork and toured the Nevada

Test Site. Though I had seen aerial images of the pockmarked landscape of Yucca Flat, I had not been able to fully conceptualize the enormity of nuclear testing until I saw the craters with my own eyes. Standing at the edge of Sedan Crater—1280 feet wide and 320 feet deep—I felt the smallness of my body in comparison to this weighty remnant of a nuclear blast, and for a moment understood the sublimity and awe, not just the fear and destruction, inspired by nuclear technologies. I also simultaneously experienced delight in the expansiveness of the desert land and wonder at the plants and animals making do in this exploded land. Being present in the place, the Nevada Test Site, shaped my understanding of it in ways I could have neither predicted nor gathered from merely studying photos or written texts.

This understanding was further complicated when I began talking to and interacting with the other people I encountered at the Nevada Test Site and other places in the Atomic West. We were in this place together. I observed how others responded to the Sedan Crater at the Test Site. Participating in a Western Shoshone sunrise ceremony at Peace Camp near the Test Site gave me insight into competing conceptions of the land and its purpose. The interviews I conducted in the field could not be separated from the landscape surrounding the interviewees and me. An interviewee could point toward a particular landmark she was referencing as she talked, for example. Once I started visiting the Atomic West and engaging in fieldwork, not only had I entered a "naturalistic" research site, but I also gained insight into the site of research as a place, with competing meanings, textures, and impacts that influenced the way I understood the rhetoric of the Atomic West.

—Danielle

Thinking of the field as place of research reveals the complexity of the place and the spatial practices that come into play in fieldwork. As Danielle experienced through her fieldwork, spending time and being physically present in the Atomic West altered her understanding of that place and attuned her to the ways that she interacted with the place, not just as a site of research but as a meaningful place. Being in the field not only gives access to emplaced rhetoric but also emplaces the critic in that rhetoric.

Field as Community of Meaning

The field can also be seen as a community of meaning. Drawing from the concepts of fields or spheres of argument,[48] the field is not just a material physical location, but also a field of meaning. In this sense, the field is a metaphor for a semi-contained rhetorical community. This conception of the field includes the discursive history, or the conversation, within which one engages; the field is informed by discourses prior to the arrival of the field researcher and part of the process of understanding emplaced rhetoric includes recognition of these ongoing discourses. Kenneth Burke's famous parlor metaphor is an apt description of entering a field of meaning:

> Imagine that you enter a parlor. You come late. When you arrive, others have long preceded you, and they are engaged in a heated discussion, a discussion too heated for them to pause and tell you exactly what it is about. In fact, the discussion had already begun long before any of them got there, so that no one present is qualified to retrace for you all the steps that had gone before. You listen for a while, until you decide that you have caught the tenor of the argument; then you put in your oar. Someone answers; you answer him; another comes to your defense; another aligns himself against you, to either the embarrassment or gratification of your opponent, depending upon the quality of your ally's assistance. However, the discussion is interminable. The hour grows late, you must depart. And you do depart, with the discussion still vigorously in progress.[49]

Viewing the field in this way highlights that it is not only a discrete location, it is also an ongoing conversation, made of both verbal and nonverbal discourses. Although this notion of the ongoing conversation in the field of meaning also applies to traditional rhetorical criticism—indeed, it might even be labeled as understanding the context—we focus in this section on how the field of community meaning impacts participatory critical rhetoric's focus on *in situ* research and emplaced rhetoric.

The field of meaning in a community is implicated by understanding rhetoric as emplaced, and more broadly human experience as emplaced. Particular places as well as sets of spatial norms contribute to a community of meaning. As Henri Lefebvre argues, each society produces its own social space, its own understanding of the role of space in society and sets of social practices that conform to that conception.[50] Capitalist society, for example, views space within the concept of modes of production, which then implicates how people understand, engage in, and construct place.[51] On a smaller scale, a field of community meaning similarly intersects with norms about space and spatial practices. Social movements, for example, take up resistance to spatial norms as a part of their purpose. Activists take over streets, disrupt traffic, move a mass of bodies through those streets, and sometimes throw bricks through buildings. These alternate uses of space not only disrupt through *spatial events*[52] that act as mind-bombs that disseminate through collective consciousness, they also challenge the dominant convention to create a designated place for protest, or free speech zone. As Endres and Senda-Cook argue, "free speech zones on college campuses often have the result of framing free speech as something that happens only in specific, designated areas. Similarly, urban and suburban zoning laws may confine protests to particular areas and times, so long as protesters obtain a permit for protest."[53] Beyond these large-scale protest actions that disrupt spatial norms, even everyday actions, as de Certeau demonstrates in his analysis of walking in the city, can transgress dominant, ordered perceptions of space.[54] Simply riding one's bike to work, for instance, can transgress normative car-centric spatial norms. Through this example of the ways that social movements resist and transgress dominant spatial practices, we have shown that social space is its own ongoing conversation, or field of community meaning, that the field-based critic must attempt to understand and engage. This is not to argue that spatial norms are the only or the most important aspect of a field of community meaning; rather, spatial norms are one part of a larger set of verbal and non-verbal aspects of community meaning.

Particular places, more localized and discrete than spatial norms, also have importance to communities of meaning. On one hand, a field of community meaning may have relationships with particular places. On the other hand, a place itself may have its own field of community meanings. Regarding the former, part of the process of engaging in the ongoing conversation of a community is understanding the places that are important to it. Sense of place is a form of attachment that groups of humans can feel toward a place.[55] Environmental (justice) social movements, for example, may feel and attempt to encourage others to feel an attachment to near and far places like the Arctic National Wildlife Reserve or one's own neighborhood. Indeed, many environmental (justice) social movements have emerged with the sole purpose of protecting a place from resource extraction, such as the Western Shoshone Defense Project's attempt to save Mt. Tenabo from gold mining. Beyond the places of importance to a field of community meaning, a particular place might have its own field of meaning, or multiple heterogeneous meanings. Mt. Tenabo in Nevada has meaning to Western Shoshone people as a sacred site. It simultaneously has meaning to Barrick Gold as a rich resource of gold and other minerals, and therefore, a potential open pit mine. These examples show the interrelationship between places and spatial practices. Barrick Gold's view of Mt. Tenabo is more in line with dominant spatial practices, making the Western Shoshone view a resistive reading of the mountain. The contested nature of place[56] is an important aspect of the field of community meaning.

Emplaced rhetoric looks at how the field of community meaning interacts with an emplaced rhetorical invention. As qualitative researchers know, it takes time and presence to get a handle on the field.[57] The emplaced participatory critical rhetorician can do a variety of things to understand the place/space elements of the ongoing conversation in the field of meaning. In examining the Step It Up rally in Salt Lake City, for example, Danielle and her research team analyzed how the location of the rally had been used previously, they paid attention to how participants talked about the place and other places during the rally, they observed how the use of the space both transgressed and reified normal spatial practices in Salt Lake City, and they revealed how dynamics of the setup of the event constructed the place in particular ways.[58] Similarly, Samantha's fieldwork in Zion National Park reveals competing fields of community meaning related to both "proper" spatial practices in a national park and expectations about how the people should engage with a particular trail in the Park.

While doing field research in Zion National Park, I learned that different parts of the park had specialized, and sometimes competing, community meanings. Some outdoor recreation practices such as hiking off trail were acceptable, even encouraged, in the eastern part of the park where the terrain was rocky. This tough surface would not likely wear down if people walked off trail in this section. The National Park Service did not mark many trails or designate natural features or campgrounds with signs in that section of the park, giving it a backcountry feel. The ability to self-direct through a backcountry natural area is attractive to some people. For example, a park ranger I interviewed said that the eastern part of the park was one of his favorite areas to visit because he could pick a direction or a spot in the distance and go. Additionally, he liked that almost no one hiked in that section because many people worry about getting lost without a trail to guide them.

But this norm of the eastern part of Zion is not acceptable in other parts of the park. In the frontcountry part of the park, where over a million people visit every year primarily during the summer, soil erosion and plant destruction are a concern so the park staff members try to keep people on trails through obvious means (e.g., signs and cairns) and more subtle measures (e.g., clearing the path of plants). The distinction is not only with regard to frontcountry and backcountry. Unlike the eastern part of the park, the backcountry areas on the western side of the park are in high demand causing degradation, for example, in spots where canyoneering is common because the ropes rub the rocks so often. Therefore, even though in the rest of the park campgrounds are first-come first-served and hiking trails are open to anyone, in these backcountry areas, hikers and campers must apply for permits. I know they enforce this rule by patrolling the backcountry because while hiking through Hop Valley, a ranger checked my permit, and rangers told me that part of their job is hiking the backcountry and being present to monitor how it is used.

These differing norms of spatial practice within the park can create conflicts. I witnessed an exchange at the backcountry desk between a group of men who wanted to hike to a particular spot and the rangers who had to tell them there were not enough permits for them all to go. The Subway, the place in question, is a well-known feature of the backcountry of Zion because it is a beautiful, water-carved, sandstone tunnel, accessible by hiking through a creek or dropping down from above by ropes after hiking across the arid landscape. The men who wanted to hike to The Subway could only purchase two permits and there were three of them. They so wanted to hike there that day that they offered to save the rangers the trouble of finding them in the backcountry and issuing them a ticket by just paying the ticket right then and there. Not surprisingly, the rangers would not comply. While this conversation demonstrates the spatial norms (and, in this case, codified rules) of a section of the park, it also illustrates the firm reputation that people bestow on some places as valuable and, in the parlance of outdoor recreation, "worth it."

Likewise, other famous places in Zion inspired pleading, poor decision-making, and defiance of authority when visitors discovered that these places were inaccessible because of their own unpreparedness or bad weather conditions. Many people had traveled hundreds or thousands of miles to the park to see the view from Angels Landing or the sheer rock faces of The Narrows. The community meaning of these places—cultivated through word-of-mouth, internet sites, and books—made it worth risking getting caught in a flash flood or getting struck by lightning to experience to them. For visitors to Zion National Park, the desire to experience a place, to understand the community meaning of it, sometimes meant that they disregarded the spatial norms that had helped to shape its meaning.

—Samantha

Samantha's vignette not only reveals how the field is a community of meaning(s), but also how the field, in her case Zion National Park, acts as an immediate context for rhetorical practices, to which we turn next.

Field as Context

The field is also a context (or situation) for rhetorical action. While we demonstrate the usefulness of thinking of the field as context, it is more useful to think of the field as both text and context. This is consistent with our embrace of emplaced rhetoric that examines both the place/space with(in) which rhetoric happens and the rhetoricity of place/space as a co-participant in rhetorical performances. In one sense, participatory critical rhetoric privileges attention to immediate context (and audience reaction), thus re-inscribing a distinction between text and context. In another sense, it blurs the distinction between text and context by recognizing that the two are always in a messy conversation in the field. In this section we primarily highlight how the field can serve as a context and we pursue how the field is a text in the following section that treats the field as a rhetorical actor.

As we discuss in chapter 1, the relationship between text and context is a significant and long-standing *topos* in rhetorical theory and criticism. A traditional notion of context sees it as the immediate or historical context in which a speech is given. Lloyd Bitzer's concept of the rhetorical situation, for example, aligns with this traditional notion of context.[59] Along with the expansion of texts and the incorporation of critical approaches, context has expanded to include ideology and discursive formations (including normative spatial practices).[60] The line between text and context has become fuzzy, and some approaches shift attention to the study of context over text.[61] Within these perspectives on context, rhetorical critics routinely examine the symbolic or discursive context of rhetorical invention.

Participatory critical rhetoric allows rhetorical critics to shift focus to aspects of emplaced material context such as the time of day, physical structures, the weather, or the sensorial experience of being there at the time and place of rhetorical invention.[62] To think of rhetoric as emplaced is to think of rhetoric as always happening in a particular place. Some may not see this statement as being much different from the idea of rhetorical context or the rhetorical situation. Yet, through looking closely at the ways in which rhetorical critics have conceived of context or rhetorical situation, there is a focus on conceptual context (i.e., the exigency that invites rhetoric or the background information that informs rhetoric) or a conceptual embodied context through imagined audiences. In other words, rhetorical critics often reconstruct contexts. When the rhetorical critic engages in fieldwork, they gain access to the immediate context. The field (both place of research and community of meaning) is a context for rhetorical invention; it is the place in which rhetoric occurs. We see value in the notion of field as context because it turns attention to a symbolic/material immediate context as opposed to a reconstructed conceptual context.[63]

Although we see value in viewing the field as context, we resist sedimentation of the field as context only. Rhetorical critics interested in space and place have made great efforts to show how place is not merely context but also can be a rhetorical text.[64] Raymie McKerrow reminds us that traditional rhetorical theory often views place and space as simply context, "as externalities influencing discourse, to be sure, but also as physical entities having no other meaning beyond what appears as commonsense evidence of one's competence in performing according to community standards," or speaking in the right place.[65] This view of place as context registers place on the level of conceptual context, and neither recognizes the value of emplaced immediate context nor imagines how place can be rhetorical.

Instead of firmly situating the field as either context or text, we argue that it is both. Participatory critical rhetoricians are comfortable in a space where context and text blur together in the field, as Senda-Cook has shown in her research on trails at Zion that are both a text to examine and a context for rhetorical practices of outdoor recreation.[66] While we argue below that the field can be a rhetorical participant, we do not see that as mutually exclusive with the notion that the field can also be context. Noting that a speech, for example, takes place in a particular setting does not necessarily deny that the place can also be a rhetorical performer. In this sense, we are playing with the stark distinctions between text and context. Instead of arguing that rhetorical critics should abandon context, we are arguing that critics need to recognize the ability of context to play a double role as both context and text in emplaced rhetoric, giving way to a more intertextual approach to rhetoric.[67] Viewing rhetoric as an emplaced phenomenon, therefore, has important implications for understanding context, text, and field in participatory critical rhetoric (and beyond).

The Step It Up Rally provides an example of how the field acts as context. The rally was enclosed with a temporary fence, which Danielle and her team learned was because beer was being served at the event. The fence was adorned with signs proclaiming "free concert." The setup within the fenced area centered a stage and a dance floor and placed informational booths on the periphery of the space. These aspects of material context supplement an understanding of the speeches that happened in between musical performers. The speeches about climate change, within a context that communicated a summer concert, were out of place. The audience paid more attention to the musical performers than to the speeches. Indeed, many participants carried on personal conversations while the speeches took place. The speeches then were seen as a break between the main musical acts in the concert. In this way the place and how it was constructed that day served as context.[68] In the following vignette, Aaron similarly reveals how his fieldwork at the "Rally to Restore Sanity and/or Fear" gave him access to emplaced rhetoric in its immediate context.

The year 2010 was an especially tough one in American politics. While President Barack Obama was still enjoying the successes of his recent campaign, Congress was engaged in a bitter fight between Republicans and Democrats who were jockeying for control. Alongside the Congressional fighting, the 24-hour news channels—especially Fox News and MSNBC—contributed heavily to a decidedly partisan tone in the country. Political divides were accented with the "everyperson" Fox News pundit Glenn Beck, a conservative commentator who encouraged his audience to hold a "Restoring Honor" rally on the steps of the Lincoln Memorial in Washington DC. The central theme of the rally, both implicitly and explicitly understood, was that Washington had lost its way, succumbing to a weakened American culture, especially accented by the election of Obama. Rally-goers, featured in news and YouTube videos, called for the return to "traditional" American values and to "take back America." While the roots of the political "Tea Party" can be traced before this event, the rally publicly showcased this new movement in the American political landscape.

A few weeks after the "Restoring Honor" rally, late-night political pundits Jon Stewart and Stephen Colbert announced that they, too, would hold a rally. At the time, Stewart was well known as a late night satirist on The Daily Show, *which targets politics in general, but especially the conservative mouthpieces at Fox News like Beck. Colbert hosted his own program,* The Colbert Report, *through a hyperbolic performance of those same conservative mouthpieces, espousing over-the-top right wing arguments always accented with comic genius. Together, they held the "Rally to Restore Sanity and/or Fear," on the opposite end of the National Mall, with the Capitol Building as a backdrop. While comedic in nature, the Rally intended to bring rationality back into political discourse, calling for cooler minds to prevail. Happening on Halloween weekend, the event drew in nearly a quarter of a million people—many dressed in costume—who flocked to the National Mall to sing, dance, and shout as Stewart and Colbert wittily performed on stage.*

My colleague and I traveled to Washington, D.C. to experience the Rally, engage with its participants, and to shoot a short documentary.[69] *We were interested in the ways that audience members perceived their actions as political at this faux rally, and asked about the relevance of humor in politics. Situated in the sea of people and surrounded by the media apparatus of Comedy Central and other news networks covering the event, the scene was complexly arranged. I had come to witness the audience reception to the central text, that is, the performance from Stewart and Colbert. Yet, at the direction of the hosts, many audience members brought their own fake protest signs, saying things like "I disagree with you, but I'm pretty sure you're not Hitler." Many of these vernacularly produced signs texturized the rally with ideas not present on stage, like Muslims asking for hugs or people seeking to legalize marijuana. The costumed protesters added to the spectacle and carnivalesque nature of the scene, showing up dressed as everything from spiders (because they are actually scary) to giant tea bags, directly referencing the "Restoring Honor" rally from weeks prior.*

Standing in the midst of signs, costumes, and songs from the stage, context and text became increasingly blurred. Attendees contextualized the event as farce, but spoke out in humorous and *political ways. The massive audience gave credence to the pundits and their message, as if to say, "Rationality in public discourse is important; I came here dressed as Dr. Seuss' Thing 1 and Thing 2 to prove it!" Interviewing attendees, I was struck by the balanced conversation about political discourse, media frames, and the need for unity. Between their interviews, the signage, and shouting in unison toward the Capitol Building on the National Mall—a place that has held so many important rallies in American history—I began to recognize that the place spoke through the people and the people through the place. It wasn't just Jon Stewart and Stephen Colbert, but all the people in attendance, in this context, that added to the text being performed on stage.*

—Aaron

As Aaron's vignette reveals, place is a significant feature of the messy and intersectional immediate context for rhetorical invention. In this case, people and place interaminated each other on the National Mall at the Rally to Restore Sanity. While his example reveals that the field can be context, it also reveals that the field can be a rhetorical actor as well.

Field as Rhetorical Actor

The field itself participates in intersectional rhetorical invention. Concurrently, thinking of rhetoric as emplaced and the field as (rhetorical) place[70] suggests that the field is not just a place of research, community meaning, and context, it is also a rhetorical actor and participant. This argument builds from the large body of research on the rhetoricity of space and place.[71] This research is well established so we do not review it here. The takeaway is that constructed places/spaces—such as memorials, shopping malls, cities, and national parks—have their own rhetorical influence and consequences.

The field in participatory critical rhetoric is also a place that exerts rhetorical influence. Senda-Cook, Middleton, and Endres argue that the "field is a physical place that is both context and text. It is influenced by the rhetorical practices of individuals who inhabit and traverse sites of rhetoric, but it also expresses rhetorical force as place."[72] Viewing the field as place attunes the participatory rhetorical critic to examine how the physical, built, material, symbolic, and practiced aspects of a particular location influence rhetorical invention. By bringing this assumption of the rhetoricity of space and place to bear in participatory critical rhetoric, observing and participating in rhetoric in the field not only involves documenting and analyzing the words spoken, bodies, and sensorial experiences, but also involves attention to the rhetoric of the place itself. Participatory critical rhetoric provides an opportunity to examine the place in which rhetoric occurs and explore how that place is also a rhetorical actor. For example, the new 9/11 memorial in New York has a rhetoricity independent of the people who visit that space. The memorial is designed to communicate loss through the two huge holes in the ground that double as reminders of the absent Twin Towers that used to be there and as mass graves. It also communicates resilience and strength through the adjacent Freedom Tower that extends well into the sky.[73] While humans made the memorial, the creators of the memorial do not need to explain it to us. The memorial communicates on its own. In a different way, place is also rhetorical in the way that it picks up residual traces of human practices (with) in it. Place is accented with discursive messages, such as banners, posters, graffiti, and decorations, that become a part of the place but cannot be traced back to an author. For example, the items left at the 9/11 Memorial, such as yellow roses and first responder patches, become a part of that place, thus signifying the processual nature of the place and the way in which the agency of place, while related to humans, does not require constant human agency. This gives rhetorical agency to place over people (since critics may not know who authored or created the place or items left in place).

While qualitative and ethnographic researchers have made moves to incorporate the study of material culture,[74] conceiving of the field as a rhetorical place is a new and important area for rhetorical scholars. Although it begins with the same assumption of current rhetorical scholarship on space and place—that place/space is rhetorical—participatory critical rhetoric's view of the field as a rhetorical actor is not solely interested in the rhetoric of place in itself, but rather in the intersectional nature of emplaced rhetoric, wherein place/space is one rhetorical form among many in *in situ* rhetoric. This perspective both centers and decenters place/space in the intersectionality of rhetorical invention.

Further, a perspective on the rhetoricity of place and space can contribute to the ethnographic and qualitative modes of research that see material culture as somewhat inert. Recall the quotation above from Pink on the emplaced nature of ethnography. In her argument for the importance of place/space to ethnography, she describes it as context. Thinking about rhetoric as intersectional and emplaced can replace the concept of material culture with a concept of how rhetorical performance always interacts with, influences, and is influenced by the place in which it occurs. A rhetorical perspective, particularly an intersectional one, reveals the ways in which material objects have rhetorical influence and consequences beyond being contextual backdrop. More specifically, by focusing in on the place/space and the embodied and emplaced nature of rhetoric in the field, it becomes clear that material objects and places cannot be separated from the multimodal experience of rhetoric in the field.

In the Step It Up example, the place is also a rhetorical actor in the intersectional rhetorical invention of the Step It Up rally. As mentioned above, the fences and "free concert" signs could be seen as context for the way the speeches were interpreted by audiences at the rally. Yet, the fence with the free concert sign also had its own rhetorical influence and consequences.

The fence along with other aspects of the setup communicated a concert. The fence also served as a physical separator between the street and the rally. This place's rhetorical force conflicted with the intended rhetoric of the organizers as a rally to address climate change and cut carbon dioxide emissions by 80 percent by 2050.[75] Participatory critical rhetoricians, similarly, can read the place/space in which they are embedded as an intersectional rhetorical form, as Michael did in his work with homeless activists in California.

Through SafeGround Sacramento's struggles against anti-camping ordinances, lack of housing for homeless persons, and other political and economic barriers to their inclusion in the city, they revealed both how place and spatial practices shape identity and function rhetorically to establish proper modes of belonging in public space, as well as how places can be altered and manipulated to "speak" new rhetorics of homelessness.

On the one hand, SafeGround Sacramento's efforts occurred against a backdrop of what Talmadge Wright refers to as "polarized topographies," or those urban places/spaces that are organized around the divisions between pleasure and refuse.[76] Pleasure place/spaces accommodate individuals whose affluence affords them the opportunity to access such places/spaces. Defined as places/spaces like shopping malls, commercial areas, and, increasingly, public parks, pleasure spaces act rhetorically to create boundaries that are then policed, while at the same time naming and valuing certain individuals, through their inclusion, as legitimate subjects/citizens of the city. On the other hand, SafeGround Sacramento's members often found themselves occupying refuse spaces, or those urban places/spaces that are on the margins, sacrificed, or in disrepair/disuse. Refuse spaces, in juxtaposition to pleasure spaces, are abandoned by the city and, as a consequence, they mark where the city's disposable populations are relegated. To be a citizen of refuse places/spaces is to be excluded from pleasure places/spaces. Through defining movement and belonging, these refuse places/spaces also rhetorically construct and enforce identities on their occupants.

But, places/spaces move, shift, and morph through the activities of their occupants. For example, members of SafeGround Sacramento, in addition to their protest activity, also organized a roving encampment, or village, that moved around the banks of the American and Sacramento Rivers and the abandoned rail yards that formed large swaths of Sacramento's refuse spaces. These villages both revealed the sensitivity of SafeGround members to the rhetorical force of place/space as such, as well as their understanding of how place/space could be manipulated, modified, and temporarily reorganized to speak in different ways about its homeless inhabitants. One way this was accomplished was through the meticulously groomed homeless villages their members constructed. Built around neatly arranged rows of evenly spaced tents, well-manicured fire pits, and careful attention to both minimizing harm to the natural environment and acting as good stewards of their encampments (i.e., carrying out trash, gear, and other human waste), the members of SafeGround used their homeless encampments to argue that they were no less capable of acting as "good citizens" of the city than their housed counterparts. At the same time, they revealed the ability to mold place/space such that it functions rhetorically in new ways. By creating and maintaining their own "pleasure spaces" within what were otherwise the sacrificed refuse spaces of the city, the homeless community introduced new rhetorical actors into the struggle over homelessness in Sacramento. In this case, their encampments were rhetorical actors that rearticulated the identities of homeless persons from a blight on the city to active citizens expanding the boundaries of inclusion for those living in Sacramento.

—Michael

The construction of SafeGround's encampments as places of active citizenship is a vital component of the rhetorical force of the movement. Michael's fieldwork with SafeGround not only gave him the access to experience these encampments as emplaced rhetoric, but also allowed him to see how they worked alongside the verbal rhetorics of the group to argue for better treatment of and rights for homeless people. As such, the field is also a rhetorical actor.

IMPLICATIONS FOR PLACE/SPACE, INTERSECTIONALITY, AND MATERIAL EXPERIENCE

We develop two interrelated arguments in this chapter. First, we argue that participatory critical rhetoric embraces the idea that rhetoric is an emplaced phenomenon, meaning that all rhetoric participates with place and space. Second, we contend that the field in participatory critical rhetoric can be conceptualized along four intersecting vectors that highlight varying ways of understanding the emplaced nature of rhetoric and the emplaced rhetorical critic. Although we recognize that emplaced rhetoric does not require a field-based rhetorical approach, participatory critical rhetoric is a particularly suitable way of accessing, documenting, interpreting, and participating with emplaced rhetoric. Our theorization of emplaced rhetoric moves beyond extant approaches to field-based rhetorical research by including more examination of the role of place/space, which we argue is inherent in any rhetorical encounter. While rhetorical field methods and critical-rhetorical ethnography center the embodied nature of rhetoric, participatory critical rhetoric also centers the emplaced nature of rhetoric. Similarly, this focus on emplaced rhetoric and the vectors of the field expand on and complicate moves in qualitative and ethnographic research, in which the focus on material culture conceives of place/space (as an element of material rhetoric) as an inert background force and not a source of potential agency,[77] to pay more attention to place/space as both part of and exceeding material culture. This move to better account for the place/space in field-based rhetorical approaches not only takes advantage of the critic's bodily presence in *in situ* emplaced moments of rhetorical invention, but also contributes to thinking about the material intersectional experience of rhetoric. Place/space, and its interrelationship with time, is part of the way beings experience the world and cannot be separated out from rhetorical invention or relegated to context. Our conception of emplaced rhetoric and the vectors of the field as place, community of meaning, context, and text offers a starting point for rhetorical critics to pay more attention to place/space in all rhetoric. The positions we take up in this chapter also contribute more broadly to several conversations in rhetorical criticism and theory.

First, emplaced rhetoric contributes to and extends the ongoing scholarly conversation about the rhetoricity of place and space. While we are indebted this scholarship, it is predominantly focused on analyzing the rhetorical qualities of particular rhetorical places, such as museums, memorials, malls, and other places. This focus has enlarged the scope of rhetorical theory and criticism to account for place and space as texts suitable for criticism, revealing how places and spaces can be rhetorical actors. Our concept of emplaced rhetoric incorporates this focus and also posits that all rhetorical invention is emplaced. Place/space, therefore, matters in all rhetoric. This does not mean that rhetorical criticism ought to shift its focus exclusively to place/space, nor that all rhetorical criticism need to attend to the emplaced aspects of rhetorical invention. There is value in examining parts of rhetorical invention and the emplaced nature of rhetoric may not be a significant aspect of a particular project. Yet, we argue that focusing on the emplaced nature of all rhetoric plays with some of the fundamental assumptions about rhetoric in our field. Emplaced rhetoric challenges conventional notions of conceptual context to be more attuned to an immediate symbolic/material context. Even more, emplaced rhetoric also sees that immediate context as inseparable from text, wherein rhetoric not only occurs in a place but also happens with place/space. This highlights how rhetoric is not just a thing to be analyzed, but is an intersectional material experience.

Second, our focus on emplaced rhetoric furthers the conversation started by Darrel Enck-Wanzer and picked up by Elinor Light about the value of an intersectional perspective on rhetoric.[78] Emplaced rhetoric necessitates seeing rhetoric as a combination of various rhetorical forms—visual, spatial, embodied, verbal—that happen with(in) a place. Further, it highlights the importance of including place/space as a rhetorical form in an intersectional theory of rhetoric. Intersectional rhetoric recognizes that a variety of rhetorical forms intersect in rhetorical invention. While there is value in critically analyzing particular rhetorical forms (e.g., visual, spatial, verbal, or embodied), an intersectional rhetoric approach not only puts these forms on an equal playing field but also sees them as fundamentally interconnected in how rhetors, audiences, and *in situ* rhetorical critics encounter rhetoric. Rhetoric is a multisensory experience of a variety of rhetorical forms coming together (seamlessly or not). In some approaches to rhetoric, this sensual experience of rhetoric is broken down into its component parts and distanced from its initial instantiation. The value in this sort of analytical work is that it hones in on better understanding the interworking of a particular rhetorical form, such as verbal or visual. An intersectional rhetorical approach that sees rhetoric as emplaced (and embodied) is valuable for examining and interpreting the multimodal, sensorial, and material experience of rhetoric, for understanding the way rhetorical forms come together in everyday rhetorical acts. Field-based rhetorical approaches, such as participatory critical rhetoric, encourage critics to use fieldwork to better access *in situ* rhetoric. The four vectors of the field that we introduce in this chapter give critics a way to engage with rhetoric as emplaced and reveal that simply doing fieldwork does not automatically open one to the complexity of intersectional rhetorical experiences.

Third, as we discuss in previous chapters, we align participatory critical rhetoric with the ongoing theorization of material rhetoric as both physical and consequential (while recognizing that the material and symbolic are always interrelated). Our notion of emplaced rhetoric encourages paying more attention to the role of place/space in the physicality of rhetoric. Although the term physical often implies bodies, it also implies the natural world. As such, a physical rhetoric is related to both bodies and place/space; it is embodied and emplaced. As we argue earlier in the chapter, an awareness of and interaction with place/space is vital to the way that beings experience their world, including rhetoric as a part of that world. Conceiving of rhetoric as emplaced can therefore contribute to scholarship on material rhetoric by nuancing the relationship between rhetoric, physicality, and place/space.

Considering emplaced rhetoric also has significant implications for how critics understand their role in relation to participants. We touched on some of the implications of thinking of the critic as emplaced in this chapter. In the next chapter, in which we primarily focus on participants, we engage with the notion of emplaced participants.

NOTES

1. Danielle Endres and Samantha Senda-Cook, "Location Matters: The Rhetoric of Place in Protest," *Quarterly Journal of Speech* 97 (2011): 257–82, doi:10.1080/00335630.2011.585167; Danielle Endres, Deborah Cox Callister, Autumn Garrison, Samantha Senda-Cook, Julie Kalil Schutten, "Step What Up?: The Rhetorical Framing of Salt Lake City's Step It Up Events," in *Social Movement to Address Climate Change: Local Steps for Global Action*, eds. Danielle Endres, Leah Sprain, and Tarla Rai Peterson (Amherst, NY: Cambria Press, 2009), 117–46.

2. Carole Blair, "Contemporary U.S. Memorial Sites as Exemplars of Rhetoric's Materiality," in *Rhetorical Bodies*, eds. Jack Selzer and Sharon Crowley (Madison: University of Wisconsin Press, 1999), 16–57.

3. We don't intend to take a purely phenomenological perspective on place and space, but rather to draw from the insights of humanist and phenomenological geography to highlight that space and place are fundamental parts of the way humans make sense of the world. Yi-Fu Tuan, *Space and Place: The Perspective of Experience* (Minneapolis: University of Minnesota Press, 2001); Edward Relph, *Place and Placelessness*, 1st ed. (London: Pion, 1976); Edward S. Casey, "How to Get from Space to Place in a Fairly Short Stretch of Time," in *Senses of Place*, eds. Steven Feld and Keith H. Basso (Santa Fe: NM: School of American Research Press, 1996), 13–52.

4. See, for example: Carole Blair, "Reflections on Criticism and Bodies: Parables from Public Places," *Western Journal of Communication* 63 (2001): 271–94; Michael L. Butterworth, "'Katie Was Not Only a Girl, She Was Terrible': Katie Hnida, Body Rhetoric, and Football at the University of Colorado," *Communication Studies* 59 (2008): 259–73, doi: 10.1080/10510970802257705; Dwight Conquergood, "Rethinking Ethnography: Towards a Critical Cultural Politics," *Communication Monographs* 58 (1991): 179–94, doi:10.1080/03637759109376222; Kevin Michael DeLuca, "Unruly Arguments: The Body Rhetoric of Earth First!, Act Up, and Queer Nation," *Argumentation and Advocacy* 36 (1999): 9–21; Norman K. Denzin and Yvonna S. Lincoln, eds., *The SAGE Handbook of Qualitative Research*, 4th ed. (Thousand Oaks, CA: Sage Publications, 2011); Mindy Fenske, *Tattoos in American Visual Culture*, 1st ed. (New York: Palgrave Macmillan, 2007); Greg Dickinson, "Joe's Rhetoric: Finding Authenticity at Starbucks," *Rhetoric Society Quarterly* 32 (2002): 5–27, doi:10.1080/02773940209391238; Christine Harold, "Tracking Heroin Chic: The Abject Body Reconfigures the Rational Argument," *Argumentation and Advocacy* 36 (1999): 65–76; Debra Hawhee, *Bodily Arts: Rhetoric and Athletics in Ancient Greece* (University of Texas Press, 2005); Thomas R. Lindlof and Bryan C. Taylor, *Qualitative Communication Research Methods*, 3rd ed (Thousand Oaks, CA: Sage Publications, 2010); Raymie E. McKerrow, "Corporeality and Cultural Rhetoric: A Site for Rhetoric's Future," *Southern Communication Journal* 63 (1998): 315–28, doi: 10.1080/10417949809373105; Samantha Senda-Cook, "Rugged Practices: Embodying Authenticity in Outdoor Recreation," *Quarterly Journal of Speech* 98 (2012): 129–52, doi:10.1080/00335630.2012.663500; Jack Selzer and Sharon Crowley, eds., *Rhetorical Bodies*, 1st ed. (Madison: University of Wisconsin Press, 1999).

5. Endres and Senda-Cook, "Location Matters," 260.

6. Thomas Rickert, *Ambient Rhetoric* (Pittsburgh: University of Pittsburgh Press, 2013), xiv.

7. Tim Cresswell, *Place: A Short Introduction* (Malden, MA: Wiley-Blackwell, 2004); Phil Hubbard, Rob Kitchin, and Gill Valentine, eds., *Key Thinkers on Space and Place* (Thousand Oaks, CA: Sage Publications, 2004).

8. We specifically chose not to use one of the common definitions of place as space that is imbued with meaning because we adhere to the concept that there is also meaning in space. As such, we prefer to think of place as particularized or localized and space as general. This has implications for how one would go about the rhetorical examination of both places and spaces, which is further elaborated in: Endres and Senda-Cook, "Location Matters," 259–60.

9. Carole Blair, Greg Dickinson, and Brian L. Ott, "Introduction: Rhetoric/Memory/Place," in *Places of Public Memory: The Rhetoric of Museums and Memorials*, eds. Greg Dickinson, Carole Blair, and Brian L. Ott (Tuscaloosa, AL: University of Alabama Press, 2010), 1–54.

10. Recent theorizing in place/space has tended to favor space over place, in line with the contemporary zeitgeist of globalization and mobility that challenges the notion of a static and contained place. However, in line with Arturo Escobar who calls for anthropologists not to throw place out with the bathwater, we see value in place as a heuristic that aligns not only with field-based rhetorical practices but also with the way that many people still make sense of their place in the world. Arturo Escobar, "Culture Sits in Places: Reflections on Globalism and Subaltern Strategies of Localization," *Political Geography* 20 (2001): 139–74, doi:10.1016/S0962–6298(00)00064–0.

11. We specifically position rhetoric as happening with place as opposed to happening in place, which implies a dynamic, processual, and agentic notion of place. To say that rhetoric happens in place implies that place is merely situation, context, or backdrop for rhetoric. See for example: Jenny Edbauer, "Unframing Models of Public Distribution: From Rhetorical Situation to Rhetorical Ecologies," *Rhetoric Society Quarterly* 35 (2005): 5–24, doi:10.1080/02773940509391320; Endres and Senda-Cook, "Location Matters"; Jeff Rice, *Digital Detroit: Rhetoric and Space in the Age of the Network* (Carbondale: Southern Illinois University Press, 2012).

12. Casey, "How to Get from Space to Place in a Fairly Short Stretch of Time"; Michel de Certeau, *The Practice of Everyday Life*, trans. Steven Rendall (Berkeley: University of California Press, 1984); Edbauer, "Unframing Models of Public Distribution"; Endres and Senda-Cook, "Location Matters"; Henri Lefebvre, *The Production of Space* (Malden, MA: Blackwell, 1992); Doreen B. Massey, *For Space*, 1st ed. (Thousand Oaks, CA: Sage Publications, 2005); Stacey Pigg, "Emplacing Mobile Composition Habits: A Study of Academic Writing in Networked Social Spaces," *College Composition and Communication* 66 (2014): 250–75; Allan Pred, "Place as Historically Contingent Process: Structuration and the Time-Geography of Becoming Places," *Annals of the Association of American Geographers* 74 (1984): 279–97, doi:10.1111/j.1467–8306.1984.tb01453.x; David Seamon, "Body-Subject, Time-Space Routines, and Place-Ballets," in *The Human Experience of Space and Place*, eds. Ann Buttimer and David Seamon (New York: St. Martin Press, 1980), 148–65.

13. Massey, *For Space.*

14. de Certeau, *The Practice of Everyday Life.*

15. Seamon, "Body-Subject, Time-Space Routines, and Place-Ballets"; de Certeau, *The Practice of Everyday Life.*

16. Tim Cresswell, *In Place/Out of Place: Geography, Ideology, and Transgression* (Minneapolis: University of Minnesota Press, 1996), 16.

17. Danielle Endres, Samantha Senda-Cook, and Brian Cozen, "Not Just a Place to Park Your Car: Park(ing) as Spatial Argument," *Argumentation and Advocacy* 50 (2014): 123.

18. Endres and Senda-Cook, "Location Matters."

19. Ibid.; Blair, "Reflections on Criticism and Bodies"; Blair, Dickinson, and Ott, "Introduction: Rhetoric/Memory/Place"; Blair, "Contemporary U.S. Memorial Sites as Exemplars of Rhetoric's Materiality"; Carole Blair and Neil Michel, "Reproducing Civil Rights Tactics: The Rhetorical Performances of the Civil Rights Memorial," *RSQ: Rhetoric Society Quarterly* 30 (2000): 31–55, doi: 10.1080/02773940009391174; Carole Blair, Marsha S. Jeppeson, and Enrico Pucci, "Public Memorializing in Postmodernity: The Vietnam Veterans Memorial as Prototype," *Quarterly Journal of Speech* 77 (1991): 263–88, doi: 10.1080/00335639109383960; Roberta Chevrette and Aaron Hess, "Unearthing the Native Past: Citizen Archaeology and Modern (Non)belonging at the Pueblo Grande Museum. *Communication and Critical/Cultural Studies* 12 (2015): 139–58, doi:10.1080/14791420.2015.1012214; Greg Dickinson, Brian L. Ott, and Eric Aoki, "Memory and Myth at the Buffalo Bill Museum," *Western Journal of Communication* 69 (2005): 85–108, doi: 10.1080/10570310500076684; Greg Dickinson, Carole Blair, and Brian L. Ott, eds., *Places of Public Memory: The Rhetoric of Museums and Memorials*, 1st ed. (Tuscaloosa: University Alabama Press, 2010); Greg Dickinson, Brian L. Ott, and Eric Aoki, "Spaces of Remembering and Forgetting: The Reverent Eye/I at the Plains Indian Museum," *Communication and Critical/Cultural Studies* 3 (2006): 27–47, doi: 10.1080/14791420500505619; Greg Dickinson, "Memories for Sale: Nostalgia and the Construction of Identity in Old Pasadena," *Quarterly Journal of Speech* 83 (1997): 1–27, doi: 10.1080/00335639709384169; Dickinson, "Joe's Rhetoric"; Raymie E. McKerrow, "Space and Time in the Postmodern Polity," *Western Journal of Communication* 63 (1999): 271, doi: 10.1080/10570319909374642; Sonja Modesti, "Home Sweet Home: Tattoo Parlors as Postmodern Spaces of Agency," *Western Journal of Communication* 72 (2008): 197–212, doi:10.1080/10570310802210106; Raka Shome, "Space Matters: The Power and Practice of Space," *Communication Theory* 13 (2003): 39–56, doi:10.1111/j.1468–2885.2003.tb00281.x; Thomas J. St. Antoine, "Making Heaven out of Hell: New Urbanism and the Refutation of Suburban Spaces," *Southern Communication Journal* 72 (2007): 127–44, doi:10.1080/10417940701316351; Jessie Stewart and Greg Dickinson, "Enunciating Locality in the Postmodern Suburb: FlatIron Crossing and the Colorado Lifestyle," *Western Journal of Communication* 72 (2008): 280–307, doi:10.1080/10570310802210148; Isaac West, "PISSAR's Critically Queer and Disabled Politics," *Communication and Critical/Cultural Studies* 7 (2010): 156–75, doi:10.1080/14791421003759174; Isaac West, "Performing Resistance In/from the Kitchen: The Practice of Maternal Pacifist Politics and La WISP's

Cookbooks," *Women's Studies in Communication* 30 (2007): 358–83, doi:10.1080/07491409.2007.10162519; Andrew F. Wood, *City Ubiquitous: Place, Communication, and the Rise of Omnitopia* (Cresskill, NJ: Hampton Press, 2009); Kenneth S. Zagacki and Victoria J. Gallagher, "Rhetoric and Materiality in the Museum Park at the North Carolina Museum of Art," *Quarterly Journal of Speech* 95 (2009): 171–91, doi:10.1080/00335630902842087.

20. Blair, "Contemporary U.S. Memorial Sites as Exemplars of Rhetoric's Materiality."

21. Aaron Hess, "Critical-Rhetorical Ethnography: Rethinking the Place and Process of Rhetoric," *Communication Studies* 62 (2011): 127–52; doi:10.1080/10510974.2011.529750.

22. Ellen Gorsevski offers a competing definition of emplaced rhetoric as: "Emplaced rhetoric is discursive and symbolic communication purveyed through public statements, visual imagery, and embodied forms of activism that emphasize the physical, lived world of earthly existence, and the numinous experience many persons gain from substantive connections to nature" (p. 293–4). We would call this place-based rhetoric (á la Endres and Senda-Cook) as opposed to emplaced rhetoric. Stacey Pigg uses emplaced rhetoric to imply that place/and space are not a mere backdrop for rhetoric in her analysis of networked writing practices. Similarly, Jenny Edbauer, Jeff Rice, Danielle Endres, and Samantha Senda-Cook note that place is not just a situation or context for rhetoric, but that place itself is processual, networked, and rhetorical. These arguments, while foundational to our concept, are only a part of the way we conceptualize emplaced rhetoric. Greg Dickinson uses the term emplaced to explain how subjects (created through rhetoric) are embodied and emplaced. Elinor Light introduces the term (em)placed vernacular as an intersectional heuristic for examining the complexity of place through materiality, images, and aesthetics. Finally, although Thomas Rickert's concept of ambient rhetoric comes closest to the way we conceptualize emplaced rhetoric, ambient rhetoric is more than emplaced. See: Edbauer, "Unframing Models of Public Distribution"; Dickinson, et al., *Places of Public Memory*; Endres and Senda-Cook, "Location Matters"; Ellen W. Gorsevski, "Wangari Maathai's Emplaced Rhetoric: Greening Global Peacebuilding," *Environmental Communication: A Journal of Nature and Culture* 6 (2012): 290–307, doi:10.1080/17524032.2012.689776; Pigg, "Emplacing Mobile Composition Habits"; Rice, *Digital Detroit*; Rickert, *Ambient Rhetoric*; Elinor Light, "The (Em)Placed Vernacular: Rhetorics of Control and Transgression in the American City" (PhD diss., University of Utah, 2015).

23. We align with Blair's take on the materiality of rhetoric that breaks down a false dichotomy between the symbolic and material and focuses on what rhetoric can do in the world. Of course, this is one position in a larger debate in the field about the materiality of rhetoric. See Blair, "Contemporary U.S. Memorial Sites."

24. A notable exception is: Light, "The (Em)Placed Vernacular."

25. We use bodies to acknowledge that rhetorical invention and interaction with place/space is not limited to human bodies.

26. Cresswell, *Place*, 37.

27. Seamon, "Body-Subject, Time-Space Routines, and Place-Ballets"; Lefebvre, *The Production of Space*.

28. Dickinson, "Joe's Rhetoric"; Blair, "Reflections on Criticism and Bodies"; Modesti, "Home Sweet Home"; Stewart and Dickinson, "Enunciating Locality in the Postmodern Suburb".

29. Dickinson, "Joe's Rhetoric," 9.

30. Sarah Pink, *Doing Sensory Ethnography* (Thousand Oaks, CA: Sage Publications, 2009), 33–34.

31. Rickert, *Ambient Rhetoric*, xviii.

32. A notable exception is Carole Blair's parables from public-placed article which attempts to remind rhetorical critics that approaches to rhetorical criticism that rely on reproduced textual accounts, while valuable, are different from the immediate material experience of rhetoric at its initial instantiation. She calls on rhetorical critics to imagine how hearing a speech in the rain would differ from reading that same speech in one's office, and how that might alter our understanding of rhetoric. See: Blair, "Reflections on Criticism and Bodies."

33. John Durham Peters, *Speaking Into the Air: A History of the Idea of Communication* (Chicago: University of Chicago Press, 2000).

34. Aaron Hess, "Critical-Rhetorical Ethnography," 127; Michael K. Middleton, Samantha Senda-Cook, and Danielle Endres, "Articulating Rhetorical Field Methods: Challenges and Tensions," *Western Journal of Communication* 75 (2011): 386–406, doi:10.1080/10570314.2011.586969; Phaedra C. Pezzullo, "Resisting 'National Breast Cancer Awareness Month': The Rhetoric of Counterpublics and Their Cultural Performances," *Quarterly Journal of Speech* 89 (2003): 345–65, doi:10.1080/0033563032000160981.

35. Kevin Michael DeLuca and Jennifer Peeples, "From Public Sphere to Public Screen: Democracy, Activism, and the 'Violence' of Seattle," *Critical Studies in Media Communication* 19 (2002): 125–51, doi:10.1080/07393180216559.

36. Adriana de Souza e Silva, "From Cyber to Hybrid: Mobile Technologies as Interfaces of Hybrid Spaces," *Space and culture* 9 (2006): 261–78, doi: 10.1177/1206331206289022; Aaron Hess and Art Herbig, "Recalling the Ghosts of 9/11: Convergent Memorializing at the Opening of the National 9/11 Memorial," *International Journal of Communication* 7 (2013): 2207–30.

37. DeLuca and Peeples, "From Public Sphere to Public Screen"; Art Herbig and Aaron Hess, "Convergent Critical Rhetoric at the 'Rally to Restore Sanity': Exploring the Intersection of Rhetoric, Ethnography, and Documentary Production," *Communication Studies* 63 (2012): 269–89, doi:10.1080/10510974.2012.674617. For example of an organization that takes up web 2.0 media in support of their cause, see Aaron Hess, "Health, Risk, and Authority in a Dysfunctional World: Online Ecstasy User Discourse," *Ohio Communication Journal* 50 (2012): 1–30.

38. Video games provide an especially interesting environment due to their immersive qualities. See Janet Horowitz Murray, *Hamlet on the Holodeck: The Future of Narrative in Cyberspace*. (New York: Simon and Schuster, 1997).

39. There are competing definitions of sense of place. We draw on the notion of the term as developed in human geography as an interrelationship between humans and their environment that is filtered through experience, feeling, and meaning. See: Edward Relph, "Sense of Place," in *Ten Geographic Ideas That Changed the World*, ed. Susan Hanson (New Brunswick, NJ: Rutgers University Press, 1997), 205–26;

Gillian Rose, "Place and Identity: A Sense of Place," in *A Place in the World? Places, Cultures, and Globalisation*, ed. Doreen B. Massey and Pat M. Jess (Oxford: The Open University Press, 1995), 87–118.

40. Endres and Senda-Cook, "Location Matters"; Endres et al., "Step What Up?: The Rhetorical Framing of Salt Lake City's Step It Up Events."

41. Carol A. Bailey, *A Guide to Qualitative Field Research*, 2nd ed. (Thousand Oaks, CA: SAGE Publications, 2006); Lindlof and Taylor, *Qualitative Communication Research Methods*; Middleton, Senda-Cook, and Endres, "Articulating Rhetorical Field Methods"; Harry F. Wolcott, *The Art of Fieldwork* (Lanham, MD: Altamira Press, 2005).

42. The definition and practices of fieldwork vary across and within academic traditions. See: Bailey, *A Guide to Qualitative Field Research.*

43. Ibid., 1.

44. David M. Fetterman, *Ethnography: Step-by-Step*, 3rd ed. (Thousand Oaks, CA: Sage Publications, 2009), 33.

45. Wolcott, *The Art of Fieldwork*, 57.

46. Bailey, *A Guide to Qualitative Field Research*, 5.

47. Charles L. Briggs, *Learning How to Ask: A Sociolinguistic Appraisal of the Role of the Interview in Social Science Research* (New York: Cambridge University Press, 1986).

48. G. Thomas Goodnight, "The Personal, Technical, and Public Spheres: A Note on 21st Century Critical Communication Inquiry," *Argumentation and Advocacy* 48 (2012): 258–67; Stephen Edelston Toulmin, *The Uses of Argument* (Cambridge, UK: Cambridge University Press, 2003).

49. Kenneth Burke, *The Philosophy of Literary Form*, 3rd ed. (Berkeley: University of California Press, 1974), 110–11.

50. Lefebvre, *The Production of Space.*

51. Ibid.

52. We are deliberately drawing an analogue to Deluca's theorization of image events. Kevin DeLuca, *Image Politics: The New Rhetoric of Environmental Activism* (New York: Guilford, 1999).

53. Endres and Senda-Cook, "Location Matters," 277.

54. Certeau, *The Practice of Everyday Life.*

55. Rose, "Place and Identity: A Sense of Place."

56. Endres and Senda-Cook, "Location Matters"; Endres, Senda-Cook, and Cozen, "Not Just a Place to Park Your Car."

57. James P. Spradley, *Participant Observation* (New York: Holt, Rinehart, Winston).

58. Endres and Senda-Cook, "Location Matters"; Endres et al., "Step What Up?: The Rhetorical Framing of Salt Lake City's Step It Up Events."

59. Lloyd F. Bitzer, "The Rhetorical Situation," *Philosophy & Rhetoric* 25 (1992): 1–14.

60. Tony Bennett, *Critical Trajectories* (Malden, MA: Blackwell Publishing Ltd, 2007), 40–53.

61. Michael Calvin McGee, "Text, Context, and the Fragmentation of Contemporary Culture," *Western Journal of Speech Communication* 54 (1990): 274–89.

62. Blair, "Reflections on Criticism and Bodies."

63. Of course, even the participatory rhetorical critic reconstructs context as they document emplaced rhetoric and write up their analysis. The key distinction we are trying to make here is that the participatory critical rhetorician has access to experiencing the immediate interrelation between text and context in the moment of rhetorical invention whereas a critic that was not present at the moment of rhetorical invention is always reconstructing context through secondary accounts or mediated experiences.

64. Edbauer, "Unframing Models of Public Distribution"; Endres and Senda-Cook, "Location Matters"; Shome, "Space Matters: The Power and Practice of Space."

65. McKerrow, "Space and Time in the Postmodern Polity," 271. See also: Edbauer, "Unframing Models of Public Distribution"; Endres and Senda-Cook, "Location Matters."

66. Senda-Cook, "Rugged Practices."

67. Martha Solomon, "The Things We Study: Texts and Their Interaction," *Communication Monographs* 60 (1993): 62, doi:10.1080/03637759309376295; Leah Ceccarelli, *Shaping Science with Rhetoric: The Cases of Dobzhansky, Schrödinger, and Wilson* (Chicago: University of Chicago Press, 2001).

68. Endres and Senda-Cook, "Location Matters"; Endres et al., "Step What Up?: The Rhetorical Framing of Salt Lake City's Step It Up Events."

69. Herbig and Hess, "Convergent Critical Rhetoric at the 'Rally to Restore Sanity.'" The video documentary produced from this project can be found here: Art Herbig, Aaron Hess, Alix Watson, and Kristy D. Hess, "Unmasking Sanity: Halloween Weekend with the Participants at the Rally to Restore Sanity and/or Fear [Short film]," (USA: Living Text Productions). http://www.youtube.com/watch?v=DE7NtFPWgw8

70. Samantha Senda-Cook, Michael Middleton, and Danielle Endres, "Interrogating the 'Field' of Rhetorical Field Methods," for *Connecting Textual Criticism and Field Work*, National Communication Association Conference, Washington D.C., November 2013.

71. See footnote 19.

72. Senda-Cook, Middleton, and Endres, "Interrogating the 'Field,'" n.p.

73. Hess and Herbig, "Recalling the Ghosts of 9/11."

74. Lindlof and Taylor, *Qualitative Communication Research Methods*.

75. Endres and Senda-Cook, "Location Matters."

76. Talmadge Wright, *Out of Place: Homeless Mobilizations, Subcities, and Contested Landscapes* (Albany: SUNY Press, 1997).

77. Lindlof and Taylor, *Qualitative Communication*; Pink, *Doing Sensory*.

78. Enck-Wanzer, "Trashing the System"; Light, "The (Em)Placed Vernacular."

Chapter 5

Participants and Perspectives

At the tenth anniversary of September 11th, thousands of people flocked to Lower Manhattan to mourn, commemorate, and mark the occasion. Presidents, tourists, and New Yorkers gazed with anticipation as the National September 11 Memorial—the official memorial for the events of 9/11—was opened. The dual memorials stand in the footprints of the Twin Towers. Aptly named Reflecting Absence, *the gaping holes create an odd opening in the New York City skyline. Critics also took to the memorial to judge and critique it, pondering its material and aesthetic significance. As I stood next to the memorial, rubbing my hands across the punched-through bronze, I took in as much of its symbolic significance as I could, including the water, trees, and aural elements. It felt contemplative, as it probably was intended.*

Standing outside the exit of the memorial, I interviewed a number of people who also spoke of its significance. Many confirmed my own sense of the memorial; it was "peaceful," "calming," and even "a little Buddhist." These judgments of the memorial lend credence to an interpretation leaning toward renewal.

As I continued to meet others, however, my view of the memorial changed significantly. They offered competing judgments about the symbolic elements and politics of the memorial that stood in contrast with many of those who attended the opening ceremony, and certainly with the ongoing narrative of 9/11.

One interviewee—a survivor who escaped death from the North Tower ten years prior—spoke of the unmarked survivor tree at the memorial, which I had walked past multiple times without realizing its significance. She indicated that the memorial served the purpose of commemorating the dead, but not the living. "Survivors are the forgotten of 9/11 and a lot of us have talked about this. We were not invited to the Memorial, we were not honored for

10 years, there is no survivor place, and this is as much of a survivor place than I've experienced in 10 years."

Similarly, another interviewee juxtaposed the events of 9/11 with the politics of the anniversary. As a first responder, he expressed great concern about the nature of the memorial and its tourist enterprise. "Yeah. The 9/11 memorial people, none of them have lived down here. None of them were at the Trade Center. None of them were in this church when the firemen, the cops, construction workers. Thinking back, guys were coming here crying their eyes out. It's...I mean, it's disgusting, the whole thing. I'm not just blaming it on them. The whole nation has made it a money-making operation. The quote '9/11, Never Forget' is now a business. It's disgusting."

—Aaron

Moving into the field recognizes that rhetoric is an exchange between people. At its core, participatory critical rhetoric invites considerations of rhetoric as living and emergent, meaning that critics will inevitably interact with other people in their research. As we discuss in the previous chapters, participatory critical rhetoric problematizes not only the nature of the critic, but also the relationship critics form with participants during the production of rhetorical artifacts. Critics' presence affects the people involved in the rhetorical field. As a *participatory* approach, participatory critical rhetoric expects interaction with individuals, whether they are audience members or rhetors. These interactions serve as primary points of understanding and interpretation—data collection. Participatory methods, such as those found in the qualitative tradition and ethnography, have long considered the relationship between researcher and participant. We intend to explore that relationship here as well, but in the context of extending these sensibilities to the study of *in situ* rhetoric. Specifically, we examine the consequences of engaging in critique with, learning from, and/or participating with individuals present in site of rhetorical invention.

We contend that engaging with participants reconfigures the nature of critical judgment from being contained within the critic (through their textual understanding of the rhetor) toward a multiperspectival form of judgment that incorporates critic, rhetor, and audience within the embodied and emplaced scene of intersectional rhetorics. As Aaron offers in the above vignette, for example, reading the 9/11 Memorial along with those who were directly affected by the events fundamentally altered his read of the bronze and light. We conceive of participants as those individuals who are involved within both the rhetorical field and in the critic's research project. They can be rhetors or audience members who are present within the immediate contexts of rhetorical practices. Given the participatory nature of our approach, engagement with participants produces a shared sense of judgment about the production, process, and reception of rhetoric. In what follows, we offer a discussion about the nature of judgment in rhetorical criticism and how it is augmented when engaged through an embodied and participatory approach. Then, we implicate multiperspectival judgment within the *telos* of rhetoric, highlighting how a participatory approach alters our understanding of texts in immediate contexts. Finally, we outline three primary conceptions for comprehending the role of participants within our approach, offering how each conception can be considered both theoretically and ethically.

IMMEDIACY, EFFECT, AND JUDGMENT

In repositioning the rhetorical act as happening within socio-spatial scenes and through embodied perspectives, participatory critical rhetoric invites consideration of the immediate effects and judgments that circulate within spaces. We define effect as the ways in which embodied and emplaced rhetoric influences and impacts audiences in terms of persuasion, identification, and meaning making. Judgment, we offer, is the process of decision making in both the forming of rhetoric, as well as the interpretation of rhetoric by audiences. Rhetors make judgments in the creation of rhetoric, while audiences make judgments about the salience of those performances. Critics offer judgments about effect, which explain why particular rhetorical attempts are effective or not, depending on criteria determined by the critic. The two concepts intersect within the immediate contexts of rhetoric, whereby investigating the rhetor's judgments about their performance and the audience's judgments in the interpretation of the performance, a critic can offer conclusions about the overall effect of the performance. Inquiring into effect illuminates an overall evaluative claim of *what happened* while examinations regarding judgment explain *why*. By being in the immediate field of invention, participatory critical rhetoricians can evaluate effect and apprehend judgment from multiple parties in ways that are difficult to ascertain from a solely textual perspective. Both effect and judgment have been long-standing concerns of rhetorical critics. Participatory critical rhetoric reconsiders the notions of effect and judgment by examining them within the context of immediacy, providing critics with new evaluative tools in the field of rhetoric.[1]

Since Herbert Wichelns's claim that the purpose of rhetorical criticism is the measurement of effect, the nature of effect and its role in rhetorical criticism has been fraught with controversy.[2] And, within Raymie McKerrow's earliest formulation, critical rhetoric has always been interested in the nature of rhetorical influence, believing that symbols have "impacts on others."[3] Concerns ranged from whether a critic can possibly determine an empirical understanding of effect—as in, the specific number of people who were impacted by a speech—to audience reception research[4] to whether an understanding of influence distracts focus away from the text itself.[5] More recently, theorists in rhetoric and public address have reintroduced the debate regarding effect, maintaining that the purpose of rhetorical inquiry is to evaluate the nature of resonance, or the ways in which speakers make impactful claims upon their audiences.[6] Ultimately, these evaluative claims made about discourse are attempting to measure *effect* in one form or another, whether seen as "resonance, or influence, or potency, or some other synonym for effect."[7] Amos Kiewe and Davis Houck challenge the discipline to revitalize the study of rhetorical effect and influence, which should be "more expansive and ought to include the interplay between speaker and audience."[8] Robert Rowland concurs, contending that examinations of influence require a discussion of how rhetorical agency is shared across audience and speaker.[9] Traditionally, understanding the nature of influence or effect has nonetheless been difficult, especially in terms of the impact that rhetoric has on its audience.[10]

However, when tied to the nature of judgment in rhetorical exchanges, the *in situ* effects of rhetoric can be understood. Judgment provides clues into the nature of rhetorical decisions, both before and after the act of speaking. Being present in the site of rhetorical invention allows critics to witness the judgments of both speaker and audience, and to invite additional perspectives into the analytical act of criticism. While judgment enters into the act of invention, audiences also provide it when they respond to a rhetor. For example, in the opening vignette of this chapter, Aaron discusses the immediate reactions to the opening of the 9/11 Memorial. The reactions from survivors, tourists, residents of Manhattan, and first responders inform a multiperspectival understanding of the memorial and its authors. Participatory critical rhetoric provides an entry point into the discussion of influence and effect by offering a new element into critical judgment: immediacy. Immediacy in judgment becomes increasingly nuanced and textured when apprehended through immanent participation by the critic.

Rhetorical methods, in one form or another, have traditionally been interested in the immediate audience of a particular speech. Wichelns offers that rhetorical criticism "regards a speech as a communication to a specific audience, and holds its business to be the analysis and appreciation of the orator's method of imparting his [*sic*] ideas to his [*sic*] hearers."[11] Rather than merely returning to this early proclamation and the implications for limiting the dissemination and force of texts, participatory critical rhetoric engages with the immediacy of interaction that occurs within a synchronic rhetorical moment. As we argue in chapter 4, the places of rhetoric are themselves rhetorical, but are also comprised of and influenced by those people who enter into the rhetorical situation. Immediacy in participatory critical rhetoric refers to the discursive and embodied interactions between people present within a particular rhetorical scene. As a temporal marker, it describes an ongoing process but also a finite moment. On the one hand, it is an ongoing process of judgment, whereby audiences and rhetors share agency regarding the impact of a particular discourse, each seeking to influence each other in nuanced ways. Given that these rhetorical moments do not occur in a vacuum, examining the historical contexts that impact present-day conflicts is an important part of examining the ongoing process of rhetorical invention. On the other hand, immediacy also recognizes that the effect of speech can and should be studied within its emplaced instantiation. As a cross-sectional moment, participatory critical rhetoric departs from the long-standing textual re-creation of rhetorical situations, believing that these moments can best be understood by the presence of the critic and through interaction with others present. In short, the here and now matters in how we evaluate rhetoric.

Immediacy is an essential element within rhetoric, especially given the long-standing conceptualization of rhetoric as situational and contingent in character. For the purposes of participatory critical rhetoric and the judgments derived from rhetorical analyses it produces, immediacy entails a critical recognition of the production and reception of rhetoric at the moment of its inception. When conducted through immanent participation, as we discuss in chapter 2, the critic is sensitized to the immediate concerns of the multiple parties involved within the spaces of rhetoric. Each concern is weighed within the immediate rhetorical context that is formed by a complex intersection of space, people, and timing. Within that intersection, critics find that the discursive drama unfolds through its players: rhetor, audience, and critic. In this case, immediacy allows the participatory critical rhetorician to engage in a direct examination of the different people linked to the rhetorical situation, each of which could be considered a participant in the research process. While this understanding is not necessarily novel, participatory critical rhetoric blurs these roles, at least partially. For example, a participatory critic who engages a social movement can be a part of the immediate audience for the message, or she or he might produce messages alongside that movement, gaining immediate knowledge of the rhetor's role, while simultaneously observing audiences for their reception of the message, as Endres and Senda-Cook did in their examination of Step It Up.[12] Furthermore, as the movement adapts its external message during internal deliberations,[13] the participatory critical rhetorician could have access to and potentially influence both exchanges. Depending on the type of message and movement, it is also possible for the critic to break from the protest to interview audience members about their reception of the message.[14]

My very first experience conducting rhetorical fieldwork occurred back in my undergraduate honors thesis research. I was curious about a very vocal controversy between the National Organization for Women (NOW) and the Promise Keepers, a Christian men's group. Under the guise of family values, the Promise Keepers were espousing masculinist claims about traditional, heterosexual families and especially about the roles of men and women in the family. NOW membership spoke frequently about how the group was promoting a traditional and patriarchal image of the family, which included suppressing women's choices in work and in life. To determine the impact and influence of the organization, I attended a Promise Keepers rally in 2000 at the Great Western Forum in Los Angeles, the stadium were the Lakers previously played. I observed and witnessed a series of speakers, including former San Diego Charger Miles McPherson, Professor Gary Oliver of the Center for Marriage and Family Studies, and most prominently, founder of the Promise Keeper movement, "Coach" Bill McCartney.

Listening to each of the speakers, I took copious notes about the types of imagery they used, the general framework of their arguments, and the ways in which audience members reacted. Some speakers, such as McPherson, were remarkably engaging, pulling the audience in by claiming, for example, that the devil desires children to be on drugs and in gangs. He called for the fathers in the audience to be "priests at home." The audience was riveted by his passionate delivery as he spoke his positive message in lay terms with an ethos of care and urgency for action. Clapping hands and standing ovations were passed back to the former football player as he exited the stage.

The main event for the Christian group in the stadium was Coach McCartney. As he was introduced to the stage by the emcee for the event, the audience's excitement grew. Certainly, this man was to be a champion of the crowd, and I awaited his speech, pen and paper in hand. Taking the stage, the Coach sounded off on the main issues pressing men in contemporary society: men losing control of their families, the "domineering homosexual" agenda, and the loss of purpose in life. Textually, his speech was exactly what NOW had feared. The founder of this movement was comparing women and children to "potted plants" that required care by the man of the family. Yet, being present for the speech, I acquired a different judgment about the Coach. His delivery lived up to his nickname, as he screamed at his audience as if it was halftime during the big game. Frankly, his monotone football-halftime delivery was remarkably unsuccessful. As I sat in the audience of thousands, observing their reception of the message, I was surprised to see members of the audience noticeably distracted during the speech, with eyes glazed over, and even falling asleep as the leader spoke. Compared to other speakers, McCartney failed to engage his audience. This judgment would not be available had I merely listened to the recorded speech or read a transcript of his words. Taking the rally as a whole, the stage presence of other speakers, such as McPherson, carried much more weight than the tiresome Coach.

—Aaron

These lessons in rhetorical production and reception that we see in Aaron's experience mirror disciplinary discussions regarding text and context that we describe in chapters 1 and 4.[15] When accented with immediacy, however, the embodied and participatory critical rhetorician gains access to contexts in ways not previously discussed by Michael McGee and allied rhetorical theorists, and learns of textual formation in ways missed by Michael Leff and other practitioners of close textual analysis.[16] Critics cannot and should not rely solely upon their own understanding of advocacy; judgment includes the immediate responses and perspectives of those present. For example, a participatory critical rhetorician will be able to experience the immediate contextual conditions pertaining to particular audiences and inquire into how they may constrain and enable a rhetorical performance. Ambient sounds, the occasional heckler, or the presence of competing messages—even audience members falling asleep during a speech—might all impact the types of judgment made by rhetor and audience. As a participatory approach, participatory critical rhetoric invites more nuanced considerations of influence as they occur across multiple levels of a rhetorical scene through the concept of immediacy. At the opening of National 9/11 Memorial, both the 9/11 Truthers and Westboro Baptist Church members were present to protest the mainstream understandings of September 11th, which changed the tenor of the event to include conspiratorial claims and narratives of theodicy regarding the events of 9/11. The oscillation between the actors within a rhetorical scene invites novel considerations of how judgment is made between each, while recognizing that judgment upon the rhetoric of a scene is shared across participants. Critics work alongside participants, learning how audiences react to messages and how speakers adapt their messages. Consequently, to form an overall critical judgment about the rhetoric produced in the field, critics will need access to multiple perspectives and vantage points on the rhetorical act. Immediate *in situ* judgment can look significantly different from an after-the-fact outsider textual perspective because it allows the critic access to competing forms of judgment among participants.

Expanding the critical approach to appreciate immediacy and the multiple perspectives in a rhetorical exchange means that the critic becomes more decentered in critical analyses. As we argue in chapter 3, the role of the critic is significantly altered within participatory critical rhetoric. There, we wrote of the particular roles and risks potentially taken up by critics as they adopt participatory roles within the rhetorical contexts under examination.

Turning now toward participants, we contend that the decentering process also requires reflexive engagement with participants and their concerns. Decentering means that the critic's judgment of the text and context is drawn down as other voices are elevated, providing insight into the vernacular exchanges found in the scene. It means being open to the ways in which ordinary voices may inform a broader read of a rhetorical field. As Davis Houck reflects on his work that includes integrating citizen responses into his read of FDR's first inaugural—of "folks writing letters"—it could be the case that their judgments could alter the critic's interpretation of the text, "[m]aybe these folks knew some things a trained rhetorical critic didn't."[17] This means that critics must account for their identity in the scene, finding instances when initial judgments are incomplete, perhaps because of inexperience with the issue at hand, or perhaps because of the nature of who they are. Snap judgments made within a rhetorical culture—whether regarding presidential address, the 9/11 Memorial, or a Christian men's movement—become significantly altered as the critic moves in and out of the spaces of rhetorical exchange, interacting with its inhabitants. Through these interactions, the critic gains new insights into its composition and encounters new ideas from its members. Additionally, the critic may need to seek out those individuals who can inform the nature of the advocacy performed, thereby supplementing the critical and interpretive act. As rhetorical informants, these individuals provide insight into the message making or receiving process. Key members of an advocacy organization or of a target audience may serve as informants into how messages are exchanged.

Ultimately, this multiperspectival approach augments efforts toward developing a materialist form of judgment. Looking back to our discussion of materiality in chapter 1, we conceptualize the materiality of rhetoric as operating on two intersecting planes, having both material consequences and existing in a physical, nondiscursive scene. We extend our discussion of materiality with the idea of judgment, as we outline in this chapter, drawing from previous theorizing about materialist judgment from John Sloop and Kent Ono, who accent materiality with a localized sensibility. In this sense, material judgment is interactional in nature, existing within "counterhegemonic decisions" in everyday life[18] and "within an economy of phenomenological experience, quite literally the *gestalt* created by the complex interaction of speaker, speech, audience, occasion, and change at a particular moment in time."[19] As we articulate in chapter 3, embodiment within the rhetorical scene leads to particularized judgments; to this, perspective—or rather, multiple perspectives—should be added to how we conceptualize judgment. Through direct participation and interaction with participants, participatory critical rhetoric invites myriad perspectives into the formation of critical and material judgment.

Drawing from Ronald Beiner's work on political judgment, James Jasinski contends that judgment "can only be comprehended in its material embodiments" and "attains conceptual solidity or substance as it is vibrated against a particular case—a materially embodied episode of discursive action and choice—and becomes refined and instantiated in an interpretation of that case."[20] To that understanding, we add that interpretation cannot be constructed by the critic in isolation from immediate participants. Judgment is shared among all members of a rhetorical scene, and participants can illuminate the nature of rhetorical action in ways that would be unknown to the critic without direct inquiry. In so doing, participatory critical rhetoric includes multiple perspectives within the process of judgment. Jasinski also indicates that the space of judgment is constituted by a number of structural antagonisms that cut across the roles, communities, politics, and temporalities inherent to public controversies.[21] For example, a rhetor who is within the space of judgment may take up a political position that is heavily invested, that of a partisan advocate, and audiences may exist in a position that is relatively impartial. At the opening of the 9/11 Memorial, first responders strongly advocated for invitations into the memorial space, while tourists traveling to the site may have been unaware of the controversy. Between these positions, a traditional textually-oriented critic may struggle to ascertain the nuance of each, given that the controversy is performed and adapted within immediate contexts that might not appear in textual reproductions. Audience members may not respond to the impassioned pleas of rhetors on the street. However, from a more participatory perspective, the motivations and orientations that participants have can be examined through interviews or direct observation. The critic, moving across perspectives, spaces, and vantage points, may learn of each element of these structural antagonisms, providing a strong doxastic understanding of the rhetoric found therein.[22] In other words, the *telos* of rhetoric is reconfigured from being a sustained critique of power relations to an active participation in the struggle.

IMMANENCE THROUGH IMMEDIACY: TOWARD A NEW *TELOS* OF RHETORIC

As we discuss in chapter 2, participatory critical rhetoric emphasizes the immanent politics of particular rhetorical fields. Understood within immediate contexts and in relation to participants, immanent politics invites critics to be affected by the localized struggles found in the field. As *telos,* the purpose of the critical act becomes invested in the struggles of people within vernacular communities, informed by the voices found within the immediate field. In critical rhetoric, McKerrow characterizes rhetoric as "symbolism which addresses publics,"[23] rather than the analysis of public address, and invites a reconsideration of the *telos* of rhetoric to include the demystification of domination and permanent criticism of freedom. Expanding this notion, Ono and Sloop encourage critical rhetoricians to pursue a "commitment toward contingent *telos*" as a "sustained critical *praxis*."[24] What is absent in these framings is the critic's presence and participation in the immediate context and the inclusion of multiple perspectives into judgments about rhetorical effects. By focusing on the embodied and emplaced qualities of rhetorical production and reception, participatory critical rhetoric can more fully engage the immanent political commitments found within the rhetorical field as they are understood by participants. Looking back on the example from the tenth anniversary of 9/11, seeking out additional voices regarding the memorial opened up political understandings of the memorial, such as the survivor narrative or over-commercialization of 9/11.

Thus, participatory critical rhetoric adds to these conceptualizations by characterizing rhetoric such that it includes discourses that address and circulate within and between publics and their agents, specifically at the moment of their inception and reception. While circulation can certainly be recognized and studied from a conventional textual perspective, being present in the immediate site of rhetorical invention allows for including judgments and shared agency that are difficult to access by textual analysis alone. The immediate and intersectional character of rhetoric, therefore, requires a *telos* that is a sustained critical praxis that includes witnessing, participating, and reflecting, which develops a robust multiperspectival judgment. Animating rhetoric in this way underscores its interactional quality, emphasizing that rhetoric is best understood within its immediate context, by including the interconnected voices of those participating in that situation, and through in-depth reflection upon the judgments and experiences encountered in these situations.

By expanding *telos* in this way, we recognize the fundamental intersubjective foundation of rhetoric.[25] Taking an insider approach to these exchanges as authored by the participants in the scene invites new epistemological considerations of rhetoric. Critics suspend their previously held role in evaluation and critical judgment as they work out details of the dialogue *in situ*. The voices of participants are elevated as they illustrate the localized judgments of meaning making. Audiences and rhetors are given opportunities to vocalize their responses to rhetoric, or to explain their choices in meaning making. In each case, the participatory critical rhetoric researcher withholds final judgment until the participants' voices have been fully contemplated. This is accomplished with due attention to the immediacy of rhetoric as an attempt to influence others through shared judgment. For example, Aaron suspended judgment about the 9/11 Memorial until more voices were incorporated into the critical act, which opened space for competing interpretations of the memorial.

Prefacing interaction within a rhetorical field also reinforces the idea that rhetoric affects multiple parties, and that those parties should be included in the critical act due to the shared agency between rhetor and audience.[26] To examine this shared agency, participatory critical rhetoricians can attend to the localized judgments proffered in the immediate context of rhetoric and explore reflections upon discursive performances. In other words, criticism in participatory critical rhetoric more closely attends to the circulation and immediacy of discourse within everyday contexts as it occurs between people. It is especially attentive to the ways that such discourse constructs and constrains the conditions for public advocacy as understood by the participants in immediate rhetorical situations. Participatory critical rhetoric is not merely an augmentation of the texts suitable for criticism; it is a direct inquiry into the processual character of discourse itself from the perspective of those involved in its creation. This means that texts are potentially understood before, during, and after their performance, thus destabilizing the boundaries of text as understood in traditional criticism. In this way, participatory critical rhetoric departs from traditional textual approaches in that it focuses on the inventional act within its immediate context and not the after-the-fact representation or dissemination of it as a text. While those approaches are valuable, the immediate context provides insight into rhetorical production and reception in ways that analyzing the text alone might miss. For example, a participatory critical rhetorician may attend planning meetings for a local social movement as members prepare for an upcoming event, witness or enact the adaptive performance of argument as it occurs, and inquire into the reception of the message as audience members receive it in the immediate context of its delivery. Moreover, participatory critical rhetoricians that are embedded and engaged within a community may also learn of the ways that communities trace the dissemination and circulation of their messages, thereby learning of the adaptations they make to their ongoing rhetorical campaigns.

The text, in this sense, is no longer contained. It cannot be. It lives and breathes, changing as participants modify their performances based on the input of critics and audiences. Rhetors may seek out advice from the critic or reframe their rhetoric in response to the critic's questioning. Moreover, the participants' framing and reframing of the message may alter the critic's understanding of rhetoric as performed, opening new spaces for theorizing about effects and judgment. By including the active voices of participants and engaging the field of rhetoric through participatory and embodied perspectives, participatory critical rhetoric opens up spaces for the apprehension of a multiperspectival and materialist form of judgment. The participants involved in participatory critical rhetoric research do not merely extend the text; they reflect on it, participate in it, and assist the critic in comprehending the nature of their vernacular advocacy. Indeed, the mere presence of the rhetorical critic may alter the nature of interactions. The questions asked during interviews may never have been considered by audiences or speakers, thereby opening up spaces for reflection. For example, Aaron's interviews about the 9/11 Memorial opened up space for critical reflection on the symbolic elements of the memorial, inviting tourists to outwardly ponder the meaning of waterfalls and symbolic absences. Furthermore, the immediate evaluation offered by the critic may have a direct impact on rhetorical performances in the future.

As we outline in chapter 1, there has been a recent trend in rhetorical scholarship that interacts with individuals and includes their voices in the act of criticism. From an observational perspective, a number of scholars have included vernacular sources that include coffee shop conversations, participant observation in social movements, interviews, and focus groups regarding existing message campaigns.[27] In many cases, these investigations seek to augment traditional textual approaches, believing that textual analysis is limited in one way or another. For example, for Watts and Orbe, the inclusion of focus groups provides another interpretive layer for determining how textual analysis is or is not able to apprehend the perspective of audiences. Such an approach opens spaces for participants to weave their voice into textual criticism, yet does so in a more clinical setting. Other more naturalistic textual recordings of coffee shop conversations or the planning of protest activities are difficult to access from any other vantage point, meaning that to most properly consider the nature of them, an insider perspective is necessary. For scholars examining counterpublic discourses, publicity may only occur in specific, visible moments (or, in moments that would be otherwise invisible except for the opportunity to glimpse them made available to the embedded critic). Reliance on outsider or textual perspectives may not allow the critic to fully appreciate the nuance of such activities as they are formed internally.

By engaging and including more voices into the critical act, participatory critical rhetoric theorizes text anew. The text becomes imbued with a performative sensibility that adapts to its surroundings and to the people involved. It is embodied, emplaced, and experiential, and often difficult to capture on the page, which invites new forms of recording rhetoric via portable media devices such as smartphone cameras, audio recordings, and video production tools.[28] Participants may guide critics to appreciate the myriad means of expression through the rhetor's body and media available, which may open up opportunities to learn of the decisions that go into vernacular media production. The text is also something that is (re)created by multiple agents involved. The critic does indeed assemble discourses suitable for criticism,[29] but this process also involves audiences and rhetors who may add their own fragments into the critical act, including spoken word, embodied and verbal reactions, and critical reflections on a more global landscape. In other words, textual composition includes judgment, not merely on what should be included in the critical invention process, but active judgments offered by those present within the field of rhetoric. The text can include both the production of protest and the visceral response from audiences present. The act of textual production and critical judgment are therefore conjoined much like how the previously distinct positions of critic, rhetor, and audience in a rhetorical situation become intersubjectively composed. When visiting the 9/11 Memorial, Aaron was at once a tourist, a critic, a documentary producer, and even a rhetor when actively performing in the commemorative activities of the day. When oscillating between audience and rhetor, the participatory critical rhetorician must consider the various ways in which participants appear in their research, along with the ethics of interacting with them, an issue we turn toward in the following section.

CONCEPTUALIZING PARTICIPANTS

As discussed above, the inclusion of other voices into a critical project is relatively infrequent in rhetorical criticism. Participatory critical rhetoric takes seriously the ways in which participants can fundamentally alter and augment the outcomes of a critical rhetorical project, as well as the ethical concerns raised by interacting with participants. Ethics in rhetorical criticism has long been a concern for critics.[30] Yet, given the limited interactions between rhetorical scholars and speakers or audience members, the ethics of interactive research practices have rarely been discussed.[31] In recent years, the turn toward interactive digital texts and certainly the rise in more participatory approaches invites considerations about how critics have an ethical responsibility to their participants.[32]

One main consideration is the potentially harmful nature of interactions with participants. Researchers' questions, inquiries, and their mere presence in a particular situation can lead to discomfort for participants. As we discuss in chapters 3 and 4, critics bear the responsibility of (potentially) influencing the rhetorical situation, meaning that they have a direct impact on the otherwise naturally occurring events in the scene. Participants who rally for causes, which are often quite personal and meaningful, will take seriously any involvement whether from an academic or a passer-by. In Michael's work with homeless populations and Danielle's work with environmental justice groups, they had to negotiate the ethics of their choices made with regard to the understaffed and under-resourced groups with whom they worked. Consequently, the notion of doing harm goes beyond a calculation of potential benefits against research discomforts; for some, harm can be inflicted in deeper ways. For example, in Aaron Hess's research on DanceSafe, his interactions included conversations with active drug-using youth, ranging from individuals talking about addiction, inquiring about contraindications between illegal substances, or seeking a treatment center for a friend.[33] These spontaneous interactions require a great deal of care. Similarly, Phaedra Pezzullo's research with breast cancer advocates who narrate their tales of pain and survival also displays the life-and-death struggle facing participants. Her investigation into this group required appreciation and concern for the seriousness of the issue.[34] In each of these cases, the potential for psychological harm exists, and participatory critical rhetoricians must attend to the ethics of the situation before engaging with participants. In this section, we outline three conceptualizations of participant interaction and discuss some of the major ethical concerns tied to each, including potential harm, the re-creation of textual practices, and the use of digital technology in the scene.

Participants as Inventors and Auditors of Discourse

Pulling out my mobile phone, I continued taking notes while the rest of the people were behind the house, drinking cider and listening to a talk about raising chickens locally. My job at this moment was guarding bikes, which created an opportunity to record what I was seeing, hearing, smelling, and feeling about this progressive dinner fundraiser called the Full Cycle Supper. During a four-mile bike ride, participants made several stops, each offering a different course of a dinner. I also recorded what I was remembering because I could not take fieldnotes while riding my bike on streets with about 35 people following me. Headnotes became essential as the competing interests of the success of the event and the opportunity to document ephemeral practices jostled for my immediate attention. I was both a volunteer with one of the hosting nonprofit organizations and a researcher, studying the rhetorical practices of local food and alternative transportation movements.

The Key Holders, a subset of volunteers within the Community Bike Project of Omaha (CBPO), plan most of the events for that organization. As a nonprofit with only one paid staff member, this organization depends on volunteers, grants, and donations to provide low-cost or no-cost bikes to community members. As a Key Holder, I not only observed the planning process unfold for the Full Cycle Supper, I also helped make decisions about what this ride would look like. At first, our idea was to bike out to a farm about 30 or 40 miles away, but after an especially harsh hail storm, it didn't seem like that farm would have any room to accommodate an event like this. We turned to Big Muddy Urban Farm, which is a three-year-old enterprise based on the idea of growing food in the city of Omaha. As a member of Big Muddy's CSA (Community Supported Agriculture) and friend of several farmers, I approached them to find out if they would be interested in partnering for this event. After they met to discuss it and agreed, our two organizations got together and started to plan where the ride would go, which chefs to invite to cook food, and what would be on the menu.

During the event, being a volunteer meant representing the organization to the diners who paid for the dinner, leading the bike ride, helping serve food, clearing dishes, and, as mentioned above, guarding bikes at some of the stops. This left little time to take fieldnotes but it provided the advantages of obtaining knowledge of organizational history and the decision-making processes. I was privy to not only what happened on the ride but the deliberations that accompanied key decisions. For example, when the chefs responsible for serving our first dish didn't show up on time, we had to decide what to do. Additionally, leading up to the event a generous community member, who rents the building that houses the CBPO and the land on which Big Muddy farms to these organizations for a dollar a year, asked if we could all stop by the end-of-the-season Gifford Park Community Garden potluck early in the evening, while it was still light, rather than after all the other stops. We had initialy refused to change the route we had in mind. But when the chefs didn't appear, we decided to alter the plans to go directly to the Community Garden. Then, when we got in touch with the chefs and learned they were only minutes away, we changed the plan again. We would stay and eat the first course but then we would still stop at the Community Garden before proceeding with the rest of the event, thus satisfying the generous community member. As an organizer, I was worried about all the changes we had made and how they would look to diners. However, talking to a co-researcher after the event, who paid for the dinner and attended as a diner only, revealed that he had no idea that a problem had existed at all. My experience and knowledge of the backchanneling of the event coupled effectively with his experience as a patron to produce a nuanced, complex understanding of the practices in play at the Fully Cycle Supper.

—Samantha

Fundamentally, participatory critical rhetoric is interested in the ways that people in a rhetorical field invent and interpret discourse. Thinking back to Rowland's claim that agency is shared between speaker and audience, and Jasinski's contention that judgment is best understood as it vibrates against a particular case, this conceptualization recognizes that rhetoric is composed and interpreted by those involved in a rhetorical field. First, as inventors of discourses, participants perform their discursive craft with care, and participatory critics can inquire into the nature of their preparation and judgments that inform the act of invention, much like Samantha's backchanneling in the Full Cycle Supper above. The contingent character of rhetoric and its connection to judgment can be engaged through a dual understanding of the larger contextual backdrop of rhetoric as well as the moment of delivery. For example, participants as inventors may take into consideration the larger historical narrative behind their movement as they take the stage to perform a specific speech. While this dimension of speech making is not new, the participatory critic can have access to the decision-making process and witness the consequences, including the spontaneous decisions to alter or adapt the message. In some cases, the critic can perform the argument as a part of the movement, learning firsthand the types of adaptive practices necessary for success.

Second, as auditors of discourses, participants can inform critics regarding their reception of a message or campaign, giving clues into the immediate effects of the rhetorical attempt. Audience members can be observed or interviewed to determine the potential impact of a message or rhetorical site. In so doing, the critic can take into consideration larger historical details that inform the reception of a message, as well as those particular details of the message that alter its meaning.[35] As we detail in the previous chapter, when Danielle and her research team interviewed participants at the Step It Up rally, they learned about how the participants cued in on different aspects of the rally, which radically altered the way they made sense of the event as concert, festival, or, less likely, as a protest for climate change. This analytic move pulls together fragments of time and space, critically examining the emplaced and temporal character of rhetoric as participants understand it. When taken together, participatory critics have a powerful evaluative tool, which enables a robust reading of how messages are produced and received within localized spaces of discourse.

Beyond the evaluation of discourse, critics can also reflect upon alternative modes of rhetorical production. Unbound from the traditional pen and paper of criticism, participatory critical rhetoricians can both engage in critical acts within the immanent politics of the scene *and* produce works that follow the mediated character of contemporary protest. For example, Kevin DeLuca and Jennifer Peeples argue that within the public screen, social movements turn toward mass communication and other media to manufacture image events, thereby commanding control of the gaze of the camera.[36] The media logics that drive contemporary protest activities extend into digital media, meaning that many movements will craft a character that exists in both online and offline worlds. This crafting takes care, and the participatory critic may learn of the ways in which vernacular organizations turn toward social media and other tools to forge identities. Moreover, the participatory critical rhetorician can also turn toward media production, such as online video, digital photography, or even social media participation, to create critical works.[37] For example, engaging social media to circulate images about a recent protest can be understood as both performing the nature of the mediated protest and an extension of more traditional critical aims. In other words, the participation of the critic in alternative text production can serve both the goals of the organization and the critic alike.

Ethically, participatory critics should consider a number of issues before interacting with vernacular organizations. If the critic intends to examine both the role of the rhetor and audience, the organization or protest group may express concern about how the critic goes about asking such questions. Members of the organization may express concern about the interview or question the loyalty of the critic to the movement. Interacting with the other side of a controversy or even with the lay public about the impact of a message may perceptually undermine the group's credibility. This concern is parallel to the varying nature of membership in qualitative research. As Patricia Adler and Peter Adler discuss, the deeper the membership role becomes, the more difficult it becomes to maintain a researcher role. Moreover, the intricacy and intimacy of relationships when engaging in full membership makes outside examinations quite difficult.[38] To quell such concerns, critics can collaborate with organizational members with a spirit of transparency about the academic aims of the project, keeping in mind that the central purpose of participatory critical rhetoric is an engagement with the immanent politics of the rhetorical situation. Displaying loyalty to the group's message can bolster the trust between organization and critic; on the other hand, it can foreclose the range of critical assessments available to the critic. Along with other qualitative researchers, the focus on loyalty is also a central concern for many participatory action researchers, who spend considerable amounts of time forging alliances between researchers and participants.[39] These alliances, while always marked by difference, still provide opportunities to display reflexivity in relation to those living under oppressive conditions, and commitment toward their goals in ameliorating such oppression.

Participatory critics who have engaged vernacular or out-law groups should also consider the internal understanding of publicity for the group.[40] What constitutes a public act may differ between groups, and some groups may only engage in tactical resistance at particular times. Bringing to light elements of the enclaved rhetoric within a group may violate their preferences for being public.[41] This concern echoes Kendall Phillips's arguments about John Sloop and Kent Ono's interrogation of out-law discourse and the rhetoric of resistance more generally.[42] Phillips believes that some out-law or vernacular groups may desire to remain hidden and out of public sight. The involvement of a critic can risk exploitation; Phillips notes that, at times, "[r]ather than academic criticism acting in service of everyday acts of resistance, everyday acts of resistance are put into the service of academic criticism."[43] The difference, in the instance of participatory critical rhetoric, is the element of reflexivity on the part of the critic in relation to the participants of a particular organization. A part of the critical exercise should include consultation at both the individual and organizational levels about the nature of publicity as vernacularly constituted. Participatory critics should take time whenever possible to understand which actions are most appropriate for the particular movement under consideration. For example, when Aaron was working with DanceSafe in the context of raves, he was engaging with an underground culture that expresses distrust of larger systems of authority. Stories of failed drug buys or instances of dealers offering drugs to DanceSafe volunteers were common out-law expressions.

Taken together, conceptualizing participants as inventors and auditors of discourse through ethically based participatory methods allows for novel insights into the nature of material and multiperspectival judgment. Interviews and other participatory methods can illustrate the planning that goes into message production. Conversely, audience members can offer vital perceptions into how a message is potentially received. As a conduit between parties, the critic can learn of the immanent practices that form judgments toward more effective speech, in whatever way they are understood by the particular organization being studied. Reflexivity, as a research practice, can assist in not only navigating the ethical requirements of research, but also as a generative force of learning for the critic. Ethical reflexivity can provide clues as to how the critic is personally implicated within embodied and emplaced scenes of rhetorical action.[44] When participants are considered within the composition of the rhetorical field, the critic can apprehend the micropolitical choices that constitute the everyday practices of rhetoric. These smaller judgments, including how to arrange pamphlets at a booth, what language choices are best for chants, and what time of day is best for protest, provide performative opportunities for the critic to directly participate in protest.

Participants as Rhetorical Bodies

Extending our discussion of embodiment from chapter 3, we also take stock of the ways in which participants' bodies operate within the rhetorical field. When participant bodies are considered as rhetorical bodies, critics can learn of the situational qualities of advocacy. This means that bodies—especially the ways in which bodies are represented, challenged, and contested—take on particular meanings. The processual character of rhetoric requires attention to the ways in which bodies move and are positioned in space. Similar to the judgments about how to craft a message, emplaced and embodied rhetorical action requires attention to the body as a part of rhetorical expression.[45] In taking up the rhetorical body, participatory critical rhetoric takes a holistic account of rhetoric as bodies and voices engaging with each other in emplaced settings. As such, the body serves as a form of rhetorical enactment, in the spirit of sit-ins or die-ins,[46] or public nudity as a sign of vulnerability.[47] As rhetorical bodies interact, the critic may seek to document their tactical and strategic use, such as the interactive and even hostile nature of protesters meeting police. When doing so, the critic should regard the body—and especially the representation of the body—as vitally connected to rhetoric. The body, then, is sacred and vulnerable as individuals interact in the rhetorical field. Before documenting participants' embodied actions, critics should carefully consider how representations of the body, whether textual or mediated, might (re)circulate or appear in the future when looking back at the moment.

This sentiment is particularly salient when recording technologies are deployed, including audio and video. Given the ubiquity of recording devices typically present in pockets, including smartphones that can record exceptionally high-quality photographs, audio, and video, participatory critical rhetoricians will likely desire to capture key moments in the field,[48] as Samantha did in her fieldwork with the Full Cycle Supper. Similarly, while Danielle often felt conspicuous taking photos in the field 10 years ago, she now takes photos on her phone and blends in with the rest of the participants who are doing the same, even in her participant observation among nuclear scientists and engineers at professional conferences. In some cases, full professional camera equipment can be used to record professional grade films and other productions. The presence of recording technology changes the nature of fieldwork. Even the most benign audio recorder can change the responses in interviews, and the presence of the camera can especially alter participants' behavior. For some, the presence of the camera and the supporting logics of spectacle can enhance and invite remarkably outspoken or even unruly behavior.[49] Participants may "perform" for the camera, seeing it as a moment for exhibitionism, or the camera might induce powerful emotions during interviews. During his work in Lower Manhattan, Aaron found that participants would quickly come to tears when asked to narrate their memories of 9/11 for the video camera. For others, photographs or video recordings might silence their voice for fear of after-the-fact reprisal. Participatory critical rhetoric research may often take place behind closed doors during internal planning for externally focused events. In these moments, great care must be taken on behalf of the privacy of those involved. Ethically, the participatory critical rhetorician must take into consideration the power of recording devices and the impact they may have on the inclusion and exclusion of participants affected by the study.

Those invested in participatory critical rhetoric will benefit through three overlapping considerations to navigate these concerns about the ethics of audio, video, or photographically recording "texts" from participants. First, current institutional practices typically require informed consent not only for interview interactions, but also for all types of recording that would not occur naturally. Of course, today's recording technology is nearly ubiquitous, where smartphones that accompany the researcher easily become powerful recording devices. Yet, the active recording of protest events or the discourse of an activist should include informed consent practices whenever possible. Second, the participatory and interactive nature of participatory critical rhetoric provides the critic with vital insider knowledge about particular rhetorical fields and vernacular organizations. When recording technology enters the mix, the critic should have gained a perspective that appreciates the types of decorum pertaining to media followed by members of the organization. For Hess, this includes due attention to *kairos* as a balanced consideration of the decorum of the scene and the opportunities for inventive practices.[50] Participatory critical rhetoricians, by the very nature of presence, participation, and immediacy, should be able to reflect upon or inquire about acceptable forms of disclosure in interviews or in media. This is similar to those engaged in ethnography or other qualitative methods. For example, Karen Stewart shared the risks of taking photography during Burning Man, a weeklong art festival located in Nevada.[51] In her case, the use of photography was disruptive to the organic elements of the festival, even while the visual elements appear to be on display for all to see. The power of recording technology cannot be underestimated by those in the field. Discretion about fieldnotes, audio/video, and other forms of recording should be learned over time and used when making a decision about recording in the scene.

The third and final consideration that the participatory critical rhetorician should also consider is the networked quality of protest in the contemporary media landscape. Often, advocates intend to capture the attention of the camera in order to extend the protest to televised or social media.[52] Participatory critical rhetoricians should also consider the ways that they are personally implicated in networked media spaces; they may find their own image plastered across social media sites or on the local news. In these cases, participatory critics should consider the ways that they may speak or appear on behalf of the movement or cause, an issue we detail in more depth below. Social media serves as an important extension for many advocates, who disseminate images of protest activities and circulate their messages beyond the physical spaces in which they occur. Consequently, as we contend in chapter 4, the field under consideration within participatory critical rhetoric extends across digital and physical places, carrying with it the dual logics of a mediated and physical presence. As a research ethic, participatory critical rhetoricians should assume that their presence and image is likely being recorded and circulated across digital networks. Frequently, these digital spaces exist on a foundational spectacular logic that attracts attention through sensationalized means.[53] As the following vignette details, decisions to photograph participants in the field are complex and implicated within diverse motivations across critic, audience, and rhetor.

I have to admit that before working on this book, I was not deeply attuned to these issues surrounding the rhetorical bodies of participants. I understood the rhetorical power of bodies and the implications of putting participants at risk through the process of fieldwork. And yet, because I don't consider myself a "body rhetoric" scholar, and I don't regularly attend to body rhetoric in my analyses, this topic has receded to the background in my rhetorical fieldwork. In the process of co-writing this book, I have been able to reflect on my past practices and understand how to better presence and attend to participants as rhetorical bodies, even within projects where I am not specifically making arguments about body rhetoric.

I am thinking about the photos I have taken at various protest events. At a public protest event, there is always the possibility that participants in that event will be photographed; indeed many participants want to be photographed in the act of protesting, either to share a "selfie" on their social networks or in the hopes of appearing in a newspaper article or other disseminated account of the protest. This public dissemination of photographs is part of what makes the analysis of visual rhetorics and body rhetorics possible. Yet, something different is going on when the critic is the one who is taking the photos and then potentially disseminating them with their rhetorical criticism. I wonder if it is on participants' minds that one of the possible implications of these photographs is to be analyzed as a form of rhetoric and included in a journal article or book on the subject. In several of my previous projects, I have included photographs taken at public events in the field and there was no possible way of tracking down the individuals in the photographs for their consent to be included in the book or journal article. Moreover, in the moment in the field when I took the photograph, it was neither practical nor feasible to track down each person for consent to take the photo. Even if I were able to do so, asking for permission could change the character of the photograph from spontaneous to posed. What responsibilities do we have as participatory rhetorical critics to the participants we capture in our photographs? While consent is not required by IRB for public photographs, it is desirable from the perspective of participatory critical rhetoric. Therefore, how do we negotiate the use of photographs that depict individual bodies in a variety of (perhaps undesirable or unflattering) ways? How do we make decisions about when to include these photographs in our research products? I don't have the definitive answers to these questions, but I do think it is crucial that each critic explicitly ask these questions as they consider the taking and use of photographs in their in situ *rhetorical criticism.*

Even more, what responsibilities do we have to take photographs that "accurately" depict the field of rhetorical invention? One project I was involved with included photos from a variety of protest events that were analyzed. As we chose photographs from the archive of photographs taken by the many participants in the project, we specifically chose one of a young child with a sign on her or his back and holding the hand of an adult (the child's face is not visible). We thought it was cute, well framed, and perhaps more importantly aligned with our *beliefs about the need for decision makers to understand the implications of environmental destruction on kids. Yet, kids were not well represented at all of the protest events examined in the project. Would we have been better off with a photograph that was more representative of the majority of participants that attended these events? Even though we did not use this photograph as evidence for a claim about the rhetorical influence about the protest event from which it was taken, we chose the photo for our own specific rhetorical purpose, revealing the power that we hold in documenting the rhetorical events and communities we work with in participatory critical rhetoric.*

—Danielle

Ultimately, the conception of the participant body as rhetorical invites a variety of considerations about localized and multiperspectival judgment. While somewhat under-theorized,[54] corporeal judgment underscores the affective intensities found in the places of rhetoric. The body becomes imbued with a performative sensibility, especially when the mere presence of protesters or a picket line challenges the normative understandings of space. When rhetors and audiences experience the rhetorical situation, they position their bodies in relation to each other, often at odds with calculated judgments about appropriateness, decorum, and civility.[55] For Danielle, the taking of photographs in the moment of protest is driven by drastically different concerns than those found in academic publishing. The participatory critical rhetorician becomes witness to the various comportments of bodies in and against each other in spaces, recognizing that representations of bodies extends their rhetorical force well beyond the immediate event. Being present in the immediate rhetorical field means that the critic is also engaging in an embodied connection to others, as we discuss in chapter 3. When conversing with participants about their embodied enactments, the critic can learn of how bodies can be positioned in protest, the choices they make in preparation and representation, and the embodiment of advocacy.

Participants as Dialogic Interlocutors

Finally, participants should be conceptualized relationally. As interlocutors within a participatory critical rhetoric project, the dynamic between "researcher" and "participant" fundamentally changes. Given the real-world consequences many advocates face, the dialogic relationship between critic and participant is quite serious. While we discuss the more integral parts of research relationships in the conclusion, for now it is important to consider the ways in which dialogic research can add to multiperspectival judgment. Michael Holquist explains that, in Mikhail Bahktin's conception of dialogue, utterances, discourses, and language work together to develop meaning rather than impose it on an otherwise undifferentiated and powerless world. He states, "A word, discourse, language or culture undergoes 'dialogization' when it becomes relativized, de-privileged, aware of competing definitions for the same things. Undialogized language is authoritative or absolute."[56] Connecting this to the critic in the field, after-the-fact criticism typically maintains such authoritative judgment about the text. In contrast, participatory critical rhetoric includes dialogues with not only other people but also fields and contexts themselves. Dialogue, in this sense, is a generative force in the formation of multiperspectival judgment, as the following vignette illustrates.

My choice to pursue research with a homeless advocacy group emerged out of an unrelenting curiosity to learn more about a story I read about the group that would later become both rhetorical informants, research participants, and trusted friends. As a doctoral student completing my exams and searching for a research opportunity that aligned with my research aims and my political commitments, I read about SafeGround Sacramento in a New York Times *story that landed on my desk as part of the morning paper. After reading the reportage offered, I was left with the questions, "what's the rest of the story, what are these activists really like?"*

Three months later, after navigating unrelenting requests from the IRB, gaining access to the field, and making some initial visits to learn about the rhetorical scene, I went to Sacramento for the first of what would be several extended visits to observe, participate, and interact with the homeless activists who would inform my research. During my initial visits, much of my time was spent sitting with members of the homeless community listening to their stories. Often, these stories were tales of what were characterized as bad, sometimes criminal, choices that led to the reality of homelessness. In other instances, members of the homeless community (especially women who had found themselves facing homelessness) would share stories of abuse and sexual assault that had been escaped only to leave them on the streets struggling to start a new life. In still others, stories of bad luck explained why this community (that had allowed me into their inner circles of conversation, camaraderie and resistance) had found themselves struggling against their present circumstances.

Months later, as my time in the field began to near an end, I was confronted with challenges I had never anticipated when my curiosity led me to the rhetorical field. Trusted friendships and important informants had fallen victim to the precarity of life on the streets and were either missing, sometimes because they had found homes, sometimes inexplicably; or, worse, others had died from accidents, exposure, and other facts of the circumstances that defined their lives. The relationships we had developed had given me the most intimate of insider knowledge about their lives, their habits, their internal conflicts, their ambitions, and their flaws. Then, and now, I struggle as a researcher deciding what stories to tell and which should remain within the safety of their backstage, vernacular communities. And each choice is neither significant enough to undo their efforts, nor insignificant enough not to potentially impact their lives and their ongoing struggle (potentially, in the most material of ways).

On the one hand, I struggle with which stories to tell and which ought to remain in the field. For instance, many of the stories told to me by informants whose homelessness was a product of abuse often shared their stories and encouraged me to tell their stories because they viewed them as a way of undoing some of the prejudices against homeless people, as well as responses to the mainstream narratives that assign the fact of homeless to the poor life choices of those living on the street. Paralleling this, the stories of past lives that, if exposed, would cast a negative light on the new lives being sought and led by homeless activists, risk undermining the credibility of the movement. On the other hand, the events I witnessed ranged from those that aligned with the commitments of the movement and enacted the politics they proclaimed to those that revealed the humanity of my activists colleagues, who like rhetors of every stripe, are "rotten with [(im)]perfection."[57] *As with the stories told to me, deciding which stories to tell about my experiences and evaluating the consequences of those choices continues to be a sometimes impossible task. Underlying both sets of choices is the very real knowledge I gained of the, sometimes, life-and-death consequences faced by their homeless bodies-at-risk. Thus far, I have found myself focusing on the more public rhetorical practices in which they engaged, including their protest marches, participation in public meetings, and other acts whose publicity was part of the strategic decision-making of the activists. Amplifying the circulation of those texts certainly is consistent with both my academic and my political commitments, but I continue to be goaded by the stories that go untold and both the risks that are avoided and the ongoing precarity of the circumstances under which their ongoing struggle exists.*

Taking to the field and experiencing the embodied forms of struggle of SafeGround Sacramento certainly told a story that could not have been included in the coverage of their efforts that first sparked my interest, but deciding how to ethically and positively honor the relationships with and dialogues between myself and the participants to the movement continues, however, to challenge me as a scholar.

—Michael

Dialogue comes with several consequences for the act of rhetorical criticism, including revealing the contingent nature of rhetorical insights by exposing the network of interactions that inform a critic's perspective, decentering the critic's authority relative to other participants in a rhetorical scene, and privileging the influence of relationships on interpretive, evaluative, and other critical claims. As offered above, Michael's decision in retelling particular stories is guided by a dialogic spirit that occurs in the streets between his body and the precarity found within people who are homeless. Making a connection between critics' bodies and participants' bodies highlights the tensions and consequences of placing the critic in dialogue with others in the rhetorical scene. Jay Dolmage defines rhetoric as "what facilitates the communication and movement between bodies—our own bodies and those around us, our own bodies and the bodies we will become."[58] Participatory critical rhetoric escapes the ossified representations of rhetorical practices (texts) by focusing on the interactions through which those rhetorics are forged, thereby opening critical judgment into a material dialogue with bodies, elevating their voices into the act of criticism, and including information formerly unavailable to textual analysis into the research project. This analytical move does not take away the expertise of the critic; rather, the additional knowledge gained through these dialogic interactions, audience reactions, and member checking provides additional evidence regarding rhetorical effects and insight into judgment.

To be witness to these events, and especially to inquire into their rhetorical force, carries a great deal of responsibility on the part of the participatory critic. Many critics can escape the very real and dire circumstances—such as the persistent traumatic memory of surviving 9/11 or having to find a safe place to sleep on the street each night—that participants face, and great care should be taken when listening to their stories. Participatory researchers should take note of how narrative ethics enter the field. Tony Adams, in a recent review of issues pertaining to narrative ethics, asks researchers to "consider who is able to tell a story and who has the ability to listen."[59] In this sense, narrative ethics entail a reflexive examination of how listeners become implicated into the storytelling act. Both asking someone to reflect on their decision to advocate and listening to their account are moral and ethical acts. Carolyn Ellis remarks, "Listening to and engaging in others' stories is a gift and sometimes the best thing we can do for those in distress."[50] Moreover, the stories individuals may tell us become a part of the critical analysis, meaning that participatory critics will, in some form, choose to represent participants in fieldnotes and final write-ups or media projects. The ethics of representation certainly apply here as well. As Della Pollock describes in oral history research, "Entwining *what is* with the normative claims of *what might be*, oral histories tell the past in order to tell the future—not to predict, to reveal, or to foreclose on it but to catch it in ethical threads drawn in the act of telling."[61] Implicated into the act of speaking and listening, the dialogic critic brings together experience in the organization, the critical impulse, and the potentialities in collaboration toward emancipatory aims.

Similarly, as we outlined above, many rhetorical critics who have turned to participatory methods did so in order to augment existing textual practices. In other words, the voices of participants are included into the study through interviews and other recordings. This element of participatory critical rhetoric brings up additional concerns about the ethics of recording in fieldwork. Augmenting textual practices carries with it concerns about what should and should not be considered a part of the study. Given that participatory critical rhetoric explores critical *topoi*, it is likely that many of the individuals sought after for inclusion in a study will be from disempowered positions, such as the members of the homeless community Michael interviewed in his project. They may exist as subaltern counterpublics, whose voices have been actively excluded from the public discourse. For some, these voices are important given their status in history. They hail from, as Ono and Sloop suggest, historically oppressed communities and are often written out of history.[62] A concern for this textual extension, therefore, is whether or not they should be included into the larger textual framework of participatory critical rhetoric research. The goals, motivations, and desires of academic communities do not always coincide with the advocacy of out-law and vernacular discourses. Moreover, the circulation of elements of a counterpublic group and their tactical rhetorical approaches may actually do harm to their overall cause, or at least expose to a dominant public their rhetorical practices that could be misconstrued. As such, critics engaging such communities through participatory critical rhetoric must take great care in balancing the needs of each. Only through reflexive consultation and dialogue should a participatory critic bring to light those (counter)public groups that wish to remain out of public sight.

In this manner, participatory critical rhetoric follows the critical turn, drawing from Wander, McGee, and McKerrow, insofar as the critic is placed in the role of the inventor of a text suitable for criticism; however, participatory critical rhetoric extends this notion to say that audiences and rhetors are also placed in the role of critic-as-inventor as well. This turn is vital, as research conducted with those clandestine and out-law discourses may violate the spirit of their concealment. Moreover, the act of making public elements of the vernacular advocacy could be tantamount to speaking for others.[63] Through consultation with those involved, the participatory critic will learn about which texts are appropriate for critical reflection, which invites rhetors and audiences members to share the responsibility of critical invention. On the one hand, the invitation for contributing to the invention process is problematic; participants may wish to keep otherwise interesting details of the processes of advocacy private, thereby negatively affecting the outcome of the research endeavor. For Michael, the stories told and untold by those in the homeless community complicated his decisions on which to include and which to exclude in his academic write up. On the other hand, the inclusion of their voice may illuminate things that were not otherwise apparent and may support a more fundamentally materialist notion of the judgments arrived at through vernacular exchange, such as the interpretations of the National 9/11 Memorial offered in the opening of this chapter. When including the voices of participants, critics can keep in mind Linda Alcoff's notion of the "rituals of speaking" which "involve not only the text or utterance but their position within a social space including the persons involved in, acting upon, and/or affected by the words."[65] She encourages critics to examine the positionality of the speaker and the context of speech in relation to larger structures of oppression. In so doing, critics choosing to speak for others should "analyze the probable or actual effects of the words on the discursive and material context."[64] Participatory critical rhetoricians might find themselves studying particularly serious issues; taking the time to consider what the impact of disseminating participant discourse might be is a pivotal step in the consideration of ethics in the rhetorical field.

Parallel to this matter is the insider-outsider dilemma in ethnography.[66] A balance must be struck between these positions, not only for the sake of knowledge produced in the participatory critical rhetoric enterprise, but also in order to protect the interests of all parties involved. Reflexive positioning of the critic alongside participants can inspire moments of clarity about when to speak in journal articles about the experiences of advocacy, and when certain elements of fieldwork are better left in the field. Put another way, participants in participatory critical rhetoric research—these living texts—are a part of the critical invention process. Participatory critics must learn to discern which elements of fieldwork are not only suitable for criticism, but which are appropriate for inclusion out of respect for participants. This means not only inquiring ahead of time to determine which practices will be acceptable, but also working with advocacy groups to learn of their general media strategy. As a standard, any detail made public should be done so only in consultation with the group and with consideration of the material consequences of doing so.

IMPLICATIONS: GAINING MULTIPERSPECTIVAL JUDGMENT

Taken together, these three conceptualizations of participants provide entry points into gaining multiperspectival judgment. Augmenting rhetorical criticism with an embodied perspective that is accented by the judgments of local speakers and audiences can kindle theorizing about the processual character of invention. Judgments about how rhetoric is produced and received can be reflected upon through dialogic moments in the field. The bodies of participants are recognized as enmeshed with one another, intersubjectively performing, enacting, and interacting. The *telos* of the participatory critical rhetorician aims toward sustained participation in the rhetorical field, thereby simultaneously engaging in the immanent politics of the field while looking to elevate more voices into the critical act. Multiperspectival judgment in the field offers theorists and critics new avenues for expanding what we know about the process, product, and contest of rhetoric. Opening up critical judgment to include participant voices challenges previous conceptions of text and context, offering intimate interpretations and insights into the composition and reception of discourse. Accented with a commitment to the immanent politics within the rhetorical field, an embodied understanding of the critical enterprise, and the emplaced character of rhetorical exchange, critics who seek out multiperspectival judgment find themselves in a sustained engagement with the immediate concerns of audiences and rhetors alike. Adding to post hoc considerations of textual practices, the participatory critic becomes more intricately and relationally implicated into textual production and reception, allowing audiences and rhetors to comment on the process as it occurs. This collaboration between critic, audience, and rhetor recognizes the shared agency within rhetoric, noting the dialogic commitments each has to the other in the field. Ethically, this means that critics must not only consider their interactions with participants, they must also offer their identities and participation up for reflexive consideration, finding ways to account for the self in service of the other. Moreover, as a larger enterprise, the immanent participatory aims coupled with participant textual production calls into question the exercise of criticism and its outputs. Critics may see the value in producing academic works that fall more in line with the groups they study, such as digital projects, films, or other media.

In considering multiple perspectives in the critical act, participatory critical rhetoric intends to open avenues for developing both theory and method in the discipline. Certainly, our discussion here opens up new methodological considerations; however, innovative theories, developed from vernacular advocacy and organizations, can be developed by allowing participant perspectives into the rhetorical research project. Rhetorical criticism has a longstanding history of theoretical development from specific cases. Interacting with participants may develop new evaluative tools for examining the effects of rhetoric. Indeed, as Davis Houck concludes, "a return to engaging with real members of an audience might help us become better scholars of public rhetoric."[67] We believe that a more participatory approach can illuminate not only the audience reception of messages produced in immediate contexts, but may also reveal the processual character of message production, thereby engaging inventional practices in a manner not seen in recent theoretical efforts within the discipline. As we outline here, and describe in more detail in the next chapter, engaging with participants before, during, and after the production of rhetoric adds nuance, augments the critical project with multivocality, and crafts judgment through new perspectives on rhetorical practices that can enable a more robust accounting for the scope, effect, and influence of rhetoric.

NOTES

1. Rhetorical effect differs from rhetorical force, which we discuss in chapter 1. While force can speak to effect, insofar as the rhetor may be able to engage rhetorical force to have an impact on the speaker, force can also speak to broader influences of rhetoric. Effect, in contrast, is typically understood as occurring upon immediate audience at hand. For more on the nature of effect, see: Amos Kiewe and Davis W. Houck, *The Effects of Rhetoric and the Rhetoric of Effects: Past, Present, Future* (Columbia, SC: University of South Carolina Press, 2015).

2. Jim A. Kuypers, "The Rhetorical River," *Southern Communication Journal* 73 (2008): 350–8, doi:10.1080/10417940802429475. See also Kiewe and Houck, *The Effects of Rhetoric.*

3. Raymie E. McKerrow, "Critical Rhetoric: Theory and Praxis," *Communication Monographs* 56 (1989): 106, doi: 10.1080/03637758909390253.

4. Leah Ceccarelli, *Shaping Science with Rhetoric: The Cases of Dobzhansky, Schrödinger, and Wilson* (Chicago: University of Chicago Press, 2001).

5. Kiewe and Houck, *The Effects of Rhetoric.*

6. Ibid. See also: Carole Blair, "'We Are All Just Prisoners Here of Our Own Device' Rhetoric in Speech Communication after Wingspread," in *The Effects of Rhetoric and the Rhetoric of Effects: Past, Present, Future,* eds. Amos Kiewe and Davis W. Houck (Columbia, SC: University of South Carolina Press, 2015), 31–58.

7. Robert C. Rowland, "Purpose, Evidence, and Pedagogy in Rhetorical Criticism," in *The Effects of Rhetoric and the Rhetoric of Effects: Past, Present, Future,* eds. Amos Kiewe and Davis W. Houck (Columbia, SC: University of South Carolina Press, 2015), 61.

8. Kiewe and Houck, *The Effects of Rhetoric,* 14.

9. Robert C. Rowland, "Purpose, Evidence, and Pedagogy in Rhetorical Criticism."

10. See Kiewe and Houck, *The Effects of Rhetoric,* for an elaborate discussion of the nature of effect and influence. This debate is one that spans across the discipline.

In particular, they and their contributors respond to the stiff charges offered from political scientist George C. Edwards III about the lack of evidence in rhetorical criticism.

11. Herbert A. Wichelns, "The Literary Criticism of Oratory," in *Readings in Rhetorical Criticism,* ed. Carl R. Burgchardt (State College, PA: Strata Publishing, 2005), 22.

12. Danielle Endres and Samantha Senda-Cook, "Location Matters: The Rhetoric of Place in Protest," *Quarterly Journal of Speech* 97 (2011): 257–82, doi: 10.1080/00335630.2011.585167.

13. See Catherine R. Squires, "Rethinking the Black Public Sphere: An Alternative Vocabulary for Multiple Public Spheres," *Communication Theory* 12 (2002): 446–68, doi:10.1111/j.1468–2885.2002.tb00278.x.

14. Danielle Endres, Leah M. Sprain, and Tarla Rai Peterson, eds., *Social Movement to Address Climate Change: Local Steps for Global Action* (Amherst, NY: Cambria Press, 2009); Art Herbig and Aaron Hess, "Convergent Critical Rhetoric at the 'Rally to Restore Sanity': Exploring the Intersection of Rhetoric, Ethnography, and Documentary Production," *Communication Studies* 63 (2012): 269–89, doi:10.1080/10510974.2012.674617; Aaron Hess, "Critical-Rhetorical Ethnography: Rethinking the Place and Process of Rhetoric," *Communication Studies* 62 (2011): 127–52, doi: 10.1080/10510974.2011.529750.

15. Michael C. Leff, "Interpretation and the Art of the Rhetorical Critic," *Western Journal of Speech Communication* 44 (1980): 337–49, doi: 10.1080/10570318009374019; Michael C. Leff, "Things Made by Words: Reflections on Textual Criticism," *Quarterly Journal of Speech* 78 (1992): 223–31, doi: 10.1080/00335639209383991; Michael Calvin McGee, "Text, Context, and the Fragmentation of Contemporary Culture," *Western Journal of Communication* 54 (1990): 274–89, doi: 10.1080/10570319009374343.

16. Michael C. Leff, "Interpretation and the Art of the Rhetorical Critic," *Western Journal of Speech Communication* 44 (1980): 337–49, doi: 10.1080/10570318009374019; Michael Calvin McGee, "Text, Context, and the Fragmentation."

17. Davis Houck, "Of 'Very Few Men' with 'Unusual Gifts' and 'Acute Sensitivity'—Whither Wichelns, Black, and Zarefsky?" in *The Effects of Rhetoric and the Rhetoric of Effects: Past, Present, Future,* eds., Amos Kiewe and Davis W. Houck (Columbia, SC: University of South Carolina Press, 2015): 287.

18. John M. Sloop and Kent A. Ono, "Out-law Discourse: The Critical Politics of Material Judgment," *Philosophy & Rhetoric* 30 (1997): 54, doi: 10.1080/14791420.2015.1071309.

19. Barbara A. Biesecker and John Louis Lucaites, *Rhetoric, Materiality, and Politics* (New York, NY: Peter Lang Publishing, 2009), 3.

20. James Jasinski, "The Status of Theory and Method in Rhetorical Criticism," *Western Journal of Communication* 65 (2001), 260, doi:10.1080/10570310109374705.

21. James Jasinski, *Sourcebook on Rhetoric: Key Concepts in Contemporary Rhetorical Studies* (Thousand Oaks, CA: Sage Publications, 2001).

22. McKerrow, "Critical Rhetoric," 103.

23. Ibid, 101.

24. Kent A. Ono and John M. Sloop, "Commitment to *Telos*—A Sustained Critical Rhetoric," *Communication Monographs* 59 (1992), 48, doi:10.1080/03637759209376248.

25. Barry Brummett, "Some Implications of 'Process' or 'Intersubjectivity': Postmodern Rhetoric," *Philosophy and Rhetoric* 9 (1976): 21–51.

26. Rowland, "Purpose, Evidence, and Pedagogy in Rhetorical Criticism."

27. Gerard A. Hauser, *Vernacular Voices: The Rhetoric of Publics and Public Spheres* (Columbia, SC: University of South Carolina Press, 1999); Eric King Watts and Mark Orbe, "The Spectacular Consumption of 'True' African American Culture: 'Whassup' with the Budweiser Guys?" *Critical Studies in Media Communication* 19 (2002): 1–20, doi:10.1080/07393180216554; Phaedra C. Pezzullo, "Resisting 'National Breast Cancer Awareness Month': The Rhetoric of Counterpublics and Their Cultural Performances," *Quarterly Journal of Speech* 89 (2003): 345–65, doi: 10.1080/0033563032000160981; Karma Chavez, *Queer Migration Politics: Activist Rhetoric and Coalitional Possibilities* (Chicago, IL: University of Illinois Press, 2013).

28. This has led many researchers to take up media as a more nuanced way of representing texts or performances. See: Herbig and Hess, "Convergent Critical Rhetoric."

29. McGee, "Text, Context, and the Fragmentation."

30. Karlyn Kohrs Campbell, "The Ontological Foundation of Rhetorical Theory," *Philosophy & Rhetoric* 3 (1970), 97–108.

31. Some exceptions include: Mindy Fenske, "The Movement of Interpretation: Conceptualizing Performative Encounters with Multimediated Performance," *Text and Performance Quarterly* 26 (2006): 138–61, doi: 10.1080/10462930500517907; Mindy Fenske, "The Aesthetic of the Unfinished: Ethics and Performance," *Text and Performance Quarterly* 24 (2004): 1–19, doi:10.1080/1046293042000239447; Samuel McCormick, "Earning One's Inheritance: Rhetorical Criticism, Everyday Talk, and the Analysis of Public Discourse," *Quarterly Journal of Speech* 89 (2003): 109–31, doi: 10.1080/00335630308176; Phaedra C. Pezzullo, "Resisting 'National Breast Cancer Awareness Month': The Rhetoric of Counterpublics and Their Cultural Performances," *Quarterly Journal of Speech* 89 (2003): 345–65, doi:10.1080/0033563032000160981; Phaedra C. Pezzullo, "Performing Critical Interruptions: Stories, Rhetorical Invention, and the Environmental Justice Movement," *Western Journal of Communication* 65 (2001): 1–25, doi:10.1080/10570310109374689; Phaedra C. Pezzullo, "Touring 'Cancer Alley,' Louisiana: Performances of Community and Memory for Environmental Justice," *Text and Performance Quarterly* 23 (2003): 226–52, doi:10.1080/10462930310001635295; Peter Simonson, "The Streets of Laredo: Mercurian Rhetoric and the Obama Campaign," *Western Journal of Communication* 74 (2010): 94–126, doi:10.1080/10570310903466045.

32. Lisa Silvestri, "A Rhetorical Forecast," *Review of Communication* 13 (2013): 127–42, doi:10.1080/15358593.2013.789121.

33. Aaron R. Hess, "Rhetorical Ethnography: Engaging the Politics of Advocacy" (PhD diss., Arizona State University, 2008).

34. Pezzullo, "Resisting 'National Breast Cancer Awareness Month.'"

35. For an example of how participants' voices can inform a critical read of a museum space, see Roberta Chevrette and Aaron Hess, "Unearthing the Native Past: Citizen Archaeology and Modern (Non)belonging at the Pueblo Grande Museum," *Communication and Critical/Cultural Studies* 12 (2015): 139–58, doi:10.1080/14791420.2015.1012214

36. DeLuca and Peeples, "From Public Sphere to Public Screen."

37. Herbig and Hess, "Convergent Critical Rhetoric."

38. Patricia A. Adler and Peter Adler, *Membership Roles in Field Research* (Thousand Oaks, CA: Sage Publications, 1987).

39. Alice McIntyre, *Participatory Action Research* (Thousand Oaks, CA: Sage Publications, 2008).

40. Sloop and Ono, "Out-law Discourse."

41. Squires, "Rethinking the Black Public Sphere."

42. Kendall R. Phillips, "Rhetoric, Resistance, and Criticism: A Response to Sloop and Ono," *Philosophy and Rhetoric* 32 (1999): 96–102.

43. Ibid, 97.

44. Marilys Guillemin and Lynn Gillam, "Ethics, Reflexivity, and 'Ethically Important Moments' in Research," *Qualitative Inquiry* 10 (2004): 261–80, doi:10.1177/1077800403262360.

45. For an interesting discussion of the connectedness between body and voice, see: Joshua Gunn, "Speech is Dead; Long Live Speech," *Quarterly Journal of Speech* 94 (2008), 343–64, doi:10.1080/00335630802210385.

46. Daniel C. Brouwer, "ACT-ing UP in Congressional Hearings," in *Counterpublics and the State*, eds. Robert Asen and Daniel C. Brouwer (Albany: State University of New York Press, 2001), 87–109; Adrienne E. Christiansen and Jeremy J. Hanson, "Comedy as Cure for Tragedy: ACT UP and the Rhetoric of AIDS," *Quarterly Journal of Speech* 82 (1996): 157–170, doi:10.1080/00335639609384148.

47. Brett Lunceford, *Naked Politics: Nudity, Political Action, and the Rhetoric of the Body* (Lanham, MD: Lexington Books, 2012).

48. Trena M. Paulus, Jessica N. Lester, and Paul G. Dempster, *Digital Tools for Qualitative Research* (Thousand Oaks, CA: Sage Publications, 2013).

49. DeLuca and Peeples, "From Public Sphere to Public Screen"; Herbig and Hess, "Convergent Critical Rhetoric."

50. Hess, "Critical-Rhetorical Ethnography."

51. Karen Stewart, Aaron Hess, Sarah Tracy, and H. L. Goodall, "Risky Research: Investigating the 'Perils' of Ethnography," in *Qualitative Inquiry and Social Justice,* eds. Norman. K. Denzin and Michael D. Giardina (Walnut Creek, CA: Left Coast Press), 198–216.

52. DeLuca and Peeples, "Public Screen."

53. Aaron Hess, "Democracy through the Polarized Lens of the Camcorder: Argumentation and Vernacular Spectacle on YouTube in the 2008 election." *Argumentation and Advocacy* 47 (2010): 106–122.

54. Gunn, "Speech is Dead."

55. Daniel C. Brouwer and Aaron Hess, "Making Sense of 'God Hates Fags' and 'Thank God for 9/11': A Thematic Analysis of Milbloggers' Responses to Reverend

Fred Phelps and the Westboro Baptist Church," *Western Journal of Communication* 71 (2007): 69–90, doi:10.1080/10570310701215388.

56. Michael Holquist, ed., *The Dialogic Imagination: Four Essays by M. M. Bakhtin*, trans. by Caryl Emerson and Michael Holquist (Austin: University of Texas Press, 1981), 427.

57. Kenneth Burke, Language as Symbolic Action: Essays on Life, Literature, and Method (Berkeley, CA: Univ of California Press, 1966), 16.

58. Jay Dolmage, *Disability Rhetoric* (Syracuse, NY: Syracuse University Press, 2013), 197.

59. Tony E. Adams, "A Review of Narrative Ethics," *Qualitative Inquiry* 14 (2008), 180, doi:10.1177/1077800407304417.

60. Carolyn Ellis, "Telling Secrets, Revealing Lives: Relational Ethics in Research with Intimate Others," *Qualitative Inquiry* 13 (2007), 26, doi:10.1177/1077800406294947.

61. Della Pollock, "Memory, Remembering, and Histories of Change: A Performance Praxis," in *The Sage Handbook of Performance Studies,* eds. D. Soyini Madison and Judith Hamera (Thousand Oaks, CA: Sage Publications, 2006): 88.

62. Kent A. Ono and John M. Sloop, "The Critique of Vernacular Discourse," *Communication Monographs* 62 (1995): 19–46, doi: 0.1080/03637759509376346.

63. Linda Alcoff, "The Problem of Speaking for Others," *Cultural Critique* 20 (1991–1992): 5–32.

64. Ibid, 12.

65. Ibid, 26.

66. For a more elaborate and foundational discussion of gaining trust in these social settings, see John Lofland, David A. Snow, Leon Anderson, and Lyn H. Lofland, *Analyzing Social Settings: A Guide to Qualitative Observation and Analysis* (Belmont, CA: Thomson and Wadsworth).

67. Houck, "Of 'Very Few Men,'" 283.

Conclusion

Theoretical Contributions, Practical Considerations, and Unresolved Questions

Participatory critical rhetoric offers a theoretical supplement to critical rhetoric and consolidates contemporary research working to theorize rhetorical analysis of *in situ,* emplaced, and embodied rhetoric. In this regard, our effort to theorize a participatory approach to rhetorical criticism is not an effort to displace other approaches to critical rhetoric, or rhetorical criticism more broadly construed. Rather, our theoretical contributions emerge from our extended engagement with the critical considerations activated by rhetorical scholarship that focuses its attention on everyday, live(d), vernacular, and intersectional rhetorical practices that are accessed through fieldwork. Our articulation of the participatory critical rhetoric approach is informed by exemplars of rhetorical criticism that examine rhetoric as *in situ* rhetoric, as well as by theorizing critical issues related to materiality, bodies, place/space, judgment, and immanent politics.

Participatory critical rhetoric's first and most fundamental theoretical contribution is to expand the archive of rhetorical practices[1] available for critical engagement, including forms of rhetorical action that exceed the more conventional texts or textual fragments that constitute the traditional objects of critical rhetorical research. Drawing together critical resources from qualitative research, ethnographic practices, and performance studies, participatory critical rhetoric focuses on collecting, participating with, and analyzing the everyday, performed, embodied, processual symbolic acts that constitute emplaced rhetorics. By virtue of embedding the critic in the field, a second contribution of participatory critical rhetoric is that it opens the space to rethink critical praxis and the *telos* of rhetorical criticism through the lens of immanent politics. We contend that this rethinking of the critical rhetorician in relation to immanent politics repositions the critic as an engaged scholar who, in addition to producing traditional scholarship, also responds to moments when critical engagement can be extended through embodied actions in the field and through the production of an expanded range of critical products, including contributing to, or creating, rhetorical campaigns, documentary films, and other forms of digital media. Finally, participatory critical rhetoric privileges a participatory epistemology that opens the critic to the intersecting corporeal, affective, embodied, emplaced, and often fleeting dimensions of rhetoric that unfold in the everyday spaces of rhetoric. This approach is unique among other approaches to critical rhetoric in that it values field-based participation in moments of rhetorical invention and engages with the ethical and methodological challenges such engagements pose. Bringing a participatory epistemology to the study of rhetoric advances understanding of the relationship between text, context, rhetor, audience, and critic. Taken together, we contend that participatory critical rhetoric both nuances the insights to be gained from rethinking how critics approach the traditional objects of critical rhetorical analysis, and brings into focus an expanded range of rhetorical practices for critical analysis.

In this chapter, we consider in further detail the implications of participatory critical rhetoric for the practice of critical rhetoric more broadly, as well as some of the critical questions it provokes that demand further consideration by rhetorical scholars. In this respect, we view this chapter as an invitation to further theorization and dialogue. We begin by highlighting what we conceptualize as some of the central theoretical contributions that can be derived from our conceptualization of this critical approach. Then, we focus directly on some of the practical considerations that inform actually undertaking the critical and methodological practices of participatory critical rhetoric. Last, we consider some unresolved questions we encountered during our theorizing of participatory critical rhetoric and call for further discussion to address them.

THEORETICAL CONTRIBUTIONS

While we organize participatory critical rhetoric into considerations of politics (chapter 2), critical embodiment (chapter 3), emplaced rhetoric (chapter 4), and participants (chapter 5) for theoretical clarity, it is the synergy between them that underpins participatory critical rhetoric's theoretical and methodological innovations. It is this synergy that highlights that participatory critical rhetoric resists a set of neatly organized procedures for doing criticism, and instead offers perspective(s) that can help attune critics to the insights available and the challenges embedded in field-based rhetorical criticism. In this section, we highlight some of these synergies and the theoretical and methodological insights they generate. In doing so, our aim is not to offer an exhaustive summary, but rather to suggest that the considerations we raise throughout the book can separately and in combination offer the means by which to gain unique insights into embodied and emplaced rhetorics.

Critical Rhetoric and Critical Praxis

As we discuss in chapter 1, participatory critical rhetoric extends the aims of critical rhetoric in terms of its focus on demystifying the discourse of power and conceptualizing rhetorical criticism as a performance by the critic aimed at participating in and/or contributing insight to efforts to pursue emancipatory ends in relation to the discourse and materiality of unjust power relations.[2] It pushes further, however, the horizon of emancipatory praxis in critical rhetoric by re-envisioning the critical rhetorician as an activist-scholar informed by a sensitivity to the practice of immanent politics that "demonstrate our central roles in enhancing democratic life."[3] In doing so, it takes up Kent Ono and John Sloop's challenge to pursue critical commitments when one puts pen to paper and extends that imperative to the presence of the researcher in the context of rhetorical practices in the field.[4] In other words, critics can make important choices in the field that signal their commitment before they even start thinking about the written products of their analysis. Consequently, participatory critical rhetoric challenges the critic to embrace the possibility of doing rhetoric in the moment, in addition to doing rhetorical criticism after the fact.

We draw this distinction to highlight that reframing critical rhetoric through the lens of immanent politics requires that critics be mindful of the embodied, emplaced dimensions of the rhetorical practices they witness, as well as the consequences of their embodied presence and relationship with participants in the rhetorical scene. Chapter 4 offers a theorization of the critical considerations implied by venturing into the field and conceptualizing rhetorical practice in relation to its immediate place of invention. In doing so, it sensitizes critics to how all rhetoric is emplaced; that is, place/space contributes to the influence and consequences of everyday rhetorical practice. Likewise, chapters 3 and 5 highlight the importance of rhetorical reflexivity and dialogue as a means of both making critical and ethical choices about what dimensions of the embodied, emplaced rhetorical practices witnessed by critics are appropriate for critical analysis, as well as how participatory critical rhetoricians can make informed choices about how to manage their presence in and relationships within the scene of rhetorical practice. We contend that if part of the enterprise of critical rhetoric (and, by extension, participatory critical rhetoric) is sharpening the political edge and consequence of rhetorical scholarship, then participatory critical rhetoric makes two important contributions to critical praxis.

First, participatory critical rhetoric provides a means by which to ground its critical praxis within the lived realities of the rhetorical practices and cultures it explores. As chapters 3 and 5 articulate, dialogue with participants in a rhetorical scene and rhetorical reflexivity about one's presence in that scene can help critics better access *phronesis*, or the culturally- and spatially-bound rhetorical logics that inform everyday rhetorical practice, and, as a consequence, identify meaningful forms of intervention that might exceed traditional forms of scholarly productivity, such as the documentary films that Aaron co-produced. In the first instance, participatory critical rhetoric's engagement with emplaced rhetorical practices better enables the critic to approach rhetors in these contexts as "thinking, theorizing, [and] culture-processing human beings" who constitute alternative frames for critical judgment, as well as rhetorical and political tactics that often "fly under the radar."[5] This is significant because it identifies a means by which critics can draw meaningful, contextually informed conclusions about local, often-undocumented rhetorical practices. As our vignettes throughout the book demonstrate, there are a range of vernacular rhetorical practices that can be witnessed and analyzed through the participatory critical rhetoric approach. Michael's work with homeless activists in Sacramento, for example, not only focuses on letting homeless people speak for themselves, but allowed Michael, in dialogue with his participants, to theorize their rhetorical tactics of resistance. This theoretical perspective avoids the critical paralysis that is sometimes the Achilles' heel of critical rhetorical inquiry by encouraging critics to align their insights with the practical, rhetorical judgment (*phronesis*) of the participants with whom they interact. In this way, participatory critical rhetoric answers Stephen John Hartnett's call for critical scholarship that recognizes the "complexities and contradictions of the communities with whom [critics] work and play,"[6] and that "pledge[s] . . . to work for social justice and for personal growth, to be both radical in our demands and gentle in our demeanor, both outraged by inequality and oppression and joyous in our commitments to end them"[7] while working within those complexities and contradictions.

In the second sense, a critical praxis informed by immanent politics and tempered by rhetorical reflexivity and a commitment to a dialogic relationship with participants in a rhetorical scene enables critics to make choices about how their time in the field can be used to develop insight into the rhetorical practices they observe, as well as to participate in acts of rhetorical invention and advocacy to test those insights in dialogue with rhetors and audiences in the field. In her work with Skull Valley Goshute and Western Shoshone anti-nuclear activist groups, Danielle was able to demonstrate her commitment, engage in immanent critical acts, and offer modest help to these groups in the form of recording and archiving their events and conducting oral histories with members. Moreover, by participating within the rhetorical practices and cultures that participatory critical rhetoric examines, critics can gain access to materials that enable them to develop forms of criticism and critical praxis that are accessible to a broader audience than traditional forms of scholarly productivity, and that support the aims of the community with whom critics conduct their research. For example, the possibility to use interviews, artifacts gathered, and other performances and texts from the field to inform one's critical praxis opens the space to embark on forms of public scholarship, like Aaron's documentary film projects at the Rally to Restore Sanity and the National 9/11 Memorial, that both amplify and further disseminate the rhetorics one researches, as well as create new spaces for critics to take tangible, material steps to align their critical efforts with and in support of the communities they study and the participants with whom they form relationships.

Critical Embodiment and Critical Authority

In addition to helping inform the political investments of participatory critical rhetoric, chapters 3 and 5, in particular, address the role of critical embodiment and critical authority for participatory critical rhetoricians in relation to their embedded engagement with rhetorics in the field. By focusing participatory rhetorical critics' attention on their own bodies and research processes, rhetorical reflexivity aims to sensitize critics to the insights available via participation and envelopment in the varied dimensions of context (symbolic, material, environmental, etc.) that animate a field of rhetorical practice. In practicing rhetorical reflexivity, critics can contribute to Dwight Conquergood's call "to seek out . . . sites of tension, displacement, and contradiction between the Being There of performed experience and the Being Here of written texts."[8] We advance three dimensions of critical embodiment and critical authority that participatory critical rhetoric encourages. First, rhetorical reflexivity cautions critics about the challenges implied by the embedded critic's ability to both (co)construct the rhetorical performance, artifact, or text for analysis based on their observations and make critical judgments about that performance. Not only does this present the critic with innumerable practical challenges, as we discuss in the next section, it also raises epistemological questions about where the boundaries between text and context are to be drawn, how those choices inform the subsequent analysis, and how the stubbornly non-textual dimensions of rhetorical practice can be apprehended for critical interrogation. Samantha's work on the construction of place/space in Omaha highlights some of the challenges she encountered with doing research in her own neighborhood, calling for moments of reflexivity in relation to how she participated in and interpreted events. Specifically, she felt the need to be critically aware of how she documented her own experiences in her neighborhood and the places that have become rhetorically significant.

Second, by considering the affective body, our discussion of critical embodiment sensitizes participatory critical rhetoricians to the relational, (often) unsayable, experiential dimensions of rhetorical practice that can only be glimpsed by giving oneself over to the experience of being in the field, forming relationships with other participants in the rhetorical scene, and *doing* their rhetorical performances alongside them. In the vignettes throughout the book, each of us described moments where of affective force that made a difference in how we engaged with the field. Danielle and Michael, in their work with activists, both found themselves in positions where they privileged their embodied, affective responses to being in the moment and the immanent choices they made to do rhetoric, to hold signs and march along with their participants.

Finally, our consideration of critical embodiment addresses the question of risk, highlighting the ways in which critics risk themselves by engaging an embodied, participatory role in the field. We also discuss the risk the rhetorical communities take when they allow critics access to their rhetorical practice and, in doing so, grant critics representational authority over their identities and their rhetorical practices. Rhetorical reflexivity, we argue, allows the critic to engage these challenges by reconceptualizing critical embodiment as an invitation to reforge the "hierarchy of observer and observed into more of a partnership" that allows participatory critical rhetoricians to, following Conquergood, "do ethnography *with*, not *of*" the rhetorical scenes and communities we enter.[9] In Aaron's work with DanceSafe, he attempted to dialogue with ravers, to take risks in his own engagement, and to think carefully about the sensitivity of analyzing and representing aspects of the drug culture and participants in that culture at play in his fieldwork.

Chapter 5 extends this insight and situates dialogue as the means by which critics can navigate the risks and challenges of critical embodiment, as well as maintain ethical relationships with participants in the rhetorical fields we examine. Specifically, we argue that participatory critical rhetoric builds relationships with participants in the field that enable the decentering of the critic, thus opening space for multiperspectival forms of rhetorical judgment. That is, by conceptualizing participants as rhetorical actors and inventors of discourse, as well as dialogic interlocutors who can inform critical perspectives, relationships with participants help provide a refined, contextually driven form of critical insight that is difficult to access from texts alone, and that is vital to moving the relevance of critical praxis from addressing future audiences toward making immediate contributions to the rhetorical efforts the critic witnesses. Within these interactions, participatory critical rhetoricians can also gain firsthand knowledge of the nature of rhetorical effects from participants, thereby providing new evaluative tools within critical rhetoric. Moreover, engaging with participants as skilled rhetoricians and competent interlocutors enables the critic to more ethically navigate the boundaries of maintaining critical integrity, enacting one's political (and critical) commitments, and avoiding practices that might unduly harm or influence the participants with whom relationships have been built. For instance, as we discuss in chapter 5, it helps the critic to more responsibly discriminate between important and insightful rhetorical performances and logics and those interactions that might have good reason to remain backstage, vernacular, and/or outside the critical spotlight. This dimension of participatory critical rhetoric provides a means to be responsive to Kendall Phillips's admonition that scholarship often makes use of everyday rhetorical practices for the benefit of scholarship (and often at the cost of those rhetorical communities) by enabling the critic to coordinate critical praxis, critical authority, and critical (dialogic) ethics.[10]

Emplaced Rhetorics and Rhetorical Spaces

Chapter 4, informed by the immanent, reflexive, dialogic dimensions of participatory critical rhetoric, theorizes how the approach offers a reconfigured conceptualization of how place/space relates to rhetorical practice. Instead of interrogating the rhetoricity of particular places and spaces as has been thoughtfully pursued in rhetorical scholarship on place/space, we move beyond this to argue that it is important to recognize that all rhetorical acts are emplaced, meaning that place/space is not just relevant in the study of particular places/spaces, but in the study of all rhetorical invention. Being present in the field through participatory critical rhetoric is a particularly good way to have access to the emplaced character of rhetoric. We begin with Tim Creswell's argument that, "Place is produced by practice that adheres to (ideological) beliefs about what is the appropriate thing to do. But place reproduces the beliefs that produce it in a way that makes them appear natural, self-evident, and common sense."[11] Then, we highlight the means by which place/space is more than a backdrop for rhetoric. Rather, we consider how place/space participates in rhetorical fields as an actor in its own right, both exerting influence on the rhetorical invention it hosts, and even speaking back against the uses that are made of particular rhetorical places/spaces.

Specifically, chapter 4 draws together the dimensions of participatory critical rhetoric we articulate in the other chapters to theorize the intersectionality of embodied and emplaced rhetorical practice. Participatory critical rhetoric contributes to existing theories of intersectionality[12] by suggesting that fieldwork affords the rhetorical critic the opportunity to embody a number of participatory roles at the intersection of rhetorical forms that make up *in situ* rhetorical practices, which grants access to the materiality of intersectional experiences. Moreover, this attention to intersectionality reveals how the places/spaces of rhetoric are always in "conversation" with the rhetorical practices they host. For example, place/space can speak in ways that overwhelm the rhetorical enactments within them, as when the attendees at the Step it Up Rally that Danielle and Samantha discuss misread a protest event held in a popular place for arts and music festivals in ways that blunt, or even silence, its intended message. By the same token, place/space can amplify, debate, challenge, reinforce, and in myriad other ways alter, for better or worse, the effect and force of emplaced rhetorical practices. Specifically, participatory critical rhetoric can enable critics to gain better insight into the multifaceted ways that emplaced rhetoric occurs in interaction with the place/space with(in) which it happens. By being present in the place/space to encounter the affective, embodied dimensions of the rhetorical performance, critics can witness how audience members relate to the place/space and the performances staged within it, apprehend the ways in which the place/space acts rhetorically, and interact with rhetorical performances in the context of those spaces. Michael and Aaron's direct participation with the SafeGround and the Rally to Restore Sanity events not only gave them access to the rhetorics of place/space, but also allowed them to experience those rhetorics alongside the other verbal, visual, embodied, and aural rhetorical forms.

By introducing the concept of emplaced rhetoric to conceptualize rhetorical place/space as a significant participant in rhetorical situations, our argument adds complexity to the way rhetoricians beginning to experiment with field-based approaches engage with their research. It shifts place/space from a container for rhetoric toward an active part of the complex intersectional rhetorical experience. This resituates place/space as one of several fragments of meaning that represents a difference that makes a difference to rhetors and audiences. Additionally, it expands already robust efforts to theorize the rhetoricity of space by reading emplaced rhetoric through a theoretical frame of intersectionality that emphasizes the amalgam of factors that lend influence to shaping rhetorical performances and determining their effectiveness. In the next section, we discuss some practical considerations that both challenge and inform critics working on emplaced, situational, interactive, field-based rhetorics, as well as how critics working in these contexts can mobilize the theoretical contributions of participatory critical rhetoric.

PRACTICAL CONSIDERATIONS OF THE FIELD

While much of this book has been dedicated to the theoretical and methodological contributions regarding participatory critical rhetoric, we would also like to address the more practical considerations faced by critics who are considering taking to the field. In the following section, we provide a general set of guidelines that are organized into sections that address challenges that arise before, during, and after fieldwork (while recognizing that there can be overlap between these phases). To be clear, these guidelines are derived from our own experiences, which we consider to be robust; however, they are not exhaustive, and nor are they prescriptive. There are a number of other sources that can augment preparation for a project that uses participatory critical rhetoric, including those scholars doing work in ethnography or performance ethnography, participant observation in the qualitative tradition, and others in critical rhetoric.[13]

Before Fieldwork

Finding a relevant scene to conduct fieldwork can be a wonderfully organic process. The types of fieldwork that we have done began with personal interests, hobbies, and fortuitous opportunities for political engagement encountered in the newspaper. To find a scene, we advise that critics first take stock of their political commitments and interests. As we discuss in chapter 2, participatory critical rhetoric engages the immanent politics of vernacular everyday discourses. Participating within these discourses might entail the direct performance of them. To be politically unaligned within these groups could be difficult for some critics or even unethical in practice, an issue we take up below. That said, advocacy work is messy; critics may agree with the overall message and *telos* of a particular cause, but find specific tactics uncomfortable. Still, we encourage critics to seek out causes to which they can dedicate their time passionately. Additionally, participatory critical rhetoricians should consider the difficulty in gaining access to particular counterpublic groups because of the types of enclaving that can occur, or because certain groups may desire to remain hidden from public sight. As we address in chapter 3, specific causes or groups may call into question the critic's subjectivity, identity, and body. In this sense, taking stock through rhetorical reflexivity is a critical praxis that is always occurring, and, importantly, begins before one enters or engages a rhetorical field.

Time is also a challenge within new participatory critical rhetoric projects. Long-term engagement within a group can lead to a rich understanding of a community and intimate relationships with its members. For example, Aaron spent two years working with DanceSafe, attending every rave and planning meeting. Similarly, Michael embedded with a homeless population for several weeklong periods over the course of eighteen months. While not as long term, Samantha's fieldwork in Zion National Park and Peter Simonson's participation in a 12-day political campaign in South Texas likewise demonstrate how researchers can benefit from a full emersion into the cultures they study.[14] Conversely, some events are contained within specific moments, such as a one-time weekend protest event. These short-term events do not offer the opportunity for immersion in a group or culture, but a critic can experience the entire existence of an event, such as Art Herbig and Aaron Hess's examination of the "Rally to Restore Sanity," Danielle Endres, Leah Sprain, and Tarla Rai Peterson's examination of national Step It Up climate change protest rallies, or Phaedra Pezzullo's examination of toxic tours.[15] Alternatively, researchers can travel to a place to experience material rhetoric *in situ*, as Carole Blair, Greg Dickinson, Brian Ott, and Eric Aoki do.[16] All of these experiences are important to conducting rhetorical fieldwork, but yield different results and stem from different questions. When critics find a specific cause or question to pursue, they should also consider the level of commitment that they can sustain. As we explore in chapter 5, some forms of advocacy address life-and-death issues. Ethically, participatory critical rhetoricians should consider the devotion they can offer to the group. More pragmatically, some organizations may have a training process or a calendar of events that does not pair with academic schedules. Critics should attempt to follow the natural progression of the group, which provides important lessons in becoming a member. Moreover, as with the life cycle of any organization, some groups may be dying or dissolving, or may collapse during the fieldwork process. Advocacy work is often difficult to sustain, and critics who seek out a project should be concerned about the longevity of an organization and how the organization's stability might impact their field research or their research questions.

As critics identify a new group or situation, they should also consider the types of methods available and how each might change the outcome of a project. Given the nature of fieldwork, it is likely that participant observation will come into play in any participatory critical rhetoric project.[17] To supplement this, interviews, oral histories, documentary film, and focus groups are available; every choice in method alters the scope of the project and the nature of the voices to be included. To begin sorting these options, participatory critical rhetoricians should take stock of their own identity, ability, and training in each method. Focus groups, for example, require specialized training and structure to produce synergistic results and will typically require being conducted in an offsite space.[18] One-on-one interviews, by contrast, can be conducted either in the field or at another location before or after specific events in the research context. There are benefits and constraints in any choice. Conducting participant interviews in spaces outside of the rhetorical field, such as a university campus or through video conferencing, can be inviting to participants who may become more reflective through distance, or the space could be institutionally cold and uninviting. Selecting to interview participants in the field can lead to other difficulties, such as the (in)ability to record or other distractions that might occur during the interview. Samantha, for example, encountered trouble in finding a power source for a recorder when she visited an oral history interviewee on a rural Native American Reservation. Aaron also struggled with ambient noise at raves, leading to audio files that were difficult to transcribe.

Finally, when initiating a new project, participatory critical rhetoricians should work with their local Institutional Review Board (IRB) to gain ethics approval for the project. While relatively infrequent in rhetorical studies, gaining certification in ethics training and IRB approval should be a part of a participatory critical rhetorician's overall research program. Certainly, the mission of the IRB has been historically designed with biomedical models and more quantitative methods in mind. However, the approval process may highlight ethical considerations for the researcher as they conceptualize their approach. Typically, the IRB will require prior certification through a training workshop. Then, the specific project will require review before fieldwork or research interaction with participants can commence. Participatory critical rhetoricians will need to think through the many possible issues that might be encountered during their project, including the scope of involvement, types of questions asked during interviews, and overall duration of the project. These procedures may appear tedious, but are also helpful insofar as they ask fundamental questions about the project before it gets underway and often help critics avoid common pitfalls as it unfolds.

During Fieldwork

When in the field, the critic will need to make numerous decisions. Indeed, every rhetorical field will be different and have its own complications, and our accounting here is necessarily incomplete. Yet, we do offer some items to contemplate as the critic enters the scene. While prior method choices may dictate planning, in the process of fieldwork, critics must remain flexible as they may need to determine and revise their choices in the process of fieldwork. On the one hand, if the critic attends a specific event, the scope of participants is determined by who shows up to the event (which may end of being smaller or larger than what the critic anticipated) and the process of choosing who to interview will need to happen rather quickly. Being in the field will reveal unanticipated factors even in the most carefully planned proposal. On the other hand, long-term immersion in a community provides more opportunities for interviewing and the critic can marinate in the scene to become more informed about what is going on, thereby building rapport and finding key informants. Yet, even these choices of informants can limit access to other members of the community or have implications on how the critic is perceived in the field. Danielle, for example, found that her engagement with and reliance on the Skull Valley Goshutes who opposed a nuclear waste site on their reservation land as informants, limited her ability to later access other factions in the divisive Skull Valley community. Although her research plan assumed she would have access to all members of the community, during her fieldwork she had to adapt and make revisions to her method choices.

Interviews, both formal and spontaneous, help critics gather background information and enhance interpretations developed from participant observation. Critics will need to be assertive in finding individuals who can inform the project. Early networking with many people will open up opportunities for interviews or sustained participant observation. As many ethnographers know, doing fieldwork means meeting and remembering many people because every interaction is a potential moment for current or future data collection. When constructing an interview guide, participatory critical rhetoricians should consider the types of knowledge they would like to learn relative to the role of the participant. For example, Aaron interviewed DanceSafe volunteers and ravers to determine the types of inventive practices performed and how they were received, questions on the interview guide for ravers inquired about DanceSafe's central message and what ravers might do with the materials and education received from the group. Likewise, in their examination of a Step It Up climate change rally in Salt Lake City, Danielle and Samantha interviewed participants and asked them what the purpose of the rally was. Those interviews revealed that the audience of the rally had a very different view of the purpose of the rally than the organizers. We suggest that critics carefully craft interview questions with an eye toward language choices in the field, argumentative strategies, the rhetoricity of bodies, or the reception and evaluation of discursive materials. As we discuss in chapter 5, participatory critical rhetoricians are seeking multiperspectival judgment through the inclusion of these forms of participant voice. Asking the right question at the right moment becomes vital to gaining said judgment. Finally, while interviews can be conceptualized in a number of ways, we believe that they are best understood as conversations guided by a spirit of inquiry and empathy.[19] They are semi-structured in form, following the interview guide developed prior to (and perhaps adapted during) fieldwork, but they should naturally flow like a conversation and be responsive to unplanned insights that emerge during conversations.

In "collecting" these conversations, participatory critical rhetoricians can use audio and video recorders, always remembering the power of such devices in altering an interview. When recorded, formal interviews can lose their spontaneity, becoming more artificial and less organic. Skilled interviewers will be able to engage their interlocutors in ways that make the recording device disappear, forgotten while conversations are enjoyed. In other cases, the use of recording devices in the rhetorical field should be carefully contemplated. As we detail in chapter 5, these devices can spark emotion, incivility, or even exhibitionism. Some participants will shy away from the camera or feel silenced by it. For example, when conducting documentary film interviews with individuals near Ground Zero at the tenth anniversary of 9/11, Aaron and his colleagues were struck by how often people were brought to tears about the event, even though they had no direct connection to those who perished. The camera was able to access the underlying affective sensations evoked by being present at that moment and adjacent to the National September 11th Memorial. Similarly, using photography, Karen Stewart describes how attendees at the Burning Man festival expressed concerns about how photography changed the experience of the event from engaged participation to voyeurism.[20] Participatory critical rhetoricians must recognize the power of the camera, not as an objective recording device, but as contributing to the rhetorical field.

For many participatory critical rhetoricians, the lessons learned through participant observation provide embodied understandings that are difficult to ascertain from a traditional textual perspective. The affective nature of embodiment and being present cannot be easily replicated, as Blair discusses when she explains her disappointment at discovering that she would not be able to take a group to see and experience a museum.[21] The smells of the field, whether from coffee, the chemical sweat pouring from dancing youth, environmental toxins, or pizza at a protest event turned concert,[22] will likely never be forgotten by the participatory critical rhetorician or the audiences with whom they shared the event. Moreover, participating with audiences in the field engages the cognitive elements of rhetoric, whereby the critic must learn the localized, adaptive strategies that will be successful in a particular scene. Consequently, as we discuss throughout this book, these moments are vitally important for the critic to record and recall. Headnotes, scratchnotes, and fieldnotes should be developed and maintained throughout the project. When initially entering the field, participatory critical rhetoricians should record as much as possible, taking in every detail. Over time, they may find that focused interactions require sustained attention that concentrates on specific dimensions of the rhetorical practices they witness. In either instance, critics should quickly transcribe scratchnotes and headnotes into larger, fuller fieldnotes. This growing document can serve as a central text for analysis, which can be conducted periodically throughout the project. Participatory critical rhetoricians should also consider journaling about their experiences in a separate document so as to record the personal qualities of the embodied experiences.

All of these practices are ethically charged. As we discuss in chapter 5, there are a multitude of ethical issues activated when interacting with participants. Critics must necessarily occupy a liminal position, embodying multiple roles simultaneously, but typically have the privilege of knowing that a safe space is not far from them. Our participants may not have such luxuries. Rhetorical reflexivity, as we outline in chapter 3, requires that critics keep these elements of identity at the forefront of their minds. As we speak with and about our participants, we become politically involved with them and responsible for our representation of them in fieldnotes and in future writing. When interacting with participants, it is also possible to face what Marilys Guillemin and Lynn Gillam call "ethically important moments" in research.[23] These moments are spontaneous and unpredictable, such as when a participant reveals deep emotional pain regarding a topic, and they surface in many forms of qualitative research. In these cases, any response, whether acknowledging the pain, providing solace or counsel, or silence, has consequences. Although difficult to write up in an IRB form, these moments are a natural part of life, and require special attention in the context of participatory research. Guillemin and Gillam contend, and we concur, that researchers should be committed to reflexivity throughout the everyday experiences of research in the field, as well as afterward when those relationships begin to fade into memories as attention is turned toward crafting academic research from the experiences had by the critic.

After Fieldwork

Leaving a rhetorical field can be especially difficult. It is likely that a participatory critical rhetorician has been significantly affected and has developed profound relationships with participants. For projects that have clear end-dates, exiting can be relatively easy; the protest is over, or event concluded. In other campaigns that require immersion over months or years, exiting can be challenging. The more of a personal or political commitment that a critic has made to the community, the more the community may come to depend on the critic's presence in the everyday enactment of the campaign. To ease the eventual exit, participatory critical rhetoricians should signal their departure ahead of time, allowing for recruitment of others to occur if the campaign will need extra help. The relationships forged through the project might persist well beyond the direct fieldwork, although there may be moments where the friendships are in conflict with the researcher's academic responsibilities. Even with due attention to privacy and confidentiality, the public presentation of fieldwork can threaten relationships when details from the field are represented.

At this stage in a project, the participatory critical rhetorician may be ready to conduct a thorough analysis of the emplaced and embodied experiences of being in the field. As we argue in chapter 4, the emplaced character of participatory critical rhetoric directly contributes to the ways that we "read" the texts of the field. Clearly, being in the places of rhetoric affects the critic and his or her perceptions of rhetorical exchanges. Conversely, stepping out of these places distances the critic in ways that invite reflection. Data analysis often requires dedicated time for reflection that is away from the rhetorical field, meaning that participatory critical rhetoricians shift their status away from insider and back toward outsider. The specifics of data analysis will depend on the questions that guided the project and the researcher's skill set, but may draw from qualitative approaches, performance studies, media production editing, and the rhetorical tradition. Scholars may be surprised, though, at the amount of data they have to analyze. Working as an individual (as opposed to part of a research team) at an ephemeral event such as a protest may produce fieldnotes and interview transcripts that are manageable. However, working for an extended period of time with a research team can yield unwieldy amounts of data to analyze, as is the case in Danielle's current research on low-carbon energy technology scientists. Therefore, the process of rhetorical criticism may look different depending on the scale of the research project. Data analysis software such as NVivo can help scholars manage these large collections of data, organize research in systematic ways, and assist in identifying themes and other insights. Making use of these tools is especially helpful when the traditional practices of close reading are confronted with the broad array of textual and other forms of data, including audio and video that can be generated during one's time in the field. Regardless, throughout the process of analysis, participatory critical rhetoricians must be attuned to the *representation* of individuals, places, situations, and behaviors. The ethics of these representations will come into focus as the critic makes active decisions about what to include, and what not to include in the final analysis.

These ethical issues will continue to surface as the participatory critical rhetorician decides how to make the experiences from the field public. Whether a traditional academic monograph, digital project, art exhibit, archive, or documentary film, all outputs require reflexive examinations regarding what critics embrace and what they excise. When including tales from the field, participatory critical rhetoricians should balance what is theoretically salient with what may appear narratively compelling, or even sensational. Sarah Tracy shares this concern regarding her own fieldwork, and believes that ethnographers take risks (both in the immediate contexts and in terms of their critical essays) in offering sensational data in their essays, which may detract from theoretical contributions.[24] Participatory critical rhetoricians should also take heed of the purpose of exemplars or other stories in their essays or other outputs. Often these stories can command attention of the viewer or reader, but should also contribute to the theoretical elements of the project. In these moments, as we discuss in chapter 5, the act of telling and retelling oral histories or other experiences is politically and ethically charged.

If producing an academic monograph, rhetoricians need to be cognizant of the ways they present their research. As with publishing other types of rhetorical criticism, critics must be familiar with the conventions of the journal and write their essays to meet those specific expectations. Although it is not customary, participatory critical rhetoricians should be prepared to offer detailed accounts of themselves, their fieldwork decisions and details, and methods of data analysis. In our own published work, we have included such accounts in different ways from devoting several paragraphs to such details to only a few sentences to putting the information in footnotes, depending not only on the conventions and audience of the journal but also on reviewer and editor comments. In addition to attention to details about the research process, participatory critical rhetoricians should also consider authoring reflexive accounts that examine the relationships between self, other, and place/space. While not often seen in published manuscripts, these reflexive moments provide insight into the politics and choices made in the field. These conscious choices during the writing process should be approached with the same care as critics would afford to making decisions about any other part of the research process and should account for the political and ethical implications embedded in fieldwork. In each instance, there are no easy answers. We believe, however, that, informed by the ethical boundaries developed in dialogue with participants and a focus on the significance of the project, participatory critical rhetoricians can balance the ethics of representation they must navigate with the critical aims of their research agenda.

This brief overview of the practical elements of conducting fieldwork represents some of the most typical considerations a rhetorician would entertain when choosing a field-based project. Throughout the process, and indeed for one's career, reflexivity is essential. This not only informs the choices that participatory critics make but also invites alternative interpretations and ideas for future projects. As participatory critical rhetoricians begin to navigate these challenges, there are an abundance of resources that offer useful guidance, as well as generative insights.[25] In the next section, we turn our attention to the problems and possibilities of participatory critical rhetoric that continue to challenge us and other critics pursuing this approach to rhetorical inquiry.

UNRESOLVED ISSUES AND FUTURE DIRECTIONS

Although this book lays out participatory critical rhetoric as a comprehensive approach to engaging in *in situ* rhetorical criticism from a critical perspective, we recognize that it also opens new questions and areas that require further thinking. We do not intend our conceptualization of participatory critical rhetoric to be a constraint on continued theorizing about field-based rhetorical criticism, but rather a starting point that enables further discussion, modification, and development of not only this approach that is specifically aligned with critical rhetoric, but also of other forms of expanding rhetorical engagement with participatory, ethnographic, and qualitative methods. In this section, we lay out three unresolved issues in participatory critical rhetoric that would benefit from further deliberation.

Re-Centering Immediacy

Participatory critical rhetoric values presence, immediacy, and attention to rhetorical invention in its initial instantiation. As we note in chapter 5, the here and now matters in participatory critical rhetoric. It matters because even as the objects of study in rhetorical criticism have expanded greatly in the past decades, there still remains a strong dependence on written texts and reproductions. In other words, as we detailed throughout the book, contemporary rhetorical criticism relies heavily on analyzing after-the-fact documented texts as its window into the complex dynamics of rhetorical invention. These texts are removed from their immediate rhetorical situation, leaving it up to rhetorical critics to reconstruct it or ignore it, depending on their approach to rhetorical criticism. Reproduced texts are removed in time-space from critics, rhetors, fields, participants, contexts, and audiences. As Blair notes in her discussion of the differences between viewing reproductions of artwork and viewing an original artwork in a museum, "we must also remember the flattening effect of such reproduction—not just the two dimensionalizing of a place and its inhabitant artworks, but also the metaphorical 'flattening' of experience."[26] We extend this notion of flattening beyond artworks to the texts that are usually studied by rhetorical critics. While, along with Blair, we recognize the value in the analysis of reproductions, we also see value in (re) turning our critical attention to the moment before reproduction, the embodied and emplaced moment of rhetorical invention. As we argue throughout the book, participatory critical rhetoric and other modes of field-based rhetorical analysis run against the grain of most contemporary rhetorical criticism because of their emphasis on being there before the reproduction is made to observe and/or participate in rhetorical invention in its immediate rhetorical situation, to gage how "real" audiences respond to and cocreate rhetorical acts, and to understand the intersectional multimodal experience of rhetoric.

Participatory critical rhetoric's emphasis on the intersectional, material experience of rhetoric in its moment of invention could be seen as a problematic, perhaps overly romantic and nostalgic, return to a traditional mode of rhetorical criticism focused too narrowly on the rhetorical influence of a particular rhetor, an immediate context, and specific audience. Critical and cultural studies' influence on rhetorical studies have encouraged a turn away from the notion that we can or should examine completed texts, intentionality, and reconstructions of immediate contexts and audiences.[27] Further, reflection on the increased reliance on social media, sound bites, and public screens in contemporary culture shifts attention to forms of rhetorical criticism interested in dissemination, force, and circulation, often absent in any discussion of the rhetor and invention.[28] This reflection of the "death of the author" and focus on dissemination and remediation is significant because it tracks how rhetoric can take on a life of its own through dissemination that removes it from the intent of the author. It could be argued that a rhetorical text takes on more persuasive force in its broad dissemination than its immediate and original instantiation. Recall Aaron's vignette in chapter 5 about the rhetoric of the head of the Promise Keepers as seen through the eyes of a participant at a Promise Keepers' rally. While the speech itself in its immediate rhetorical situation was uninspiring, the dissemination and circulation of the text of that speech could still have strong rhetorical influence. Similarly, the judgment of a protest event in the moment may differ strongly from the dissemination of image events or sound bites from that event through the public screen. Even if the protest event itself is unimpressive or unpersuasive to an immediate audience, the dissemination of one key image could have rhetorical force that outweighs the impacts of the protest event itself. Some might argue that participatory critical rhetoric's insistence on examining rhetoric in its initial instantiation could over-privilege the embodied and emplaced elements of rhetorical invention and under-privilege a focus on the dissemination and unintended force of a rhetorical act.

We argue, first, that given the preponderance of analysis of reproductions in rhetorical criticism, there is inherent value in participatory critical rhetoric and other forms of *in situ* rhetorical analysis simply because they offer a different vantage point through which to understand the way that rhetoric does work in the world. This does not call for an end to analysis of reproductions, but instead calls for evening the balance of focus in rhetorical criticism. Second, participatory critical rhetoric's focus on examining rhetoric in its immediate, *in situ*, nonreproduced instantiation is not mutually exclusive with the "death of the author," dissemination, and social media. We are not arguing that dissemination, remediation, and circulation of rhetorical texts outside the initial instantiation do not matter. Indeed, these forces can be very persuasive. We are arguing instead that there is important knowledge to be had from the examination of immediate rhetorical invention. This information can be combined with investigation of dissemination, reproduction, and remediation for a fuller picture of the complexity of rhetorical experience. Analysis of *in situ* rhetoric alongside the remediation and dissemination of that rhetoric provides significant insight into the ways in which our everyday lives are appended to technology, media, and public screens. Further, as we discuss in chapter 4, the examination of virtual fields of rhetorical invention could allow for embodied and emplaced understanding of rhetorical dissemination in social networks. There is abundant space for more engagement with these topics and others that arise from participatory critical rhetoric's centering of immediate embodied and emplaced experiences of rhetoric over the analysis of reproductions and their dissemination.

Critics' Relations with Rhetorical Fields and Participants

Participatory critical rhetoric offers an opportunity for a different relationship with the artifacts that scholars study than conventional forms of rhetorical criticism that rely on already documented texts. In this mode of criticism, critics are closer to and sometimes even (co)create the rhetorical artifacts they analyze (e.g., interviews and fieldnotes). Critics also engage closely and personally with participants in the field who create the texts they analyze. The preceding chapters are a testament to participatory critical rhetoric's ability to expand the range of texts suitable for criticism, provide more access to vernacular and minor rhetorics that might not otherwise be documented, highlight the importance of reflexivity and dialogue in the critic's interpretation of their time in the field, and put critics in personal relationships with the rhetors and audiences they study. Yet, some might challenge how participatory critical rhetoric reconfigures the relationship between critics and their objects of study through participation.

First, the closeness and relationships that participatory critical rhetoricians develop in the field might raise eyebrows in terms of how those relationships impact the critic's analysis and interpretation of the texts that were built from the sometimes intimate and always personal experiences in the field. Further, when the critic contributes to the creation of texts in the field, then she or he becomes to some degree invested in those texts. These forms of personal closeness with rhetorical texts, while valuable, could also be seen as biased. Given the interpersonal attachments that critics feel as a result of their interaction and relationships in the field, it could be more likely to create biased—positive or apologist, for example—interpretations of the rhetorical practices brought back from the field. Admittedly, there is potential for critics to hedge their claims because they not only know and care about the rhetors personally, but they also know the implications a negative critique could have on the community. When critics have interpersonal relationships with rhetors and audiences, interact with them regularly, and appreciate their willingness to be studied, they might struggle with how to make arguments, especially critical arguments, about their rhetoric. The stakes of a highly critical interpretation are raised when participatory critical rhetoricians plan to or are asked to share their findings with the community. In contrast, the broader practice of rhetorical criticism often analyzes rhetors who are well known but unknown to the critic, such as rhetors at the highest levels of government or other people that the critic has little chance of meeting.

It could be argued, therefore, that performing criticism about someone who is not personally known by a critic would be less biased because there is no need to actually interact with that person at a later date. Although discussions about qualitative and ethnographic methods provide resources to address issues of negotiating the researcher role with the participant role, they are somewhat new to rhetorical criticism, a field that has not traditionally put critics in relationship with the producers of texts.[29] Yet, we would suggest that while there is potential for bias in participatory critical rhetoric, there is also potential for bias in more conventional rhetorical criticism of texts. Even though the critic does not know the producer of the rhetoric, there are still a variety of factors that could bias the interpretation. Indeed, we argue that there is always subjectivity and the potential for bias in any form of rhetorical criticism; recognition of that potential is crucial. Given the nuanced negotiations, engagement with rhetorical reflexivity, and conversations with participants in field-based rhetorical criticism, we contend that participatory critical rhetoric is better equipped to acknowledge and address potential biases.

Second, some might argue that more than just being too close to the texts they study, participatory critical rhetoricians may actually lose some control and expertise over texts and analysis when they yield power and authority to their participants. Indeed, in the process of fieldwork, critics may struggle with how to maintain control over their artifacts and analysis, and may find themselves surrendering some control to participants. We contend that, in the main, this sort of struggle is a benefit of participatory critical rhetoric; as we argue in chapter 5, multiperspectival judgment brings participants' perspectives and forms of judgment into conversation with critics' perspectives and judgment, which generates the potential for a more robust set of critical insights. Yet some may argue that ceding judgment and control to participants also makes the expertise of the critic nonunique. We, however, do not see an either/or proposition between multiperspectival judgment and critical expertise. Rhetorical critics still bring an important set of instruments to the field that are not undermined, but are rather strengthened by participation with rhetors and audiences. Rhetoricians will negotiate this in different ways and differences exist in the levels of critical control given to participants depending on the particular combination of critic, participants, and research context. We see this variation as a strength, not a weakness of participatory critical rhetoric. Within qualitative research, many approaches exist to negotiate power, control, and authority. In oral history, for example, shared authority is used to negotiate the relationship between the researcher and the interviewee in the interview text that is produced.[30]

Although these new relationships with texts and the participants who produce them may seem challenging, scholars who use participatory critical rhetoric see them as advantages because they allow for documentation of rhetorical situations that are otherwise excised from our understanding of rhetorical action and interaction. When critics examine after-the-fact rhetorical texts, they depend on reproductions, and therefore rely on whoever reproduced them to have done a thorough and ethical job forging that reproduction.[31] In participatory critical rhetoric, the critic is the one who collects, documents, and creates texts for analysis. Without participatory critical rhetoric, those events not documented by others would remain ephemeral and inaccessible. These issues represent some of the challenges that participatory critical rhetoricians face given their close proximity to rhetorical texts and participants. Further discussion would help to clarify and extend these themes in relation to participatory critical rhetoric.

Working with(in) Disagreement

As we theorize in chapter 1, participatory critical rhetoric is a particular form of field-based rhetorical criticism that is strongly aligned with a critical approach to rhetoric. In that chapter we argue that participatory critical rhetoric hinges on the critic's politics and advocates an activist-scholar stance in which critics engage alongside participants and, at times, put their research on hold to engage in immanent politics. This perspective, then, could assume that critics do research with communities that align with their politics and with whom they generally agree. This raises an important question about whether participatory critical rhetoric includes room for field-based rhetorical research with a community with which one disagrees. For example, Danielle's political commitments predispose her toward advocacy against nuclear power, but she is now engaged in a field-based rhetorical project examining the rhetoric of nuclear power advocates. How does this sort of project fall within participatory critical rhetoric's alignment with a critical sensibility? Similarly, if a critic believes that current immigration and border policies are socially unjust and inhumane, what are the implications of joining the Minutemen as a field researcher?

One of the more unresolved questions raised by participatory critical rhetoric is this: Can a participatory critical rhetorician study a group with whom he or she disagrees? This is a concern given that the participatory and immanence-oriented directives in the approach suggest that in the process of fieldwork, critics will find themselves in the position of being a part of the group, possibly advocating alongside the group, and engaging in on-the-ground forms of rhetorical action that support the group. This can be difficult to do and justify if you disagree with the fundamental goals of the group. Yet, there is also immense value in both openness to discovery and an ability to learn the perspective of another or multiple sides of an issue. While participatory critical rhetoricians often choose to embed themselves within rhetorical communities because of a political commitment or interest in that community, like all good researchers, they remain open to argument and change through the process of fieldwork. It is possible that the commitments that brought the critic to the field may change over time. It is possible that critics will be persuaded by what they observe in the field. And, indeed, to do good field research, the critic must not only remain open to these possibilities, but also be able to learn from and understand the community through its member meanings and practices. In other words, while critics inevitably bring commitments to the field and have opportunities to act on those commitments, they also bring research practices that seek to understand the community with whom they participate, even if those understandings do not conform to their initial commitments. There has to be a flexibility and openness in the field that allows the critic to undergo an evolving and dynamic relationship with the field, participant, and the critic's commitments. In this sense, it is always possible that the critic may begin in agreement with the community, but develop disagreement.

Moreover, there is value in learning and understanding another perspective. Classical rhetorical training included the *dissoi logoi* as an exercise in gaining a better understanding of an opposing perspective through learning about or actually advocating that perspective. While the *dissoi logoi* assumes two sides to an issue, we extend it to multiple sides, also keeping in mind that advocacy work is often messy. A participatory critical rhetorician may disagree with a cause, but agree with its rhetorical practices or performances or vice versa. The important point is that learning and participating in the rhetorical practices of an oppositional group with which the critic disagrees could also be seen as a crucial form of rhetorical engagement that is still aligned with the critic's political commitments. In understanding the perspective of another side, it is possible to better refute (or strengthen) oppositional perspectives. In that sense, critics who embed themselves within groups to which they are opposed are undertaking an important analysis of the strategies that sustain structures of control and oppression. Or, the *dissoi logoi* can also lead to developing shared starting points for discussion and debate that might not have otherwise been recognized, expanding the possibility of conflict resolution between the opposing sides. To be clear, we believe that participatory critical rhetoric should be used in instances that can advance understanding and conflict resolution in ethical ways; we do not advocate that participatory critical rhetoricians approach opposing groups with a spirit of sabotage. As a *participatory* approach, it calls on its practitioners to engage, and not actively obstruct, the efforts of groups that extend their trust in allowing critics into their rhetorical cultures. That said, the dialogic character of the approach could invite new interpretations of the group under investigation. In other words, engaging in dialogue, not damage or disruption, with participants is consistent with the immanent political aims found in participatory critical rhetoric.

This discussion of whether participatory critical rhetoric works in a community with which the critic disagrees may also lead into a related question of whether participatory critical rhetoric is an inherently left-leaning form of scholarship because of its reliance on the critical turn's focus on emancipatory politics and unmasking oppression. The critical turn in rhetorical studies has emphasized the analysis of vernacular rhetorics of resistance with a goal of intervening (in some small way) into discourses of oppression and domination. One of the appeals of participatory rhetoric is the ability to access minor and vernacular rhetorics that are usually left out of the official accounts of those in power. Further, our advocacy of activist-scholarship and immanent politics implies that the participatory critical rhetorician is working toward a conception of social justice that runs against the grain of dominant, oppressive logics. To some, this implies that it is only leftist political commitments that can be aligned with a participatory critical rhetoric project. Without falling into a relativistic trap, is it possible to argue that there are movements on the right that not only resist dominant norms, but also espouse adherence to social justice? In discussing this vexing issue among ourselves, we quickly agreed that it would be possible for someone from the right-wing to engage in participatory critical rhetoric based on an assumption that the critic would embed with a community with which he or she agrees, thus avoiding what we thought was the more difficult question of embedding with an oppositional community. However, perhaps we dismissed that topic too quickly and it would be worthy of more discussion. Ultimately, we do not have a neat resolution to this issue, but call on future practitioners to continue this conversation to better nuance our discussion of the role that the political commitments of the critic play in relation to the political commitments of the community under study.

PARTICIPATORY CRITICAL RHETORIC: FUTURE DIRECTIONS

In this chapter, we articulated the contributions participatory critical rhetoric makes to rhetorical theory and methodology, presented some of the practical considerations of fieldwork, and highlighted unresolved issues that invite future discussions and theorization. We suggest that participatory critical rhetoric provides new ways of advancing critical rhetoric and pushes critics to answer the challenges of this project. By becoming sensitized to multiple perspectives, critics can also more fully engage in reflexivity. Additionally, we build theories of material intersectionality by advancing the idea of embodied and emplaced rhetorics. Choosing to engage in fieldwork means that critics should consistently orient themselves to the ethical challenges of their research engagements before, during, and after participant-observations and interviews. And, finally, although participatory critical rhetoric could be seen as a romantic return to concerns of the specific effects for a specific audience, a problematic reconfiguring of the relationship between critics, texts, and participants, or an approach that excludes the possibility of studying groups with which one disagrees, we contend that the ability to gain multiple perspectives and document ephemeral situations is worthwhile. We emphasize that our efforts with this book have been aimed at theorizing the foundational concepts already being experimented with by critics who utilize emergent forms of field-based rhetorical study. In this way, this book recognizes the productive and difficult work that scholars have been doing for more than a decade and contributes to a theoretical conversation about this work directly.

We open this book by briefly describing some of the rhetorical situations that reflect a participatory critical rhetorical approach, and we deploy vignettes throughout the text in an effort to ground rhetorical theories in *phronetic* experiences. To understand place construction and embodied practices that build some cultures and resist others, we felt compelled to participate in protests; observe dancing, conversations, and hiking; go into people's homes (of all sorts) and talk with them about not only the rhetorical strategies that they invent, but also about their daily lives and struggles for the causes they both support and live. For our participants, and for us, these constructions matter. Social oppressions and opportunities have come into being through embodied and emplaced rhetoric. And, we approached these projects with curiosity about people, places, and practices. Our understanding has been and continues to be that rhetoric is more than words on the page; our desire is to be there at the site of rhetorical invention, performance, and dissemination. We wanted to see the moments when thoughts become words and actions, and, indeed, we wanted to say (and sing) those words and participate in those actions ourselves, to feel what our participants felt. For us, constituting reality happens through documents, but it also happens in a thousand other ways, some of which we are trying to understand through participatory critical rhetoric.

At the heart of this book is at once a call to action—urging critics to embrace embodied and emplaced rhetorics by engaging *in situ* rhetoric—but also a caution—urging critics to consider the foundations and consequences of our critical choices before rushing into the field. We appreciate and admire the critics who have blazed a path and dared to challenge conventional forms of text-based rhetorical criticism by integrating field-based experiences into their own work. We use their insights throughout this book as the warrants and grounds for our claims. Our call to action is not simply that more rhetorical critics take up participatory critical rhetoric, but rather we challenge rhetorical theorists to recognize what participatory critical rhetoric reveals about the foundations of our discipline. We ask critics to consider topics such as materiality and reflexivity as they go forward with their projects. And, of course, we invite conversation and debate about these topics. Through these discussions, we begin the process of reflecting about our commitments and conceits in the field. As Dwight Conquergood observes, "It is ironic that the discipline of communication has been relatively unreflexive about the rhetorical construction of its own disciplinary authority."[32] Participatory critical rhetoric addresses this criticism in relation to rhetorical criticism generally, and (field-based) critical rhetoric specifically. At the same time, it highlights how critical rhetoric's commitments can be used to examine the nature of rhetoric as a discipline, as well as how it can be deployed in ways that encourage critics to apply to themselves the same critical eye they bring to the rhetorical practices they examine.

As we are sure as has happened with many other critics, we have been inspired and outraged by our experiences in the field. Instead of pushing those emotions to the side, we have wondered where they came from and sought answers through rhetorical criticism. While we may integrate the tools of other bodies of research, we are grounded in and indebted to rhetorical criticism. Through participatory critical rhetoric, scholars can access places and people formerly unavailable through the textocentric model that informs much rhetorical scholarship, they can extend the politics set forth by critical rhetoric, and they can understand their embodied roles in the critical process, experience emplaced rhetoric, and engage in multiperspectival judgment. In this respect, it opens new theoretical opportunities for and sustains the impulse of rhetoric's critical turn to use rhetoric in the service of challenging discourses and practices that sustain unjust power relations, as well as sharpening the sometimes marginalized rhetorical practices that seek out new forms of freedom.

NOTES

1. Pierre Bourdieu, *Outline of a Theory of Practice*, trans. Richard Nice (Cambridge, University of Cambridge Press, 1977 [1972]); Michel de Certeau, *The Practice of Everyday Life*, trans. Steven Rendall (Berkeley: University of California Press, 1984); Michel de Certeau, Luce Giard, and Pierre Mayol, *The Practice of Everyday Life, Volume 2: Living and Cooking*, trans. Timothy J. Tomasik (Minneapolis: University of Minnesota Press, 1998); Kevin DeLuca, "Articulation Theory:

A Discursive Grounding for Rhetorical Practice," *Philosophy and Rhetoric* 32 (1999): 334–48; Elizabeth Fleitz, "Cooking Codes: Cookbook Discourses as Women's Rhetorical Practices," *Present Tense: A Journal of Rhetoric in Society* 1, (2010): 1–8; Marouf Hasian, Jr., "Communication Law as a Rhetorical Practice: A Case Study of the Masses Decision," *Communication Law & Policy* 1 (1996): 497–532, doi: 10.1080/10811689609368614; Phaedra C. Pezzullo, *Toxic Tourism: Rhetorics of Pollution, Travel, and Environmental Justice* (Tuscaloosa: University of Alabama Press, 2009); Robert Stephen Reid, "Faithful Preaching: Preaching Epistemes, Faith Stages, and Rhetorical Practice," *Journal of Communication and Religion* 21 (1998): 164–99; Samantha Senda-Cook, "Rugged Practices: Embodying Authenticity in Outdoor Recreation," *Quarterly Journal of Speech* 98, (2012): 129–52, doi:10.1080/00335630.2012.663500.

2. Raymie McKerrow, "Critical Rhetoric: Theory and Praxis," *Communication Monographs* 56 (1989): 91–92, doi:10.1080/03635639109383945.

3. Stephen John Hartnett, "Communication, Social Justice, and Joyful Commitment," *Western Journal of Communication* 74 (2010): 75, doi: 10.1080/10570310903463778

4. Kent A. Ono and John M. Sloop, "Commitment to Telos–A Sustained Critical Rhetoric," *Communications Monographs* 59 (1992): 48–60, doi: 10.1080/03637759209376248.

5. E. Patrick Johnson, *Appropriating Blackness: Performance and the Politics of Authenticity* (Durham: Duke University Press, 2003), 10.

6. Hartnett, "Communication, Social Justice, and Joyful Commitment," 78.

7. Ibid., 71–75.

8. Dwight Conquergood, "Rethinking Ethnography: Towards a Critical Cultural Politics," *Communication Monographs* 58 (1991): 193, doi:10.1080/03637759109376222.

9. Dwight Conquergood, "Book Reviews: Ethnography, Rhetoric, and Performance," *Quarterly Journal of Speech*, 78 (1992): 87.

10. Kendall R. Phillips, "Rhetoric, Resistance, and Criticism: A Response to Sloop and Ono," *Philosophy and Rhetoric* 32 (1999): 96–102.

11. Tim Cresswell, *In Place/Out of Place: Geography, Ideology, and Transgression* (Minneapolis: University of Minnesota Press, 1996), 16.

12. Darrel Enck-Wanzer, "Trashing the System: Social Movement, Intersectional Rhetoric, and Collective Agency in the Young Lords Organization's Garbage Offensive," *Quarterly Journal of Speech* 92 (2006): 174–201, doi:10.1080/00335630600816920; Elinor Light, "The (Em)Placed Vernacular: Rhetorics of Control and Transgression in the American City." PhD diss., University of Utah, 2015.

13. Robert M. Emerson, Rachel I. Fretz, and Linda L. Shaw, *Writing Ethnographic Fieldnotes*, 2nd ed. (Chicago, University of Chicago Press, 2011); H. L. Goodall, Jr., *Writing Qualitative Inquiry: Self, Stories, and Academic Life* (Walnut Creek, CA: Left Coast Press, Inc., 2008); Thomas R. Lindlof and Bryan C. Taylor, *Qualitative Communication Research Methods*, 3rd ed. (Los Angeles: Sage Publications, 2011); John Lofland, David Snow, Leon Anderson, and Lyn H. Lofland, *Analyzing Social Settings: A Guide to Qualitative Observation and Analysis*, 4th ed. (Belmont, CA: Wadsworth, 2006); D. Soyini Madison, *Critical Ethnography: Method, Ethics, and Performance*

(Thousand Oaks, CA: Sage Publications, 2011); Barbara W. Sommer and Mary Kay Quinlan, *The Oral History Manual* (Walnut Creek, CA: AltaMira Press, 2002); Sarah J. Tracy, *Qualitative Research Methods: Collecting Evidence, Crafting Analysis, Communicating Impact* (Malden, MA: Wiley-Blackwell, 2013).

14. Samantha Senda-Cook, "Rugged Practices"; Samantha Senda-Cook, "Materializing Tensions: How Maps and Trails Mediate Nature," *Environmental Communication: A Journal of Nature and Culture* 7 (2013): 355–71, doi:10.1080/17524032.2013.792854; Peter Simonson, "The Streets of Laredo: Mercurian Rhetoric and the Obama Campaign," *Western Journal of Communication* 74 (2010): 94–126, doi:10.1080/10570310903466045.

15. Danielle Endres, Leah Sprain, and Tarla Rai Peterson eds., *Social Movement to Address Climate Change: Local Steps for Global Action* (Amherst, NY: Cambria Press, 2009); Herbig and Hess, "Convergent Critical Rhetoric;" Phaedra C. Pezzullo, *Toxic Tourism: Rhetorics of Pollution, Travel, and Environmental Justice*. 1st ed. (Tuscaloosa: University of Alabama Press, 2007).

16. Carole Blair, "Reflections on Criticism and Bodies: Parables from Public Places," *Western Journal of Communication* 65 (2001): 271–94, doi: 10.1080/10570310109374706; Carole Blair, Marsha S. Jeppeson, and Enrico Pucci Jr., "Public Memorializing in Postmodernity: The Vietnam Veterans Memorial as Prototype," *Quarterly Journal of Speech* 77 (1991): 263–88, doi: 10.1080/00335639109383960; Greg Dickinson, "Memories for Sale: Nostalgia and the Construction of Identity in Old Pasadena," *Quarterly Journal of Speech* 83 (1997): 1–27, doi: 10.1080/00335639709384169; Greg Dickinson, "Joe's Rhetoric: Finding Authenticity at Starbucks," *Rhetoric Society Quarterly* 32 (2002): 5–27, doi: 10.1080/02773940209391238; Greg Dickinson, Brian L. Ott, and Eric Aoki, "Memory and Myth at the Buffalo Bill Museum," *Western Journal of Communication* 69 (2005): 85–108, doi: 10.1080/10570310500076684; Greg Dickinson, Brian L. Ott, and Eric Aoki, "Spaces of Remembering and Forgetting: The Reverent Eye/I at the Plains Indian Museum," *Communication and Critical/Cultural Studies* 3 (2006): 27–47, doi: 10.1080/14791420500505619.

17. Carol A. Bailey, *A Guide to Qualitative Field Research*. 2nd ed. (Thousand Oaks, CA: Sage Publications, 2006).

18. Linda C. Lederman, *Focus Group Research Manual* (New Brunswick, NJ: Center for Communication and Health Issues, 2006). See also: Edward F. Fern, *Advanced Focus Group Research* (Thousand Oaks, CA: Sage Publications, 2001).

19. Steinar Kvale, *InterViews: An Introduction to Qualitative Research Interviewing* (Thousand Oaks, CA: Sage Publications, 1996); Lindlof, and Taylor, *Qualitative Communication Research Methods*.

20. Karen Ann Stewart, "In Dust We Trust: A Narrative Journey into the Communal Heart of Public Art at the Burning Man Festival" (PhD diss., Arizona State University, 2010).

21. Blair, "Reflections on Criticism and Bodies."

22. Dickinson, "Joe's Rhetoric"; Endres et al., "Step What Up?"; Aaron Hess, "Critical-Rhetorical Ethnography: Rethinking the Place and Process of Rhetoric," *Communication Studies* 62 (2011): 127–52, doi:10.1080/10510974.2011.529750; Pezzullo, *Toxic Tourism*.

23. Marilys Guillemin and Lynn Gillam, "Ethics, Reflexivity, and 'Ethically Important Moments' in Research," *Qualitative Inquiry* 10 (2004): 261–80, doi:10.1177/1077800403262360.

24. Karen A. Stewart, Aaron Hess, Sarah J. Tracy, and H. L. Goodall, Jr., "Risky Research: Investigating the 'Perils' of Ethnography," in *Qualitative Inquiry and Social Justice: Toward a Politics of Hope*, eds. Norman K. Denzin and Michael D. Giardina. (Walnut Creek, CA: Left Coast Press, 2009), 198–218.

25. See footnote 13 for some texts useful when navigating the practical questions raised by participatory critical rhetorical research.

26. Blair, "Reflections on Criticism and Bodies," 275.

27. Michael Calvin McGee, "Text, Context, and the Fragmentation of American Culture," *Western Journal of Communication* 54 (1990): 274–89, doi:10.1080/10570319009374343.

28. Kevin Michael DeLuca and Jennifer Peeples, "From Public Sphere to Public Screen: Democracy, Activism, and the 'Violence' of Seattle," *Critical Studies in Media Communication* 19 (2002): 125–51, doi:10.1080/07393180216559; Kevin DeLuca, Sean Lawson, and Ye Sun, "Occupy Wall Street on the Public Screens of Social Media: The Many Framings of the Birth of a Protest Movement," *Communication, Culture & Critique* 5 (2012): 483–509, doi:10.1111/j.1753–9137.2012.01141.x.

29. Lindlof and Taylor, *Qualitative Communication Research Methods*; Lofland, et al., *Analyzing Social Settings.*

30. Michael Frisch, *A Shared Authority: Essays on the Craft and Meaning of Oral and Public History* (Albany: State University of New York Press, 1990).

31. See, for example, Black's discussion of how historical Native American texts may not have been accurately translated. Jason Edward Black, "Native Authenticity, Rhetorical Circulation, and Neocolonial Decay: The Case of Chief Seattle's Controversial Speech," *Rhetoric & Public Affairs* 15 (2012): 635–45, doi: 10.1353/rap.2012.004.

32. Conquergood, "Rethinking Ethnography," 193.

Bibliography

Achter, Paul. "Unruly Bodies: The Rhetorical Domestication of Twenty-First-Century Veterans of War." *Quarterly Journal of Speech* 96 (2010): 46–68, doi: 10.1080/00335630903512697.

Ackerman, John M., and David J. Coogan, eds. *The Public Work of Rhetoric: Citizen-Scholars and Civic Engagement.* Columbia: University of South Carolina Press, 2010.

Adams, Tony E. "A Review of Narrative Ethics." *Qualitative Inquiry* 14 (2008): 175–94, doi:10.1177/1077800407304417.

Adler, Patricia A., and Peter Adler. *Membership Roles in Field Research.* Thousand Oaks, CA; Sage Publications, 1987.

Alcoff, Linda. "The Problem of Speaking for Others." *Cultural Critique* 20 (1991–1992): 5–32, doi: 10.2307/1354221.

Alexander, Bryant Keith. "Fading, Twisting, and Weaving: An Interpretive Ethnography of the Black Barbershop as Cultural Space." *Qualitative Inquiry* 9 (2003): 105–28, doi:10.1177/1077800402239343.

Alexander, Bryant Keith. "Performance Ethnography: The Reenacting and Inciting of Culture." *The Sage Handbook of Qualitative Research* 3 (2005): 411–42.

Alexander, Bryant Keith. *Performing Black Masculinity: Race, Culture, and Queer Identity.* Lanham, MD: AltaMira Press, 2006.

Andersen, Peter. "Beyond Criticism: The Activist Turn in the Ideological Debate." *Western Journal of Communication* 57 (1993): 247–56, doi: 10.1080/10570319309374447.

Asen, Robert, and Daniel C. Brouwer, eds. *Counterpublics and the State.* Albany: SUNY Press, 2001.

Bailey, Carol A. *A Guide to Qualitative Field Research.* 2nd ed. Thousand Oaks, CA: Sage Publications, 2006.

Benjamin, Walter. "The Work of Art in the Age of Mechanical Reproduction." In *Illuminations: Essays and Reflections*, edited by Hannah Arendt, translated by Harry Zohn, 217–54. New York: Schocken Books, 1969.

Bennett, Tony. *Critical Trajectories*. Malden, MA: Blackwell Publishing Ltd., 2007.

Biesecker, Barbara A., and John Louis Lucaites. *Rhetoric, Materiality, & Politics*. New York: Peter Lang Publishing, 2009.

Biesecker, Barbara. "Michel Foucault and the Question of Rhetoric." *Philosophy & Rhetoric* 25 (1992): 351–64.

Bitzer, Lloyd F. "The Rhetorical Situation." *Philosophy & Rhetoric* 1 (1968): 1–14.

Black, Edwin. *Rhetorical Criticism: A Study in Method.* Madison: University of Wisconsin Press, 1978.

Black, Jason Edward. "Native Authenticity, Rhetorical Circulation, and Neocolonial Decay: The Case of Chief Seattle's Controversial Speech." *Rhetoric & Public Affairs* 15 (2012): 635–45, doi: 10.1353/rap.2012.0041.

Blair, Carole, and Neil Michel. "Reproducing Civil Rights Tactics: The Rhetorical Performances of the Civil Rights Memorial." *Rhetoric Society Quarterly* 30 (2000): 31–55, doi: 10.1080/02773940009391174.

Blair, Carole, Greg Dickinson, and Brian L. Ott. "Introduction: Rhetoric/Memory/Place." In *Places of Public Memory: The Rhetoric of Museums and Memorials*, edited by Greg Dickinson, Carole Blair, and Brian L. Ott, 1–54. Tuscaloosa, AL: University of Alabama Press, 2010.

Blair, Carole, Marsha S. Jeppeson, and Enrico Pucci Jr. "Public Memorializing in Postmodernity: The Vietnam Veterans Memorial as Prototype." *Quarterly Journal of Speech* 77 (1991): 263–88, doi: 10.1080/00335639109383960.

Blair, Carole. "'We Are All Just Prisoners Here of Our Own Device' Rhetoric in Speech Communication after Wingspread." In *The Effects of Rhetoric and the Rhetoric of Effects: Past, Present, Future,* edited by Amos Kiewe and Davis W. Houck, 31–58. Columbia, SC: University of South Carolina Press, 2015.

Blair, Carole. "Contemporary US Memorial Sites as Exemplars of Rhetoric's Materiality." In *Rhetorical Bodies,* edited by Jack Selzer and Sharon Crowley, 16–57. Madison: University of Wisconsin Press, 1999.

Blair, Carole. "Reflections on Criticism and Bodies: Parables from Public Places." *Western Journal of Communication* 65 (2001): 271–94, doi: 10.1080/1057031010 9374706.

Booth, Wayne C. *The Company We Keep: An Ethics of Fiction.* Berkeley, CA: University of California Press, 1988.

Bourdieu, Pierre. *Outline of a Theory of Practice*. Translated by Richard Nice. Cambridge, University of Cambridge Press, 1977 [1972].

Bowman, Michael S. "Killing Dillinger: A Mystery." *Text and Performance Quarterly* 20 (2000): 342–74, doi: 10.1080/10462930009366309.

Braun, M. J. "Against Decorous Civility: Acting as if you Live in a Democracy." In *Activism and Rhetoric: Theories and Contexts for Political Engagement*, edited by Seth Kahn and JongHwa Lee, 137–46. London: Routledge, 2011.

Briggs, Charles L. *Learning How to Ask: A Sociolinguistic Appraisal of the Role of the Interview in Social Science Research.* New York: Cambridge University Press, 1986.

Brouwer, Daniel C. "ACT-ing UP in Congressional Hearings." In *Counterpublics and the State*, edited by Robert Asen and Daniel C. Brouwer, 87–109. Albany: State University of New York Press, 2001.

Brouwer, Daniel C. "Counterpublicity and Corporeality in HIV/AIDS Zines." *Critical Studies in Media Communication* 22 (2005): 351–71, doi: 10.1080/07393180500342860.

Brouwer, Daniel C., and Aaron Hess. "Making Sense of 'God Hates Fags' and 'Thank God for 9/11': A Thematic Analysis of Milbloggers' Responses to Reverend Fred Phelps and the Westboro Baptist Church." *Western Journal of Communication* 71 (2007): 69–90, doi:10.1080/10570310701215388.

Brummett, Barry. "Some Implications of 'Process' or 'Intersubjectivity': Postmodern Rhetoric." *Philosophy & Rhetoric* 9 (1976): 21–51.

Burke, Kenneth. *Language as Symbolic Action: Essays on Life, Literature, and Method.* Berkeley, CA: University of California Press, 1966.

Burke, Kenneth. *A Grammar of Motives.* Los Angeles: University of California Press, 1969.

Burke, Kenneth. *A Rhetoric of Motives, Vol. 1.* Los Angeles: University of California Press, 1969.

Burke, Kenneth. *The Philosophy of Literary Form.* 3rd ed. Berkeley: University of California Press, 1974.

Butterworth, Michael L. "'Katie was Not Only a Girl, She was Terrible': Katie Hnida, Body Rhetoric, and Football at the University of Colorado." *Communication Studies* 59 (2008): 259–73, doi: 10.1080/10510970802257705.

Campbell, Karlyn Kohrs, and Kathleen Hall Jamieson. "Form and Genre in Rhetorical Criticism: An Introduction." In *Form and Genre: Shaping Rhetorical Action,* edited by Karlyn Kohrs Campbell and Kathleen Hall Jamieson, 9–32. Falls Church, VA: Speech Communication Association, 1978.

Campbell, Karlyn Kohrs. "Criticism: Ephemeral and Enduring." *The Speech Teacher* 23 (1974): 9–14, doi:10.1080/03634527409378050.

Campbell, Karlyn Kohrs. "Response to Forbes Hill." *Central States Speech Journal* 34 (1983): 126–27, doi:10.1080/10510978309368130.

Campbell, Karlyn Kohrs. "The Ontological Foundation of Rhetorical Theory." *Philosophy & Rhetoric* 3 (1970): 97–108.

Casey, Edward S. "How to Get from Space to Place in a Fairly Short Stretch of Time." In *Senses of Place*, edited by Steven Feld and Keith H. Basso, 13–52. Santa Fe, NM: School of American Research Press, 1996.

Ceccarelli, Leah. *Shaping Science with Rhetoric: The Cases of Dobzhansky, Schrödinger, and Wilson.* Chicago: University of Chicago Press, 2001.

Certeau, Michel de, Luce Giard, and Pierre Mayol. *The Practice of Everyday Life, Volume 2: Living and Cooking*. Translated by Timothy J. Tomasik. Minneapolis: University of Minnesota Press, 1998.

Certeau, Michel de. *The Practice of Everyday Life*. Translated by Steven Rendall. Berkeley: University of California Press, 1984.

Charland, Maurice. "Constitutive Rhetoric: The Case of the Peuple Quebecois." *Quarterly Journal of Speech* 73 (1987): 133–50, doi:10.1080/00335638709383799.

Charland, Maurice. "Finding a Horizon and *Telos*: The Challenge to Critical Rhetoric." *Quarterly Journal of Speech* 77 (1991): 71–74, doi:10.1080/00335639109383944.

Charmaz, Kathy. *Constructing Grounded Theory: A Practical Guide through Qualitative Analysis*. Thousand Oaks, CA: Sage Publications, 2006.

Chavez, Karma. *Queer Migration Politics: Activist Rhetoric and Coalitional Possibilities*. Chicago, IL: University of Illinois Press, 2013.

Chevrette, Roberta, and Aaron Hess. "Unearthing the Native Past: Citizen Archaeology and Modern (Non)belonging at the Pueblo Grande Museum. *Communication and Critical/Cultural Studies* 12 (2015): 139–58, doi:10.1080/14791420.2015.10 12214

Christiansen, Adrienne E., and Jeremy J. Hanson. "Comedy as Cure for Tragedy: ACT UP and the Rhetoric of AIDS." *Quarterly Journal of Speech* 82 (1996): 157–70, doi:10.1080/00335639609384148.

Cloud, Dana L. "The Materiality of Discourse as Oxymoron: A Challenge to Critical Rhetoric." *Western Journal of Communication* 58 (1994): 141–63, doi: 10.1080/10570319409374493.

Cloud, Dana L. "*The Matrix* and Critical Theory's Desertion of the Real." *Communication and Critical/Cultural Studies* 3 (2006): 329–54.

Cloud, Dana L. "The Only Conceivable Thing to Do: Reflections on Academics and Activism." In *Activism and Rhetoric: Theories and Contexts for Political Engagement*, edited by Seth Kahn and JongHwa Lee, 11–24. London: Routledge, 2011.

Condit, Celeste Michelle. "The Critic as Empath: Moving Away from Totalizing Theory." *Western Journal of Communication* 57 (1993): 178–90, doi: 10.1080/10570319309374441.

Condit, Celeste. "Contemporary Rhetorical Criticism: Diverse Bodies Learning New Languages." *Rhetorical Review* 25 (2006): 368–72.

Connolly, William E. *A World of Becoming*. Durham: Duke University Press, 2011.

Conquergood, Dwight. "Performing as a Moral Act: Ethical Dimensions of the Ethnography of Performance," *Text and Performance Quarterly* 5 (1985): 1–13, doi: 10.1080/10462938509391578

Conquergood, Dwight. "Rethinking Ethnography: Towards a Critical Cultural Politics." *Communication Monographs* 58 (1991): 179–94, doi: 10.1080/03637759109376222.

Conquergood, Dwight. "Ethnography, Rhetoric, and Performance." *Quarterly Journal of Speech* 78 (1992): 80–97, doi: 10.1080/00335639209383982.

Conquergood, Dwight. "Performance Studies: Interventions and Radical Research." *TDR/The Drama Review* 46 (2002): 145–56, doi:10.1162/105420402320980550.

Corey, Frederick C., and Thomas K. Nakayama. "Sextext." *Text and Performance Quarterly* 17 (1997): 58–68, doi: 10.1080/10462939709366169.

Cox, Robert. "Nature's 'Crisis Disciplines': Does Environmental Communication have an Ethical Duty?" *Environmental Communication: A Journal of Nature and Culture* 1 (2007): 5–20, doi: 10.1080/17524030701333948.

Crenshaw, Carrie. "Resisting Whiteness' Rhetorical Silence." *Western Journal of Communication* 61 (1997): 253–78, doi: 10.1080/10570319709374577.

Cresswell, Tim. *In Place/Out of Place: Geography, Ideology, and Transgression*. Minneapolis: University of Minnesota Press, 1996.

Cresswell, Tim. *Place: A Short Introduction*. Malden, MA: Wiley-Blackwell, 2004.

Crick, Nathan. "Rhetoric, Philosophy, and the Public Intellectual." *Philosophy & Rhetoric* 39 (2006): 127–39.

Darr, Christopher. "Civility as Rhetorical Enactment: The John Ashcroft 'Debates' and Burke's Theory of Form." *Southern Communication Journal* 70 (2005): 316–28, doi: 10.1080/10417940509373337.

Deleuze, Gilles and Felix Guattari. *Essays Critical and Clinical.* London: Verso, 1998.

DeLuca, Kevin Michael, and Jennifer Peeples. "From Public Sphere to Public Screen: Democracy, Activism, and the 'Violence' of Seattle." *Critical Studies in Media Communication* 19 (2002): 125–51, doi: 10.1080/07393180216559.

DeLuca, Kevin Michael. "Unruly Arguments: The Body Rhetoric of Earth First!, Act Up, and Queer Nation." *Argumentation and Advocacy* 36 (1999): 9–21.

DeLuca, Kevin, Sean Lawson, and Ye Sun. "Occupy Wall Street on the Public Screens of Social Media: The Many Framings of the Birth of a Protest Movement." *Communication, Culture & Critique* 5 (2012): 483–509, doi:10.1111/j.1753–9137.2012.01141.x.

DeLuca, Kevin. "Articulation Theory: A Discursive Grounding for Rhetorical Practice." *Philosophy & Rhetoric* 32 (1999): 334–48.

DeLuca, Kevin. *Image Politics: The New Rhetoric of Environmental Activism.* New York: Guilford, 1999.

Denzin, Norman K. *Interpretive Ethnography: Ethnographic Practices for the 21st Century.* Thousand Oaks, CA: Sage Publications, 1997.

Denzin, Norman K., and Yvonna S. Lincoln, eds., *The SAGE Handbook of Qualitative Research.* 4th ed. Thousand Oaks, CA: Sage Publications, 2011.

Dickinson, Greg, Brian L. Ott, and Eric Aoki. "Memory and Myth at the Buffalo Bill Museum." *Western Journal of Communication* 69 (2005): 85–108, doi: 10.1080/10570310500076684.

Dickinson, Greg, Brian L. Ott, and Eric Aoki. "Spaces of Remembering and Forgetting: The Reverent Eye/I at the Plains Indian Museum." *Communication and Critical/Cultural Studies* 3 (2006): 27–47, doi: 10.1080/14791420500505619.

Dickinson, Greg, Carole Blair, and Brian L. Ott, eds. *Places of Public Memory: The Rhetoric of Museums and Memorials.* Tuscaloosa, University Alabama Press, 2010.

Dickinson, Greg. "Joe's Rhetoric: Finding Authenticity at Starbucks." *Rhetoric Society Quarterly* 32 (2002): 5–27, doi: 10.1080/02773940209391238.

Dickinson, Greg. "Memories for Sale: Nostalgia and the Construction of Identity in Old Pasadena." *Quarterly Journal of Speech* 83 (1997): 1–27, doi: 10.1080/00335639709384169.

Dickinson, Greg. "The Pleasantville Effect: Nostalgia and the Visual Framing of (White) Suburbia." *Western Journal of Communication* 70 (2006): 212–33, doi: 10.1080/10570310600843504.

Dolmage, Jay. *Disability Rhetoric.* Syracuse, NY: Syracuse University Press, 2013.

Dubisar, Abby M. "Embodying and Disabling Antiwar Activism: Disrupting YouTube's 'Mother's Day for Peace.'" *Rhetoric Review* 34 (2015): 56–73, doi: 10.1080/07350198.2015.976305.

Edbauer, Jenny. "Unframing Models of Public Distribution: From Rhetorical Situation to Rhetorical Ecologies." *Rhetoric Society Quarterly* 35 (2005): 5–24, doi:10.1080/02773940509391320.

Ellis, Carolyn. "Telling Secrets, Revealing Lives: Relational Ethics in Research with Intimate Others." *Qualitative Inquiry* 13 (2007): 3–29, doi:10.1177/1077800406294947.

Emerson, Robert M., Rachel I. Fretz, and Linda L. Shaw. *Writing Ethnographic Fieldnotes.* 2nd ed. Chicago: University of Chicago Press, 2011.

Enck-Wanzer, Darrel. "Decolonizing Imaginaries: Rethinking 'the People' in the Young Lords' Church Offensive." *Quarterly Journal of Speech* 98 (2012): 1–23, doi: 10.1080/00335630.2011.638656.

Enck-Wanzer, Darrel. "Race, Coloniality, and Geo-Body Politics: *The Garden* as Latin@ Vernacular Discourse." *Environmental Communication: A Journal of Nature and Culture* 5 (2011): 363–71, doi: 10.1080/17524032.2011.593535.

Enck-Wanzer, Darrel. "Trashing the System: Social Movement, Intersectional Rhetoric, and Collective Agency in the Young Lords Organization's Garbage Offensive." *Quarterly Journal of Speech* 92 (2006): 174–201, doi: 10.1080/0033563060081 6920.

Endres, Danielle, and Samantha Senda-Cook. "Location Matters: The Rhetoric of Place in Protest." *Quarterly Journal of Speech* 97 (2011): 257–82, doi: 10.1080/ 00335630.2011.585167.

Endres, Danielle, Brian Cozen, Megan O'Byrne, and Andrea Feldpausch-Parker, "Putting the U in Carbon Capture and Storage: Performances of Rupture within the CCS Scientific Community." In *Communication for the Commons: Revisiting Participation and Environment,* edited by Mark S. Meisner, Nadarajah Sriskandarajah, and Stephen P. Depoe (Turtle Island: The International Environmental Communication Association, 2015), 320–31.

Endres, Danielle, Deborah Cox Callister, Autumn Garrison, Samantha Senda-Cook, and Julie Kalil Schutten. "Step What Up?: The Rhetorical Framing of Salt Lake City's Step It Up Events." In *Social Movement to Address Climate Change: Local Steps for Global Action*, edited by Danielle Endres, Leah Sprain, and Tarla Rai Peterson, 117–46. Amherst, NY: Cambria Press, 2009.

Endres, Danielle, Leah M. Sprain, and Tarla Rai Peterson, eds. *Social Movement to Address Climate Change: Local Steps for Global Action.* Amherst, NY: Cambria Press, 2009.

Endres, Danielle, Leah Sprain, and Tarla Rai Peterson. "The Imperative of Praxis-Based Environmental Communication Research: Suggestions from the Step It Up 2007 National Research Project." *Environmental Communication: A Journal of Nature and Culture* 2 (2008): 237–45, doi: 10.1080/17524030802141794.

Endres, Danielle, Samantha Senda-Cook, and Brian Cozen. "Not Just a Place to Park Your Car: Park(ing) as Spatial Argument." *Argumentation and Advocacy* 50 (2014): 121–40.

Endres, Danielle. "Environmental Oral History." *Environmental Communication: A Journal of Nature and Culture* 5 (2011): 485–498, doi: 10.1080/17524032.2011. 610810.

Escobar, Arturo. "Culture Sits in Places: Reflections on Globalism and Subaltern Strategies of Localization," *Political Geography* 20 (2001): 139–74, doi:10.1016/ S0962–6298(00)00064–0.

Fairclough, Norman. "Critical Discourse Analysis as a Method in Social Scientific Research." In *Methods of Critical Discourse Analysis*, edited by Ruth Wodak and Michael Meyer, 121–38. London: Sage Publications, 2001.

Felski, Rita. *Beyond Feminist Aesthetics: Feminist Literature and Social Change*. Cambridge: Harvard University Press, 1989.

Fenske, Mindy. "Movement and Resistance: (Tattooed) Bodies and Performance." *Communication and Critical/Cultural Studies* 4 (2007): 51–73, doi: 10.1080/14791420601138302.

Fenske, Mindy. "The Aesthetic of the Unfinished: Ethics and Performance." *Text and Performance Quarterly* 24 (2004): 1–19, doi: 10.1080/1046293042000239447.

Fenske, Mindy. "The Movement of Interpretation: Conceptualizing Performative Encounters with Multimediated Performance." *Text and Performance Quarterly* 26 (2006): 138–61, doi: 10.1080/10462930500517907.

Fenske, Mindy. *Tattoos in American Visual Culture*. 1st ed. New York: Palgrave Macmillan, 2007.

Fern, Edward F. *Advanced Focus Group Research.* Thousand Oaks, CA: Sage Publications, 2001.

Fetterman, David M. *Ethnography: Step-by-Step*. 3rd ed. Thousand Oaks, CA: Sage Publications, 2009.

Fleitz, Elizabeth. "Cooking Codes: Cookbook Discourses as Women's Rhetorical Practices." *Present Tense: A Journal of Rhetoric in Society* 1 (2010): 1–8.

Foucault, Michel. "Questions of Method." In *The Foucault Effect: Studies in Governmentality,* edited by Graham Burchell, Colin Gordon, and Peter Miller, 73–86. Chicago: University of Chicago Press, 1991.

Foucault, Michel. *The History of Sexuality: Volume 1: An Introduction*. Translated by Robert Hurley. New York: Vintage Books, 1978.

Fox, Ragan. "'Ragan Fox is a Gay Slam Poet': An Autobiographical Exploration of Performance Poetry's Performative Implications." *Text and Performance Quarterly* 30 (2010): 420–29, doi:10.1080/10462937.2010.508535.

Fox, Ragan. "Re-membering Daddy: Autoethnographic Reflections of My Father and Alzheimer's Disease" *Text and Performance Quarterly* 30 (2010): 3–20, doi:10.1080/10462930903366969.

Fox, Ragan. "Skinny bones# 126–774-835–29: Thin Gay Bodies Signifying a Modern Plague." *Text and Performance Quarterly* 27 (2007): 3–19, doi: 10.1080/10462930601045956.

Fox, Ragan. "Tales of a Fighting Bobcat: An "Auto-archaeology" of Gay Identity Formation and Maintenance." *Text and Performance Quarterly* 30 (2010): 122–42, doi: 10.1080/10462931003650153.

Fraser, Nancy. "Politics, Culture, and the Public Sphere: Toward a Postmodern Conception." In *Social Postmodernism: Beyond Identity Politics*, edited by Linda Nicholson and Steve Seidman, 287–312. Cambridge: Press Syndicate of the University of Cambridge, 1995.

Fraser, Nancy. "Rethinking the Public Sphere: A Contribution to the Critique of Actually Existing Democracy." *Social Text* 25/26 (1990): 56–80.

Frey, Lawrence R. "Communication and Social Justice Research: Truth, Justice, and the Applied Communication Way." *Journal of Applied Communication Research* 26 (1998): 155–64, doi: 10.1080/00909889809365499.

Frey, Lawrence R., W. Barnett Pearce, Mark A. Pollock, Lee Artz, and Bren A. O. Murphy. "Looking for Justice in All the Wrong Places: On a Communication Approach to Social Justice." *Communication Studies* 47 (1996): 110–27, doi: 10.1080/10510979609368467.

Frisch, Michael. *A Shared Authority: Essays on the Craft and Meaning of Oral and Public History*. Albany: State University of New York Press, 1990.

Fuller, Steve. "The Public Intellectual as Agent of Justice: In Search of a Regime." *Philosophy & Rhetoric* 39 (2006): 147–56.

Gaonkar, Dilip Parameshwar. "Performing with Fragments: Reflections on Critical Rhetoric." In *Argument and the Postmodern Challenge: Proceedings of the Eighth SCA/AFA Conference on Argumentation*, edited by Raymie E. McKerrow, 149–55. Annandale, VA: SCA, 1993.

Giard, Luce. "Plat Du Jour." In *The Practice of Everyday Life: Volume 2: Living & Cooking*, edited by Luce Giard, translated by Timothy J. Tomasik, 171–98. Minneapolis: University of Minnesota Press, 1998.

Goodall, Jr., H. L. *Writing Qualitative Inquiry: Self, Stories, and Academic Life*. Walnut Creek, CA: Left Coast Press, Inc., 2008.

Goodnight, G. Thomas. "The Personal, Technical, and Public Spheres: A Note on 21st Century Critical Communication Inquiry." *Argumentation and Advocacy* 48 (2012): 258–67.

Gorsevski, Ellen W. "Wangari Maathai's Emplaced Rhetoric: Greening Global Peacebuilding." *Environmental Communication: A Journal of Nature and Culture* 6 (2012): 290–307, doi:10.1080/17524032.2012.689776.

Greene, Ronald Walter. "Another Materialist Rhetoric." *Critical Studies in Media Communication* 15 (1998): 21–40, doi: 10.1080/15295039809367031.

Greene, Ronald Walter. "The Aesthetic Turn and the Rhetorical Perspective on Argumentation." *Argumentation and Advocacy* 35 (1998): 19–29.

Gregg, Melissa, and Gregory J. Seigworth. *The Affect Theory Reader*. Durham, NC: Duke University Press, 2010.

Griffin, Leland M. "The Rhetorical Structure of the 'New Left' Movement: Part I." *Quarterly Journal of Speech* 50 (1964): 113–35, doi: 10.1080/0033563640 9382652.

Guillemin, Marilys, and Lynn Gillam. "Ethics, Reflexivity, and 'Ethically Important Moments' in Research." *Qualitative Inquiry* 10 (2004): 261–80, doi:10.1177/10778 00403262360.

Gunn, Joshua, and Jenny Edbauer Rice. "About Face/Stuttering Discipline." *Communication and Critical/Cultural Studies* 6 (2009): 215–19, doi:10.1080/ 14791420902868029.

Gunn, Joshua. "Speech is Dead; Long Live Speech." *Quarterly Journal of Speech* 94 (2008): 343–64, doi:10.1080/00335630802210385.

Happe, Kelly. "The Body of Race: Toward a Rhetorical Understanding of Racial Ideology." *Quarterly Journal of Speech* 99 (2013): 131–55, doi: 10.1080/00335630. 2013.775700.

Hariman, Robert. "Critical Rhetoric and Postmodern Theory." *Quarterly Journal of Speech* 77 (1991): 67–70, doi:10.1080/00335639109383943.

Harold, Christine. "On Target: Aura, Affect, and the Rhetoric of 'Design Democracy.'" *Public Culture* 21 (2009): 599–618, doi:10.1215/08992363–2009-010.

Harold, Christine. "Tracking Heroin Chic: The Abject Body Reconfigures the Rational Argument" *Argumentation and Advocacy* 36 (1999): 65–76.

Hartnett, Stephen John. "'Tibet is Burning': Competing Rhetorics of Liberation, Occupation, Resistance, and Paralysis on the Roof of the World." *Quarterly Journal of Speech* 99 (2013): 283–316, doi: 10.1080/00335630.2013.806819.

Hartnett, Stephen John. "Communication, Social Justice, and Joyful Commitment." *Western Journal of Communication* 74 (2010): 68–93, doi: 10.1080/105703109034 63778.

Hasian, Jr., Marouf. "Communication Law as a Rhetorical Practice: A Case Study of the Masses Decision." *Communication Law & Policy* 1 (1996): 497–532, doi:10.1080/10811689609368614.

Hasian, Marouf, and Rulon Wood. "Critical Museology, (Post)Colonial Communication, and the Gradual Mastering of Traumatic Pasts at the Royal Museum for Central Africa (RMCA)." *Western Journal of Communication* 74 (2010): 128–49, doi: 10.1080/10570311003614484.

Hauser, Gerard A. "Forum: The Nature and Function of Public Intellectuals." *Philosophy & Rhetoric* 39 (2006): 125–26, doi: 10.1353/par.2006.0014.

Hauser, Gerard A. *Vernacular Voices: The Rhetoric of Publics and Public Spheres.* Columbia, SC: University of South Carolina Press, 1999.

Hawhee, Debra. "Rhetorics, Bodies, and Everyday Life" *Rhetoric Society Quarterly* 36 (2006): 155–64, doi: 10.1080/02773940600605487.

Hawhee, Debra. *Bodily Arts: Rhetoric and Athletics in Ancient Greece.* Austin: University of Texas Press, 2005.

Herbig, Art, Aaron Hess, Alix Watson, and Kristy D. Hess. *Unmasking Sanity: Halloween Weekend with the Participants at the Rally to Restore Sanity and/or Fear.* 2012. Short Film/YouTube video. Directed by Art Herbig. USA: Living Text Productions. http://www.youtube.com/watch?v=DE7NtFPWgw8.

Herbig, Art, Aaron Hess, and Alix Watson. *Never Forget: Public Memory & 9/11.* Motion Picture directed by Art Herbig (2014; USA, Living Text Productions), Digital Video.

Herbig, Art, and Aaron Hess. "Convergent Critical Rhetoric at the 'Rally to Restore Sanity': Exploring the Intersection of Rhetoric, Ethnography, and Documentary Production." *Communication Studies* 63(2012): 269–89, doi:10.1080/10510974.2012.674617.

Hess, Aaron R. "Rhetorical Ethnography: Engaging the Politics of Advocacy." PhD diss., Arizona State University, 2008.

Hess, Aaron, and Art Herbig. "Recalling the Ghosts of 9/11: Convergent Memorializing at the Opening of the National 9/11 Memorial." *International Journal of Communication* 7 (2013): 2207–2230, doi: 10.1080/10570310109374706.

Hess, Aaron. "Critical-Rhetorical Ethnography: Rethinking the Place and Process of Rhetoric." *Communication Studies* 62 (2011): 127–52, doi: 10.1080/10510974.2011.529750.

Hess, Aaron. "Democracy through the Polarized Lens of the Camcorder: Argumentation and Vernacular Spectacle on YouTube in the 2008 election." *Argumentation and Advocacy* 47 (2010): 106–122.

Hess, Aaron. "Health, Risk, and Authority in a Dysfunctional World: Online Ecstasy User Discourse." *Ohio Communication Journal* 50 (2012): 1–30.

Hill, Forbes. "Conventional Wisdom—Traditional Form—the President's Message of November 3, 1969." *Quarterly Journal of Speech* 58 (1972): 373–86, doi:10.1016.

Hodder, Ian. "The Interpretation of Documents and Culture." In *Collecting and Interpreting Qualitative Materials*, edited by Norman K. Denzin and Yvonna S. Lincoln, 110–29. Thousand Oaks, CA: Sage, 1998.

Holquist, Michael, ed. *The Dialogic Imagination: Four Essays by M. M. Bakhtin.* Translated by Caryl Emerson and Michael Holquist. Austin: University of Texas Press, 1981.

Houck, Davis. "Of 'Very Few Men' with 'Unusual Gifts' and 'Acute Sensitivity'—Whither Wichelns, Black, and Zarefsky?" In *The Effects of Rhetoric and the Rhetoric of Effects: Past, Present, Future,* edited by Amos Kiewe and Davis W. Houck, 282–96. Columbia, SC: University of South Carolina Press, 2015.

Howard, Robert Glenn. "The Vernacular Web of Participatory Media." *Critical Studies in Media Communication* 25 (2008): 490–513, doi: 10.1080/15295030802468065.

Hubbard, Bryan, and Marouf A. Hasian Jr. "Atomic Memories of the Enola Gay: Strategies of Remembrance at the National Air and Space Museum." *Rhetoric & Public Affairs* 1 (1998): 363–85, doi: 10.1353/rap.2010.0084.

Hubbard, Phil, Rob Kitchin, and Gill Valentine, eds. *Key Thinkers on Space and Place*. Thousand Oaks, CA: Sage Publications, 2004.

Ingalsbee, Timothy. "Earth First! Activism: Ecological Postmodern Praxis in Radical Environmentalist Identities." *Sociological Perspectives* 39 (1996): 263–76, doi: 10.2307/1389312.

Ivie, Robert L. "Productive Criticism." *Quarterly Journal of Speech* 81 (1995): 2, doi: 10.1080/00335639509384093.

Jack, Jordynn. "Acts of Institution: Embodying Feminist Rhetorical Methodologies in Space and Time." *Rhetoric Review* 28 (2009): 285–303, doi: 10.1080/0735019090 2958909.

Jasinski, James. "The Status of Theory and Method in Rhetorical Criticism." *Western Journal of Communication* 65 (2001): 249–70, doi:10.1080/10570310109374705.

Jasinski, James. *Sourcebook on Rhetoric: Key Concepts in Contemporary Rhetorical Studies*. Thousand Oaks, CA: Sage Publications, 2001.

Johnson, E. Patrick. *Appropriating Blackness: Performance and the Politics of Authenticity*. Durham, NC: Duke University Press, 2003.

Katriel, Tamar. "'Our Future is Where our Past Is': Studying Heritage Museums as Ideological and Performative Arenas." *Communication Monographs* 60 (1993): 69–75, doi:10.1080/03637759309376296.

Katriel, Tamar. "Rhetoric in Flames: Fire Inscriptions in Israeli Youth Movement Ceremonials." *Quarterly Journal of Speech* 73 (1987): 444–59, doi: 10.1080/0033 5638709383818.

Kiewe, Amos, and Davis W. Houck. *The Effects of Rhetoric and the Rhetoric of Effects: Past, Present, Future*. Columbia, SC: University of South Carolina Press, 2015.

Klumpp, James F., and Thomas A. Hollihan. "Rhetorical Criticism as Moral Action." *Quarterly Journal of Speech* 75 (1989): 84–96, doi: 10.1080/00335638909383863.

Kuypers, Jim A. "The Rhetorical River." *Southern Communication Journal* 73 (2008): 350–58, doi:10.1080/10417940802429475.

Kvale, Steinar. *InterViews: An Introduction to Qualitative Research Interviewing.* Thousand Oaks, CA: Sage Publications, 1996.

Lederman, Linda C. *Focus Group Research Manual.* New Brunswick, NJ: Center for Communication and Health Issues, 2006.

Lefebvre, Henri. *The Production of Space.* Malden, MA: Blackwell, 1992.

Leff, Michael C. "Interpretation and the Art of the Rhetorical Critic." *Western Journal of Speech Communication* 44 (1980): 337–49, doi: 10.1080/10570318009374019.

Leff, Michael C. "Things Made by Words: Reflections on Textual Criticism." *Quarterly Journal of Speech* 78 (1992): 223–31, doi: 10.1080/00335639209383991.

Leff, Michael, and Andrew Sachs. "Words the Most Like Things: Iconicity and the Rhetorical Text." *Western Journal of Speech Communication* 54 (1990): 252–73, doi:10.1080/10570319009374342.

Light, Elinor. "The (Em)Placed Vernacular: Rhetorics of Control and Transgression in the American City." PhD diss., University of Utah, 2015.

Lindlof, Thomas R., and Bryan C. Taylor. *Qualitative Communication Research Methods.* 3rd ed. Thousand Oaks, CA: Sage Publications, 2010.

Lofland, John, David Snow, Leon Anderson, and Lyn H. Lofland. *Analyzing Social Settings: A Guide to Qualitative Observation and Analysis.* 4th ed. Belmont, CA: Wadsworth, 2006.

Lunceford, Brett. *Naked Politics: Nudity, Political Action, and the Rhetoric of the Body.* Lanham, MD: Lexington Books, 2012.

Madison, D. Soyini. *Critical Ethnography: Method, Ethics, and Performance.* Thousand Oaks, CA: Sage Publications, 2011.

Mailloux, Steven. "Thinking in Public with Rhetoric." *Philosophy & Rhetoric* 39 (2006): 140–46, doi: 10.1353/par.2006.0016.

Mansbridge, Jane. "Cracking Through Hegemonic Ideology: The Logic of Formal Justice." *Social Justice Research* 18 (2005): 335–47, doi: 10./007/s11211-005-6828-0.

Massey, Doreen B. *For Space.* 1st ed. Thousand Oaks, CA: Sage Publications, 2005.

Massumi, Brian. "The Autonomy of Affect." *Cultural Critique* 31 (1995): 83–109, doi: 10.2307/1354446.

Mayol, Pierre. "Propriety." *The Practice of Everyday Life: Volume 2: Living & Cooking*, edited by Luce Giard, translated by Timothy J. Tomasik, 15–34. Minneapolis: University of Minnesota Press, 1998.

McCormick, Samuel. "Earning One's Inheritance: Rhetorical Criticism, Everyday Talk, and the Analysis of Public Discourse." *Quarterly Journal of Speech* 89 (2003): 109–31, doi: 10.1080/00335630308176.

McGee, Michael Calvin. "Text, Context, and the Fragmentation of Contemporary Culture." *Western Journal of Speech Communication* 54 (1990): 274–89, doi: 10.1080/10570319009374343.

McHendry Jr., George F., Michael Middleton, Danielle Endres, Samantha Senda-Cook, and Megan O'Byrne. "Rhetorical Critic(ism)'s Body." *Southern Journal of Communication,* 79 (2014), 293–310, doi:10.1080/1041794X.2014.906643.

McIntyre, Alice. *Participatory Action Research.* Thousand Oaks, CA: Sage Publications, 2008.

McKerrow, Raymie E. "Corporeality and Cultural Rhetoric: A Site for Rhetoric's Future." *Southern Communication Journal* 63 (1998): 315–28, doi: 10.1080/10417949809373105.

McKerrow, Raymie E. "Critical Rhetoric and the Possibility of the Subject." In *The Critical Turn: Rhetoric and Philosophy in Postmodern Discourse*, edited by Ian Angus and L. Langsdorf, 51–67. Carbondale: Southern Illinois Press, 1993.

McKerrow, Raymie E. "Critical Rhetoric in a Postmodern World." *Quarterly Journal of Speech* 77 (1991): 75–78, doi:10.1080/00335639109383945.

McKerrow, Raymie E. "Critical Rhetoric: Theory and Praxis." *Communication Monographs* 56 (1989): 91–111, doi: 10.1080/03637758909390253.

McKerrow, Raymie E., and Jeffrey St. John. "Critical Rhetoric and Continual Critique." In *The Art of Rhetorical Criticism*, edited by Jim A. Kuypers, 345–66. Boston: Allyn & Bacon, 2005.

McLaren, Peter. "Field Relations and the Discourse of the Other: Collaboration in Our Own Ruin." In *Experiencing Fieldwork*, edited by William B. Shaffir and Robert A. Stebbins, 149–63. Thousand Oaks, CA: Sage Publications, 1991.

Medhurst, Martin J. "The Contemporary Study of Public Address: Renewal, Recovery, and Reconfiguration." *Rhetoric & Public Affairs* 4 (2001): 495–511, doi: 10.1353/rap.2001.0048.

Mendelson, Michael. "The Rhetoric of Embodiment." *Rhetoric Society Quarterly* 28 (1998): 29–50, doi: 10.1080/02773949809391129.

Merchant, Jamie. "Immanence, Governmentality, Critique: Toward a Recovery of Totality in Rhetorical Theory." *Philosophy & Rhetoric* 47 (2014): 227–50, doi: 10.5325/philrhet.47.3.0227.

Middleton, Michael K. "'SafeGround Sacramento' and Rhetorics of Substantive Citizenship." *Western Journal of Communication* 78 (2014): 1–15, doi:10.1080/10570314.2013.835064.

Middleton, Michael K. "Housing, Not Handcuffs: Homeless Misrecognition and 'SafeGround Sacramento's' Homeless Activism." *Communication, Culture & Critique* 7 (2014): 320–37, doi: 10.1111/cccr.12055.

Middleton, Michael K., Samantha Senda-Cook, and Danielle Endres. "Articulating Rhetorical Field Methods: Challenges and Tensions." *Western Journal of Communication* 75 (2011): 386–406, doi: 10.1080/10570314.2011.586969.

Modesti, Sonja. "Home Sweet Home: Tattoo Parlors as Postmodern Spaces of Agency." *Western Journal of Communication* 72 (2008): 197–212, doi:10.1080/10570310802210106.

Morris III, Charles E. "Performing/Rhetorical Studies: Differential Belonging Across Intradisciplinary Borders." *Text and Performance Quarterly* 34 (2014): 104–07, doi: 10.1080/10462937.2013.849813.

Murray, Janet Horowitz. *Hamlet on the Holodeck: The Future of Narrative in Cyberspace.* New York: Simon and Schuster, 1997.

Ono, Kent A. and John M. Sloop. "Commitment to *Telos*: A Sustained Critical Rhetoric." *Communication Monographs* 59 (1992): 48–60, doi: 10.1080/03637759209376248.

Ono, Kent A. and John M. Sloop. "The Critique of Vernacular Discourse." *Communication Monographs* 62 (1995): 19–46, doi: 10.1080/03637759509376346.

Ono, Kent A., and John M. Sloop. "Critical Rhetorics of Controversy." *Western Journal of Communication* 63 (1999): 526–38, doi: 10.1080/10570319909374657.

Ono, Kent A., and John M. Sloop. *Shifting Borders: Rhetoric, Immigration, and California's Proposition 187*. Philadelphia: Temple University Press, 2002.

Ott, Brian L. "(Re)Locating Pleasure in Media Studies: Toward an Erotics of Reading." *Communication and Critical/Cultural Studies* 1 (2004): 194–212, doi: 10.1080/1479142041000 1685386.

Ott, Brian L. "The Visceral Politics of *V for Vendetta*: On Political Affect in Cinema." *Critical Studies in Media Communication* 27 (2010): 39–54, doi:10.1080/15295030903554359.

Owen, A. Susan, and Peter Ehrenhaus. "Animating a Critical Rhetoric: On the Feeding Habits of American Empire." *Western Journal of Communication* 57 (1993): 169–77, doi: 10.1080/10570319309374440.

Paulus, Trena M., Jessica N. Lester, and Paul G. Dempster. *Digital Tools for Qualitative Research.* Thousand Oaks, CA: Sage Publications, 2013.

Peters, John Durham. *Courting the Abyss: Free speech and the Liberal Tradition.* Chicago: University of Chicago Press, 2005.

Peters, John Durham. *Speaking Into the Air: A History of the Idea of Communication.* Chicago: University of Chicago Press, 2000.

Peterson, Eric E., and Kristin M. Langellier. "The Politics of Personal Narrative Methodology." *Text and Performance Quarterly* 17 (1997): 135–52, doi: 10.1080/10462939709366178.

Pezzullo, Phaedra C. "Performing Critical Interruptions: Stories, Rhetorical Invention, and the Environmental Justice Movement." *Western Journal of Communication* 65 (2001): 1–25, doi:10.1080/10570310109374689.

Pezzullo, Phaedra C. "Resisting 'National Breast Cancer Awareness Month': The Rhetoric of Counterpublics and Their Cultural Performances." *Quarterly Journal of Speech* 89 (2003): 345–65, doi:10.1080/0033563032000160981.

Pezzullo, Phaedra C. "Touring 'Cancer Alley,' Louisiana: Performances of Community and Memory for Environmental Justice." *Text and Performance Quarterly* 23 (2003): 226–52, doi:10.1080/10462930310001635295.

Pezzullo, Phaedra C. "Tourists and/as Disasters: Rebuilding, Remembering, and Responsibility in New Orleans." *Tourist Studies* 9 (2009): 23–41, doi: 10.1177/1468797609360591.

Pezzullo, Phaedra C. *Toxic Tourism: Rhetorics of Pollution, Travel, and Environmental Justice*. Tuscaloosa: University of Alabama Press, 2007.

Phillips, Kendall R. "Rhetoric, Resistance, and Criticism: A Response to Sloop and Ono." *Philosophy & Rhetoric* 32 (1999): 96–102.

Pigg, Stacey. "Emplacing Mobile Composition Habits: A Study of Academic Writing in Networked Social Spaces." *College Composition and Communication* 66 (2014): 250–75.

Pineau, Elyse. "Nursing Mother and Articulating Absence." *Text and Performance Quarterly* 20 (2000): 1–19, doi: 10.1080/10462930009366280.

Pink, Sarah. *Doing Sensory Ethnography*. Thousand Oaks, CA: SAGE Publications, 2009.

Pollock, Della. "Memory, Remembering, and Histories of Change: A Performance Praxis." In *The Sage Handbook of Performance Studies,* edited by D. Soyini Madison and Judith Hamera, 87–105. Thousand Oaks, CA: Sage Publications, 2006.

Pred, Allan. "Place as Historically Contingent Process: Structuration and the Time-Geography of Becoming Places." *Annals of the Association of American Geographers* 74 (1984): 279–97, doi:10.1111/j.1467–8306.1984.tb01453.x.

Pruchnic, Jeff, and Kim Lacey. "The Future of Forgetting: Rhetoric, Memory, Affect." *Rhetoric Society Quarterly* 41 (2011): 472–94, doi:10.1080/02773945.2011.597818.

Rand, Erin. "An Appetite for Activism: The Lesbian Avengers and the Queer Politics of Visibility." *Women's Studies in Communication* 36 (2013): 121–41, doi: 10.1080/07491409.2013.794754.

Reid, Robert Stephen. "Faithful Preaching: Preaching Epistemes, Faith Stages, and Rhetorical Practice." *Journal of Communication and Religion* 21 (1998): 164–99.

Relph, Edward. "Sense of Place." In *Ten Geographic Ideas That Changed the World,* edited by Susan Hanson, 205–26. New Brunswick, NJ: Rutgers University Press, 1997.

Relph, Edward. *Place and Placelessness*. 1st ed. London: Pion, 1976.

Renegar, Valerie R. "Critical/Cultural Scholarship and the Responsibility for Building Theory: Enduring Criticism Revisited." *Western Journal of Communication* 77 (2013): 509–13, doi:10.1080/10570314.2013.804194.

Rice, Jeff. *Digital Detroit: Rhetoric and Space in the Age of the Network*. Carbondale: Southern Illinois University Press, 2012.

Rickert, Thomas. *Ambient Rhetoric*. Pittsburgh: University of Pittsburgh Press, 2013.

Rogers, Richard. "Overcoming the Objectification of Nature in Constitutive Theories: Toward a Transhuman, Materialist Theory of Communication." *Western Journal of Communication* 62 (1998): 244–72, doi: 10.1080/10570319809374610.

Rose, Gillian. "Place and Identity: A Sense of Place." In *A Place in the World? Places, Cultures, and Globalisation*, edited by Doreen B. Massey and Pat M. Jess, 87–118. Oxford: The Open University Press, 1995.

Rowland, Robert C. "Purpose, Evidence, and Pedagogy in Rhetorical Criticism." In *The Effects of Rhetoric and the Rhetoric of Effects: Past, Present, Future,* edited by Amos Kiewe and Davis W. Houck, 59–81. Columbia, SC: University of South Carolina Press, 2015.

Salvador, Michael, and Tracylee Clarke. "The Weyekin Principle: Toward an Embodied Critical Rhetoric." *Environmental Communication* 5 (2011): 243–60, doi: 10.1080/17524032.2011.586713.

Seamon, David. "Body-Subject, Time-Space Routines, and Place-Ballets," In *The Human Experience of Space and Place*, edited by Ann Buttimer and David Seamon, 148–65. New York: St. Martin Press, 1980.

Seigworth, Gregory J., and Melissa Gregg. "An Inventory of Shimmers." In *The Affect Theory Reader*, edited by Melissa Gregg and Gregory J. Seigworth, 1–28. Durham: Duke University Press, 2010.

Selzer, Jack, and Sharon Crowley, eds. *Rhetorical Bodies*. Madison: University of Wisconsin Press, 1999.

Senda-Cook, Samantha, and Danielle Endres. "A Place of One's Own." In *Environmental Rhetoric and Ecologies of Place*, ed. Peter Goggin (London: Routledge, 2013), 143–54.

Senda-Cook, Samantha, Michael Middleton, and Danielle Endres. "Interrogating the 'Field' of Rhetorical Field Methods." For *Connecting Textual Criticism and Field Work*, National Communication Association Conference, Washington D.C., November 2013.

Senda-Cook, Samantha, Michael Middleton, and Danielle Endres. "Rhetorical Cartographies: (Re)Mapping Urban Spaces." Conference on Communication and the Environment, Boulder, CO, June 2015.

Senda-Cook, Samantha. "Materializing Tensions: How Maps and Trails Mediate Nature." *Environmental Communication: A Journal of Nature and Culture* 7 (2013): 355–71, doi:10.1080/17524032.2013.792854.

Senda-Cook, Samantha. "Rugged Practices: Embodying Authenticity in Outdoor Recreation." *Quarterly Journal of Speech* 98 (2012): 129–52, doi: 10.1080/0033 5630.2012.663500.

Shome, Raka. "Space Matters: The Power and Practice of Space." *Communication Theory* 13 (2003): 39–56, doi:10.1111/j.1468–2885.2003.tb00281.x.

Shugart, Helene. "An Appropriating Aesthetic: Reproducing Power in the Discourse of Critical Scholarship." *Communication Theory* 13 (2003): 275–303, doi: 0.1111/ j.1468–2885.2003.tb00293.x.

Silva, Adriana de Souza e. "From Cyber to Hybrid: Mobile Technologies as Interfaces of Hybrid Spaces." *Space and Culture* 9 (2006): 261–78, doi: 10.1177/1206331206289022.

Silvestri, Lisa. "A Rhetorical Forecast." *Review of Communication* 13 (2013): 127–42, doi:10.1080/15358593.2013.789121.

Simonson, Peter. "The Streets of Laredo: Mercurian Rhetoric and the Obama Campaign." *Western Journal of Communication* 74 (2010): 94–126, doi:10.1080/10570310903466045.

Singer, Ross. "Anti-Corporate Argument and the Spectacle of the Grotesque Rhetorical Body in *Super Size Me*." *Critical Studies in Media Communication* 28 (2011): 135–52, doi: 10.1080/15295036.2011.553724.

Sloop, John M., and Kent A. Ono. "Out-law Discourse: The Critical Politics of Material Judgment." *Philosophy & Rhetoric* 30 (1997): 50–69, doi: 10.1080/14791420.2015.1071309.

Smith, Daniel. W. "'A Life of Pure Immanence': Deleuze's 'Critique et Clinique' Project." In *Essays Critical and Clinical*, edited by Gilles Deleuze and Felix Guattari, xi–lv. Minneapolis: University of Minnesota Press, 1997.

Solomon, Martha. "The Things We Study: Texts and Their Interaction." *Communication Monographs* 60 (1993): 62–68, doi:10.1080/03637759309376295.

Sommer, Barbara W., and Mary Kay Quinlan. *The Oral History Manual*. Walnut Creek, CA: AltaMira Press, 2002.

Spradley, James P. *Participant Observation.* New York: Holt, Rinehart, Winston, 1980.

Sprain, Leah, Danielle Endres, and Tarla Rai Peterson. "Research as a Transdisciplinary Networked Process: A Metaphor for Difference-Making Research." *Communication Monographs* 77 (2010): 441–44, doi: 10.1080/03637751.2010.523600.

Squires, Catherine R. "Rethinking the Black Public Sphere: An Alternative Vocabulary for Multiple Public Spheres." *Communication Theory* 12 (2002): 446–68, doi: 10.1111/j.1468–2885.2002.tb00278.x.

St. Antoine, Thomas J. "Making Heaven out of Hell: New Urbanism and the Refutation of Suburban Spaces." *Southern Communication Journal* 72 (2007): 127–44, doi:10.1080/10417940701316351.

Stewart, Jessie, and Greg Dickinson. "Enunciating Locality in the Postmodern Suburb: FlatIron Crossing and the Colorado Lifestyle." *Western Journal of Communication* 72 (2008): 280–307, doi: 10.1080/10570310802210148.

Stewart, Karen Ann. "In Dust We Trust: A Narrative Journey into the Communal Heart of Public Art at the Burning Man Festival." PhD diss., Arizona State University, 2010.

Stewart, Karen, A., Aaron Hess, Sarah J. Tracy, and H. L. Goodall, Jr. "Risky Research: Investigating the 'Perils' of Ethnography." In *Qualitative Inquiry and Social Justice: Toward a Politics of Hope*, edited by Norman K. Denzin and Michael D. Giardina, 198–216. Walnut Creek, CA: Left Coast Press, 2009.

Strine, Mary S. "Articulating Performance/Performativity: Disciplinary Tasks and the Contingencies of Practice." In *Communication: Views from the Helm for the Twenty-First Century,* edited by Judith Trent , 312–17. Boston: Allyn and Bacon, 1998.

Stromer-Galley, Jennifer, and Edward Schiappa. "The Argumentative Burdens of Audience Conjectures: Audience Research in Popular Culture Criticism." *Communication Theory* 8 (1998): 27–62, doi: 10.1111/j.1468–2885.1998.tb00210.x.

Taylor, Bryan C. "The Bodies of August: Photographic Realism and Controversy at the National Air and Space Museum." *Rhetoric & Public Affairs* 1 (1998): 331–62, doi: 10.1353/rap.2010.0070.

Toulmin, Stephen Edelston. *The Uses of Argument*. Cambridge, UK: Cambridge University Press, 2003.

Tracy, Sarah J. "Fieldwork Horse-Assery: Making the Most of Feeling Humiliated, Rebuffed, and Offended During Participant Observation Research." *Management Communication Quarterly* 28 (2014): 458–65, doi: 10.1177/0893318914536965.

Tracy, Sarah J. *Qualitative Research Methods: Collecting Evidence, Crafting Analysis, Communicating Impact.* Malden, MA: Wiley-Blackwell, 2013.

Tuan, Yi-Fu. *Space and Place: The Perspective of Experience*. Minneapolis: University Of Minnesota Press, 2001.

Turner, Victor. *From Ritual to Theater: The Human Seriousness of Play*. New York: PAJ Publications, 1982.

Vatz, Richard. "The Myth of the Rhetorical Situation." *Philosophy & Rhetoric* 6 (1973): 154–61.

Wander, Philip. "The Ideological Turn in Modern Criticism." *Central States Speech Journal* 34 (1983): 1–18, doi: 10.1080/10510978309368110.

Wander, Philip. "The Third Persona: An Ideological Turn in Rhetorical Theory." *Central States Speech Journal* 35 (1984): 197–216, doi: 10.1080/10510978409368190.

Warnick, Barbara. "Leff in Context: What is the Critic's Role?" *Quarterly Journal of Speech* 78 (1992): 232–37, doi: 10.1080/00335639209383992.

Watts, Eric King, and Mark Orbe. "The Spectacular Consumption of 'True' African American Culture: 'Whassup' with the Budweiser Guys?" *Critical Studies in Media Communication* 19 (2002): 1–20, doi:10.1080/07393180216554.

Welsh, Scott. "Coming to Terms with the Antagonism between Rhetorical Reflection and Political Agency." *Philosophy & Rhetoric* 45 (2012), 1–23.

Welsh, Scott. "Deliberative Democracy and the Rhetorical Production of Political Culture." *Rhetoric & Public Affairs* 5 (2002): 679–707, doi: 10.1353/rap.2003.0020.

West, Isaac. "Performing Resistance In/from the Kitchen: The Practice of Maternal Pacifist Politics and La WISP's Cookbooks." *Women's Studies in Communication* 30 (2007): 358–83, doi:10.1080/07491409.2007.10162519.

West, Isaac. "PISSAR's Critically Queer and Disabled Politics." *Communication and Critical/Cultural Studies* 7 (2010): 156–75, doi:10.1080/14791421003759174.

Whitson, Steve, and John Poulakos. "Nietzsche and the Aesthetics of Rhetoric." *Quarterly Journal of Speech* 79 (1993): 131–45, doi:10.1080/00335639309384025.

Whitson, Steve, and John Poulakos. "Rhetoric Denuded and Redressed: Figs and Figures." (1995): 378–85, doi: 10.1080/00335639509384121.

Wichelns, Herbert A. "The Literary Criticism of Oratory." In *Readings in Rhetorical Criticism,* edited by Carl R. Burgchardt, 3–27. State College, PA: Strata, 2005.

Wilkins, Richard, and Karen Wolf. "The Role of Ethnography in Rhetorical Analysis: The New Rhetorical Turn." *Empedocles: European Journal for the Philosophy of Communication* 3 (2012): 7–23, doi: http://dx.doi.org/10.1386/ejpc.3.1.7_1.

Williams, James. "Immanence." In *The Deleuze Dictionary*, edited by Adrian Parr, 125–27. New York: Columbia University Press, 2010.

Williams, Raymond. "Culture is Ordinary." In *Cultural Theory: An Anthology*, edited by Imre Szeman and Timothy Kaposy, 53–59. Malden, MA: Wiley-Blackwell, 2011.

Wolcott, Harry F. *The Art of Fieldwork*. Lanham, MD: Altamira Press, 2005.

Wood, Andrew F. *City Ubiquitous: Place, Communication, and the Rise of Omnitopia*. Cresskill, NJ: Hampton Press, 2009.

Wright, Talmadge. *Out of Place: Homeless Mobilizations, Subcities, and Contested Landscapes*. Albany: SUNY Press, 1997.

Zagacki, Kenneth S., and Victoria J. Gallagher. "Rhetoric and Materiality in the Museum Park at the North Carolina Museum of Art." *Quarterly Journal of Speech* 95 (2009): 171–91, doi:10.1080/00335630902842087.

Index

About the Authors

Michael K. Middleton (PhD, University of Utah) is an assistant professor of argumentation & public discourse, and the director of the John R. Park Debate Society in the Department of Communication at the University of Utah. Michael's research focuses on rhetoric, argumentation, public discourse, and cultural studies in the contexts of political advocacy and social movements. His work has been published in the *Western Journal of Communication, Southern Communication Journal,* and *Communication, Culture, Critique.* His current research examines how homeless populations in Sacramento, CA have carved out spaces of democratic participation within their surrounding communities. Michael teaches courses in rhetoric, argumentation, and communication theory. In addition, Michael has nearly 20 years of experience with competitive academic debate and public speaking where he has coached numerous students to the highest ranks of national competition.

Aaron Hess (PhD, Arizona State University, Tempe) is an assistant professor of rhetoric in the College of Letters and Sciences at the Arizona State University, Downtown Phoenix campus. His research interests focus on rhetorical expression and advocacy in vernacular and local communities as well as in digital contexts. His work has been published in the *International Journal of Communication, Critical Studies in Media Communication, Media, Culture & Society, Communication and Critical/Cultural Studies,* and *Argumentation and Advocacy.* Additionally, along with other colleagues, Aaron has embraced media production tools to produce documentary films and other digital humanities projects as outcomes of his research. Using this approach, he examined public memory rhetoric during the tenth anniversary of September 11th while in Lower Manhattan in a feature length documentary and in local presentations in the community. Currently, his work is exploring the intersections between physical spaces and digital or locative media as simultaneous sites for rhetorical expression by social movements or other advocacy groups. Outside of academia, Aaron enjoys hiking and climbing the desert mountains of Arizona.

Danielle Endres (PhD, University of Washington) is an associate professor of rhetoric in the Department of Communication and affiliated faculty in the Environmental Humanities program at the University of Utah. She examines the rhetorical dynamics of contemporary controversies over nuclear technologies, energy policy, climate change, Native American mascots, and dominant spatial practices. She also has expertise in rhetorical methods, particularly the use of ethnography, oral history, interviewing and other participatory approaches into the practice of rhetorical criticism. Her research has been published in the *Quarterly Journal of Speech, Rhetoric & Public Affairs, Communication and Critical/Cultural Studies, Western Journal of Communication, Argumentation and Advocacy, Environmental Communication*, and others. Her co-edited book, *Social Movement to Address Climate Change: Local Action for Global Change* (Cambria Press, 2009) was awarded the Christine L. Oravec book award from the Environmental Communication division of the National Communication Association. Her current work is focused on examining the rhetoric of nuclear energy scientists and engineers through participant observation and interviewing toward an understanding of the role of scientists and engineers' discourse in the creation of energy policy.

Samantha Senda-Cook (PhD, University of Utah) is an assistant professor of rhetoric in the Department of Communication Studies and an affiliated faculty member with the Environmental Science and Sustainability programs at Creighton University. She studies rhetorical theory and analyzes environmental communication and materiality in the contexts of social movements, outdoor recreation, and urban spaces/places. Her work has been published in the *Quarterly Journal of Speech*, *Environmental Communication*, *International Journal of Wilderness*, *Southern Journal of Communication*, and *Argumentation and Advocacy*. Her current research focuses on constructions of space/place in urban environments, specifically in Omaha, NE, and tactical acts of resistance. To help make this scholarship relevant to community members, she has given public presentations at a monthly open meeting of the Gifford Park Neighborhood Association and the Bemis Center for Contemporary Arts. She teaches courses in rhetoric, environmental communication, intercultural communication, and communication practices. Additionally, she serves on the boards of the Community Bike Project Omaha and the Friends of KIOS. When she is not researching, teaching, or volunteering, she can usually be found reading a mystery novel, trying out a new recipe, or riding the hills of Omaha on her bike.

CPSIA information can be obtained
at www.ICGtesting.com
Printed in the USA
LVHW031928120319
610380LV00002B/205/P

9 781498 530774